BRANDING TELEVISION

Branding Television examines why and how the UK and US television industries have turned towards branding as a strategy in response to the rise of satellite, cable and digital television, and new media, such as the internet and mobile phone.

This is the first book to offer a sustained critical analysis of this new cultural development. *Branding Television* examines the industrial, regulatory and technological changes since the 1980s in the UK and the USA that have led to the adoption of branding as broadcasters have attempted to manage the behaviour of viewers and the values associated with their channels, services and programmes in a world of increased choice and interactivity. Wide-ranging case studies drawn from commercial, public service, network and cable/satellite television (from NBC and HBO to MTV, and from BBC and Channel 4 to UKTV and Sky) analyse the role of marketing and design in branding channels and corporations, and the development of programmes as brands.

Exploring both successful and controversial uses of branding, this book asks what problems there are in creating television brands and whether branding supports or undermines commercial and public service broadcasting.

Branding Television extends and complicates our understanding of the changes to television over the past 30 years and of the role of branding in contemporary Western culture. It will be of particular interest to students and researchers in television studies, but also in creative industries and media and cultural studies more generally.

Catherine Johnson lectures in Film and Television Studies at the University of Nottingham, UK. Her research examines the Western television industries and the impact of industrial shifts on the cultural artefacts that they produce. She is the author of *Telefantasy* (2005) and co-editor of *ITV Cultures* (2005).

COMEDIA

Series Editor: David Morley

Comedia titles available from Routledge:

ADVERTISING INTERNATIONAL
The Privatisation of Public Space
Armand Mattelart translated by Michael Chanan

BLACK BRITISH CULTURE AND SOCIETY
A Text Reader
Edited by Kwesi Owusu

THE CONSUMERIST MANIFESTO
Advertising in Postmodern Times
Martin Davidson

CULTURAL SNIPING
The Art of Transgression
Jo Spence

CULTURE AFTER HUMANISM
History, Culture, Subjectivity
Iain Chambers

CULTURE IN THE COMMUNICATION AGE
Edited by James Lull

CULTURES OF CONSUMPTION
Masculinities and Social Space in Late Twentieth-Century Britain
Frank Mort

CUT 'N' MIX
Culture, Identity and Caribbean Music
Dick Hebdige

THE DYNASTY YEARS
Hollywood Television and Critical Media Studies
Jostein Gripsrud

FAMILY TELEVISION
Cultural Power and Domestic Leisure
David Morley

A GAME OF TWO HALVES: FOOTBALL, TELEVISION AND GLOBALISATION
Cornel Sandvoss

HIDING IN THE LIGHT
On Images and Things
Dick Hebdige

HOME TERRITORIES
Media, Mobility and Identity
David Morley

IMPOSSIBLE BODIES
Femininity and Masculinity at the Movies
Chris Holmlund

THE KNOWN WORLD OF BROADCAST NEWS
Stanley Baran and Roger Wallis

MEDIA/THEORY
Thinking About Media and Communications
Shaun Moores

MIGRANCY, CULTURE, IDENTITY
Iain Chambers

THE PHOTOGRAPHIC IMAGE IN DIGITAL CULTURE
Edited by Martin Lister

THE PLACE OF MEDIA POWER
Pilgrims and Witnesses of the Media Age
Nick Couldry

THE POLITICS OF HERITAGE
The Legacies of 'Race'
Edited by Jo Littler and Roshi Naidoo

SPECTACULAR BODIES
Gender, Genre and the Action Cinema
Yvonne Tasker

STUART HALL
Critical Dialogues in Cultural Studies
Edited by Kuan-Hsing Chen and David Morley

TEACHING THE MEDIA
Len Masterman

TELEVISION AND COMMON KNOWLEDGE
Edited by Jostein Gripsrud

TELEVISION, AUDIENCES AND CULTURAL STUDIES
David Morley

TELEVISION, ETHNICITY AND CULTURAL CHANGE
Marie Gillespie

TIMESHIFT
On Video Culture
Sean Cubitt

TIMES OF THE TECHNOCULTURE
From the Information Society to the Virtual Life
Kevin Robins and Frank Webster

TO BE CONTINUED …
Soap Opera Around the World
Edited by Robert C. Allen

TRANSNATIONAL CONNECTIONS
Culture, People, Places
Ulf Hannerz

VIDEO PLAYTIME
The Gendering of a Leisure Technology
Ann Gray

WATCHING WITH THE SIMPSONS
Television, Parody, and Intertextuality
Jonathan Gray

MEDIA, MODERNITY AND TECHNOLOGY
The Geography of the New
David Morley

MEDIA EVENTS IN A GLOBAL AGE
Nick Couldry, Andreas Hepp and Friedrich Krotz

RELOCATING TELEVISION
Television in the Digital Context
Edited by Jostein Gripsrud

BRANDING TELEVISION
Catherine Johnson

Available in hardback:

TRANSMEDIA TELEVISION
Audiences, New Media and Daily Life
Elizabeth Evans

TELETECHNOLOGIES, PLACE, AND COMMUNITY
Rowan Wilken

BRANDING TELEVISION

Catherine Johnson

LONDON AND NEW YORK

First published 2012
by Routledge
2 Park Square, Milton Park, Abingdon, Oxon OX14 4RN

Simultaneously published in the USA and Canada
by Routledge
711 Third Avenue, New York, NY 10017

Routledge is an imprint of the Taylor & Francis Group, an informa business

British Library Cataloguing in Publication Data
A catalogue record for this book is available from the British Library

Library of Congress Cataloging in Publication Data
Johnson, Catherine.
Branding television / Catherine Johnson.
p. cm. – (Comedia)
Includes bibliographical references and index.
1. Television broadcasting – United States. 2. Television broadcasting – Great Britain. 3. Branding (Marketing) – United States. 4. Branding (Marketing) – Great Britain. I. Title.
HE8700.8.H56 2011
384.55068'8 – dc22
2011016514

ISBN: 978-0-415-54842-7 (hbk)
ISBN: 978-0-415-54843-4 (pbk)
ISBN: 978-0-203-59703-3 (ebk)

Typeset in Garamond
by Taylor & Francis Books

Printed and bound in Great Britain by
TJ International Ltd, Padstow, Cornwall

FOR ROB

CONTENTS

TABLES

ACKNOWLEDGEMENTS

I first became interested in the relationship between branding and television when working on my PhD (which was subsequently published as *Telefantasy*, London: BFI, 2005). After years of working in other areas it was the writing of Celia Lury, John Thornton Caldwell and Mark C. Rogers, Michael Epstein and Jimmie L. Reeves that redirected my attention and interest towards branding, and their work has provided an excellent starting point for the research presented in this book. Of course, this research would never have materialized if it wasn't for two lots of research leave granted to me by the Department of Media Arts at Royal Holloway, University of London: the first of which allowed me to dip my toes in the water and try out initial ideas; the second, four years later, gave me the much-needed space to work my research up into a book, and was greatly enhanced by a period of research leave supported and funded by the Arts & Humanities Research Council. The teaching relief provided by the University of Nottingham when I moved there from Royal Holloway and, in particular, the friendly welcome I received from the staff of the Department of Culture, Film and Media provided a warm and collegiate environment within which to put the finishing touches to this book.

Over the course of researching this book I have presented my work at various conferences and symposia, including at the University of Southampton, the Society for Cinema and Media Studies in Los Angeles, De Montfort University, Leicester, the British Film Institute (BFI) and the University of Nottingham, where I received useful feedback as my ideas were developing. Special thanks must go to the members of the Southern Broadcasting History Group (now too numerous to list individually!) who have provided a consistently warm, engaging, stimulating and enjoyable place to share research and ideas, and who have patiently put up with me talking rather incessantly about branding for the past few years. I would also like to thank the industry professionals (including Victoria Jaye, Charlie Mawer and Ian Grutchfield) who generously gave up their time to answer my questions about television branding. This research would not have been possible without the help of a number of archives and archivists. In particular,

I would like to thank Kathleen Luckey and Steve Bryant at the BFI's National Archive, Andy O'Dwyer at the BBC, Brian Otnes at the Instructional Media Centre of the University of Texas at Austin and Mark Quigley at the Film and Television Archives of the University of California, Los Angeles (UCLA), who have all given generously of their time as I've attempted to seek access to and information about the more ephemeral and largely overlooked texts of television. I would also have been unable to complete this book if it wasn't for the help of American friends and colleagues (Jonathan Gray, Max Dawson, Avi Santo and Madeleine Nolan) who generously recorded evenings of off-air US network television for me.

My thanks also to Jonathan Gray and Paul Grainge for their suggestions on the book at proposal stage, to David Morley for his useful comments on the final manuscript and for supporting the book in the first place, and to Natalie Foster and Ruth Moody at Routledge for their patient support. And my apologies must go to my friends for not always being at my most chipper during the tougher periods of book writing. This book is dedicated to Rob Turnock, for many, many things, from his insightful comments on drafts of my work, to putting up with me over the last few months of working on the book when I had little space in my head for anything else – particularly housework – to supporting me whole-heartedly in everything I've wanted to do. I couldn't have written this book without him and now that it's finished I can't find the words to thank him enough.

ABBREVIATIONS

A&E	Arts & Entertainment
ABC	American Broadcasting Company
BARB	Broadcasters' Audience Research Board
BBC	British Broadcasting Corporation
BDB	British Digital Broadcasting
BFI	British Film Institute
CBS	Columbia Broadcasting System
DBS	direct broadcast satellite
DOG(s)	digital on-screen graphic(s)
DTB	digital terrestrial broadcasting
DTN	Digital Television Network
DVD	digital versatile disk
DVR	digital video recorder
FCC	Federal Communications Commission
GPO	General Post Office
GPS	global positioning system
HBO	Home Box Office
HBOIP	HBO Independent Productions
IBA	Independent Broadcasting Authority
ID(s)	ident(s)
IPP(s)	in programme pointer(s)
ITC	Independent Television Commission
ITV	Independent Television
LWT	London Weekend Television
MTV	Music Television
NBC	National Broadcasting Company
NFC	National Football Conference
NFL	National Football League
NTL	National Transcommunications Limited
PSB(s)	public service broadcasting
SBS	Special Broadcasting Service
S-DMB	satellite digital multimedia broadcasting

The WB	Warner Bros TV
UCLA	University of California, Los Angeles
UHF	ultra-high frequency
UK	United Kingdom
UNM	United News and Media
UPN	United Paramount Network
URL	Uniform Resource Locator
US/ A	United States/ of America
VCR	videocassette recorder
VH1	Video Hits One
VHS	video home system
VOD	video on demand
WASE	Warner Amex Satellite Entertainment
WGA	Writers Guild of America

INTRODUCTION – BUT TELEVISION'S NOT SOAP!

Approaching television branding

In 2009 Channel 4 produced a trailer for its on-demand service 4oD. In the advert a young man entered a convenience store whose shelves were filled with popular Channel 4 programmes represented as branded consumer goods. Working-class comedy drama *Shameless* (2004–) appeared as a four-pack of lager, cooking show *Come Dine with Me* (2005–) as flour, teen drama *Skins* (2007–) as Pot Noodle, and older shows such as *Brookside* (1982–2003) and *Vic Reeves' Big Night Out* (1990–91) as frozen produce. The advert made explicit the dramatic changes that television had undergone over the previous three decades. Once a broadcast medium dominated by a handful of national channels broadcasting linear schedules into the home, by 2009 there were hundreds of channels and, if you did not want to watch a programme when it was broadcast, you could download it and watch it later on your computer or portable media device. The positioning of television programmes as branded consumer products in this trailer for one of these new on-demand services is perhaps unsurprising given the emergence of branding as a strategy to respond to the challenges and complexities of this new television landscape. John Thornton Caldwell has argued that '"Branding" has emerged as a central concern of the television industry in the age of digital convergence' (2004: 305), while Rogers *et al.* (2002: 48) claim that the new 'digital era' of television 'must be considered the age of brand marketing'. Television corporations now have brand strategies and television channels are being constructed with brand identities that are conveyed through logos, slogans and trailers. Even programmes are now being constructed as brands designed to encourage audience loyalty and engagement with the text beyond the act of television viewing.

However, despite the proclamations that television has entered a 'world full of brands' (Ellis 2000: 165), the adoption of branding by the television industries is by no means straightforward or uncontested. If we return to the 4oD trailer, it is striking that, even though an awning with the URL 'Channel4.com' does fall open as the man leaves the shop at the end of the advert, the store that contains all these branded programmes is simply named 'Convenience'. If television programmes are branded here, the new television service being promoted is not a branded supermarket chain, but a generic (and slightly down-at-heel) local convenience store or corner shop. In some ways this mirrors Simone Murray's (2005: 422) argument that media conglomerates have attempted to shift public perception of them from being a 'household brand' to being a 'house of brands' in order to obscure increasingly concentrated ties of ownership. Here, Channel 4 situates itself as a local, small and accessible business, rather than a large corporate branded supermarket chain. Yet the 4oD trailer also reveals an anxiety about how branding should be applied to television in the digital era. Sanjay Nazerali (former marketing director for MTV Europe) argues that there is little evidence to justify the money spent on branding channels and that television has specific attributes that make branding less useful than in the consumer goods industries: 'Television channels aren't really products. Our consumers aren't really consumers – they're viewers. They don't directly pay for us (except in rare pay-per-view cases), don't watch us (they watch our programmes) and they don't use us to describe themselves.' (Nazerali 2003: 30). While the television programme, therefore, seems relatively open to being recast as a branded consumer good within an on-demand environment, 'television' itself seems resistant to the logics of branding. If the digital era of television is the 'age of brand marketing', we need to ask what is being branded here, and how. Indeed, despite the increasingly widespread references to branding in both the industry press and academia, the uses and meanings of 'television branding' are often taken for granted. A central aim of this book is to correct this by offering a sustained examination of how and why branding has been used by the television industries in the USA and the UK.

What Is branding?

Celia Lury (2004) argues that the role of branding in contemporary industrialized societies can be traced back to the mid-nineteenth century, when branding began to be used by soap manufacturers as a means of product differentiation. The branding of soap through packaging was a strategy designed to convey a set of attributes that distinguished the branded soap from other generic soap products. Effectively, consumers were not simply buying soap, but were purchasing a set of attributes created by the packaging of the soap. As such, the brand conveyed certain qualities to the consumer and acted as a guarantee of the origin of the product, providing product differentiation and offering reliability and enhanced consumer loyalty. These early examples of branding were intended to enable the producer to circumvent the retailer and speak directly to the consumer, although soon enough retail outlets began to emerge as brands in themselves, sometimes with their own branded products.[1]

Broader shifts within the retail industries over the second half of the twentieth century altered the ways in which branding was used and increased the importance of branding as an industrial strategy. Lury notes that in the post-war period, marketing became increasingly integrated into production, legitimated by the development of marketing science and consumer research and the rise of self-service outlets (such as supermarkets) in which the product needed to speak directly to the consumer (2004: 22–23). Marketing is particularly concerned with communicating directly with the consumer, and the integration of marketing into the production process therefore altered the understanding of the relationship between producers and consumers. Emphasis shifted towards designing and marketing products based on research into the experiences of the consumer. The design and style of the product became as important as its functionality as a way of communicating the value and identity of the product to the consumer (see Lury 2004: 24–25). The function of branding in this new environment shifted from simply indicating product origin and inviting consumer loyalty, to communicating shared values between producer, product and consumer. The purchase of a branded product, therefore, did not simply provide reliability, but also became a way in which the consumer adopted the values conveyed through the brand. For example, if I were to purchase a Nike trainer, I would not simply be getting a reliable piece of footwear; I would also be buying into a set of values about individuality, determination, dynamism and cool conveyed by the brand. Hence, branding emerged as a means of managing the complex relationships between the consumer, the product purchased and the producer (and sometimes retailer) of that product.

Adam Arvidsson argues that the development of these new marketing practices was tied to the emergence of electronic media and, in particular, television (2006: 23–25). Television and other electronic media provided a means through which consumers could learn about the symbolic and use value of new products (Jansson 2002: 10). At the same time, and particularly over the 1950s and 1960s, the use of consumer goods to construct social relationships and identities became more visible, whether in the development of youth cultures or the pressures on the suburban family to 'keep up with the Joneses'. Arvidsson argues that media culture fills consumer goods with meanings that have the potential to 'enable their user to think him- or herself different' (2006: 39). However, as the increased mediatization of consumption placed more emphasis on the symbolic dimensions of consumer goods and their productive uses by consumers, it also opened up the meanings associated with products to contestation. As a consequence, constructing and maintaining a 'brand image' that communicated the symbolic dimensions of the product became more central to the marketing of consumer goods.

However, for branding to be successful, these symbolic dimensions added to the product have to be accepted by the consumer. Thus, branding depends on interactivity, two-way communication, between the consumer and producer. Yet this interactivity is not open or equal. Rather, branding attempts to shape, control and/or manage the values attributed to products and, through this, the uses to which the product is put. Branding is therefore much more than simply an element of design and packaging added to a product. Rather, the brand needs to be understood as a 'new media object' (Lury 2004: 6): a form of mediated and dynamic communication that constantly frames and reframes the relationships between producers, products and consumers. As Lury argues, 'the account of activities of the marketers ... does not adequately describe the brand' (2004: 51). Indeed, Lury argues that accounting for the activities of all of the different constituencies that might engage with the interface of the brand (designers, marketers, producers, consumers) would not adequately describe the brand because it would fail to acknowledge the brand as 'a complex, indeterminate or open object' (ibid.). While it might not be possible to pinpoint a specific determining definition of a brand, however, we can trace the different and changing ways in which the brand functions as an interface within culture in order to understand how it operates as a cultural artefact.

Yet, if television was central in the development of the branding of consumer goods, what about the branding of television itself? One of the difficulties with applying branding to television is the nature of television as a medium. Sylvia M. Chan-Olmsted argues that 'On the surface, ... branding and brand management notions ... appear to be not as applicable to the broadcasting industry due to the diverse and continuous nature of its product (programming) and lack of specific product attributes as well as easily identifiable product logos' (2001: 78). Broadcast television produces programmes that are ordered and transmitted as a schedule through television channels by specific broadcasters. Essentially what is provided is the *experience* of watching television. Within the consumer goods industries branding emerged to manage the relationships between the producer, product and consumer. In the television industry the channel that aggregates the consumer's experience of the television programme adds an additional layer to the relationships between producer, product and viewer. While in the consumer goods industry it is the product (and occasionally the corporation) that is branded, within the television industry the product is potentially both the television programme and the channel (or other service/medium) through which that programme is viewed. As such, we can think of three areas where branding might be adopted by television broadcasters: corporations, channels/services and programmes.[2]

Practices associated with branding have been used in the USA and UK from the start of television broadcasting in each of these areas. The BBC adopted a coat of arms shortly after receiving its first Royal Charter in 1927 that symbolized its public purpose and acted as a form of corporate branding. It utilized the colours associated with the three non-English national regions of the UK (blue for Scotland, red for Wales and green for Northern Ireland) and depicted two eagles with bugles around their necks between a shield with a globe and stars to symbolize the breadth of the corporation's public broadcasting. Along the bottom of the coat of arms is the motto: 'nation shall speak peace unto nation', exemplifying the national purpose upon which the BBC's charter was based. Films designed to communicate the work of the BBC to the public were also produced in this period, such as the General Post Office Film Unit's impressionistic documentary *The Voice of Britain* (1935) and the BBC-produced promotional film *This is the BBC* (1959), which followed the corporation's activities for a day.

It was not until the early 1950s that the BBC developed a logo specifically for its television service. Indeed, the use of logos for television channels only really emerged in the UK in 1955, when the arrival of ITV provided competition for the BBC's television service for the first time. ITV was made up of a number of regional companies which used idents (short films transmitted in between programmes that animated their channel logos) to distinguish their services. In the USA, the national networks and local stations also developed channel logos (referred to as station IDs) to distinguish themselves from their rivals.[3] However, the characteristics of the television industries in the USA and the UK at this time limited the usefulness of channel branding. In the USA from the mid-1950s to the mid-1980s the national networks had an oligopoly on broadcasting. The networks endeavoured to attract undifferentiated mass audiences and it was common practice for a network to imitate the programming innovations of its rivals. Any brand identity that was too specific or too defined could potentially alienate viewers, and so branding functioned primarily as a shorthand device for indicating the general identity of a network. Similarly, the same period in the UK was characterized by a duopoly between the BBC and ITV, both regulated by a similar public service remit. Within the US network oligopoly and UK duopoly there was little competition between television channels, and so little value in conceiving of and promoting the television channel as a branded product. In this context, branding emerged primarily as the adoption of channel logos that functioned to differentiate and distinguish each channel.[4]

The public service ethos behind British television at this time also militated against the adoption of branding as a cultural form that emerged within the marketplace (Lury 2004: 4). The associations of branding and marketing with the promotion of products within a marketplace to enhance profits pulls against the public service ethos of broadcasting as a social good provided by broadcasters as trustees of the airwaves. Indeed, the negative associations of branding with marketization even extended to the US networks. John Thornton Caldwell argues that the networks promoted themselves to the US government as caretakers of the airwaves as part of a strategic move to protect the government-sanctioned network oligopoly.[5]

> Early on the networks exploited one side of their dualistic identity (lobbying for trusteeship with regulators), even though they

> effectively and simultaneously sold themselves to viewers (as branded producers of entertainment). This tension between branding and trusteeship has existed in American network television from the start.
> (Caldwell 2004: 306)

The ephemeral nature of broadcasting also militated against the adoption of programme branding. Much early television was produced and transmitted live, and so did not exist separately from its broadcast on a television channel. Even when broadcasters adopted recording technologies over the 1950s and 1960s, a significant proportion of television production (particularly in the UK) was as-live, and the BBC famously wiped vast swathes of its own archives in the 1960s and 1970s (see Fiddy 2001). The trade in rights to television programmes from the 1940s and (from the mid-1950s) the trade in programmes on film (and later on videotape) did construct the programme itself as a product that could be branded (see Johnson 2009 and Santo 2010).[6] However, at this time such practices were not central to the television industries in the USA and UK whose primary source of revenue was the sale of spot advertising (or the licence fee in the case of the BBC).

Therefore, although it is possible to identify practices associated with branding from the 1940s to the 1970s, and although this is the period within which branding emerges as key to the consumer goods industries in the USA and the UK, the nature of broadcast television and the industries within which it was produced worked against the adoption of television branding. Yet, by the mid-1990s the trade press in the USA and the UK were proclaiming branding as essential to the television industry. The first two parts of this book will examine in detail the reasons why branding was adopted in the USA and the UK from the 1980s. In doing so, it will examine the impact of the deregulation and marketization of television, the rise of new technologies that displaced broadcasting as the central experience of television and the emergence of branding as a broader cultural strategy that extended well beyond the consumer goods industries into areas of public life.

Television history and periodization

The changes that have taken place in the US and UK television industries since the late 1970s raise the thorny problem of periodization. To what extent is it possible to argue that over the 1980s television entered a new and distinct period in its history? There are a number of different models for understanding the periodic shifts in television history. John Ellis (2000) argues that television has developed over three distinct eras: those of scarcity, availability and plenty. In the era of scarcity television developed as a key component of consumer society, but was characterized by a relatively small number of channels and broadcasters. The growth of satellite and cable in the late 1970s and early 1980s ushered in a new era of availability, in which television services were expanded. This expansion was intensified in the era of plenty that emerged at the end of the 1990s when digital technologies vastly increased viewers' choices and the old model of broadcasting came under threat.

If Ellis's model highlights the gradually increasing channels and platforms through which television has been distributed, Rogers, Epstein and Reeves's (2002) model of TVI, TVII and TVIII (developed in relation to US television and largely corresponding to Ellis's periodizations) focuses on how television is funded and distributed. In the era of TVI, the three-network oligopoly dominated the production, distribution and transmission of television programmes. Television was a mass medium funded through the sale of advertising based on total audience ratings. Over the 1970s certain demographics started to emerge as particularly valuable for advertisers and broadcasters (such as the youth market). The turn towards demographics was accentuated with the emergence of cable and satellite television over the 1980s as significant competition for the networks, partly as a consequence of deregulation. This ushered in the era of TVII in which the network oligopoly was broken and new niche cable networks introduced demographics as core to the ways in which advertisers paid for airtime. However, Rogers *et al.* argue that the eras of TVI and TVII were both characterized by the dominance of second-order commodity relations, in which most television was paid for indirectly by consumption of the products advertised on air. They argue that the era of TVIII, from the late 1990s, can be characterized by the emergence of first-order commodity relations in which viewers can pay directly for television, either through premium subscription channels or through new on-demand services.

While the eras of TVI, TVII and TVIII usefully outline key changes to US television, a perhaps more descriptive way of periodizing the same shifts is that adopted by Amanda Lotz, who describes these changes as a move from the 'network era' (late-1950s to mid-1980s), to a period of 'multi-channel transition' (mid-1980s to mid-2000s), into the 'post-network era' that began in the mid-2000s. As with Rogers *et al.*, Lotz sees continuities between the network era and the period from the mid-1980s onwards when the network oligopoly was challenged. However, she argues that from the mid-2000s a new era has begun to emerge in which 'different industrial practices are becoming dominant and replacing those of the network era' (2007a: 7–8). One difficulty with the models of both Rogers *et al.* and Lotz is that they are based solely on the US context and so cannot account for a key shift in most public service contexts, which is the emergence of the first non-public service channels in the 1980s and 1990s. By contrast, Ellis' model tends to flatten out nationally specific developments in television while drawing largely from British public service broadcasting.

One of the ways in which this book attempts to avoid being too parochial on the one hand or too generalist on the other is to adopt a comparative approach. Focusing on the USA and the UK enables comparison between two different models of organizing and funding television – commercial and public service – from two nations with advanced television industries. There are some limitations with this approach, not least the Western-centric focus of looking solely at the USA and the UK. Yet, there are some benefits in that these two industries faced a very similar set of changes over the 1980s and 1990s. They therefore offer useful cases for comparing the impact of these changes in commercial and public service contexts. This is particularly important for a study of branding in television because branding, as we have seen, is associated with the increasing conflation of consumerism and marketization. As a consequence, while the adoption of branding might seem a logical strategy in the commercially competitive environment of US television, it is potentially more problematic for the UK's public service broadcasters. This raises the question of what functions branding might serve in the different contexts of US and UK television and the extent to which branding strategies can be used to serve commercial and/or public service aims.

The difficulty for such an approach is to develop a historical model that enables comparison between the UK and US contexts while simultaneously allowing exploration of the national specificities of each industry. It is for this reason that I have chosen to adopt a fourth model in circulation within histories of television that argues for the development of television through three eras: broadcast, cable/satellite, and digital. The primary reason for choosing this terminology lays with the focus in this book on the television industries, and specifically television broadcasters, themselves. Thus, while Ellis' model of scarcity, availability and plenty usefully describes many of the changes outlined here, the terminology reveals his driving interest in the social function and place of television. By contrast, the focus of this book is on examining how and why television broadcasters in the USA and UK have adopted a particular industrial strategy – branding. Although this will involve examining brands as new media objects (as argued above), this book is particularly interested in asking why the television industries in each context adopted this particular strategy at this particular moment in history and what this might tell us about how the television industry and the products and services that they produce are changing.

However, in adopting periodizations drawn from technological shifts (the move from television as a medium of broadcasting to the rise of cable, satellite and then digital technologies), the intention is not to posit a technologically determinist understanding of the historical development of television. Technology does not determine historical change, because the socio-cultural and industrial significance of any technology is shaped by policy, market conditions and broader social and cultural factors. Yet, at the same time, television is a technology and its historical development has been fundamentally affected by technological developments. Indeed, attempts to delineate the specificity of television are always bound by an understanding of the technological possibilities (or limits) of the medium (see Carroll 2003). While, therefore, television is a cultural medium of communication, it is also, essentially, a piece of technology. As such, this book uses the broadcast, cable/satellite and digital eras to refer to the political, industrial and socio-cultural factors shaping the changes brought about by the adoption of new technologies that altered the nature of television and the industries that produce it.

A key reason for my emphasis on the technological basis of television as a medium lies in my hypothesis that the fundamental shift that began in the 1980s was the gradual challenge to the centrality of broadcasting to our understanding of television as a medium. As argued above, from its introduction (in the 1930s in the UK, the 1940s in the USA and later across much of the rest of the world), television was conceptualized as a medium of broadcasting.[7] This has shaped the ways in which television has been studied, regulated, produced and consumed. The challenge to broadcasting began in the 1980s with the increasing dominance of cable television in the USA and the emergence of satellite as competition to the public service broadcasters in the UK. As will be explored in more depth in the first two parts of this book, cable and satellite undermine some of the fundamental assumptions about television as a broadcast medium: that television cannot be paid for at the point of reception, that television is a medium of the masses, that television is a national medium. These challenges are amplified with the emergence of digital television. By 2010 television was no longer the set in the corner of the living room broadcasting an ephemeral linear schedule to an undifferentiated mass audience. The emergence of new platforms and technologies that allow viewers to download programmes on demand and circumvent the traditional channels and broadcasters seems to threaten the future of television altogether. While the range of academic publications exploring the 'end of television' have usefully challenged the extent to which these changes will be the death knell of broadcasting, in the digital era broadcasting is no longer adequate as a way of describing television.[8]

This book is therefore centrally concerned with exploring this fundamental change in the very nature of television as a medium, arguing that branding, as a key industrial shift over the period, offers a useful lens for examining the changes that threaten to undermine our conceptualization of this once-familiar technology. However, it is important to raise a number of caveats here. First, it is worth returning to the issue of periodization. The emergence of cable, satellite and digital technologies is significantly different in the US and UK contexts. This is particularly the case with cable and satellite. In the USA, cable began to offer competition to the broadcast networks over the 1980s. By contrast, in the UK it was not until the very end of the 1980s that satellite services emerged to compete with the terrestrial channels, and cable has taken far longer to develop as a mature industry. Furthermore, the development of satellite and cable in the UK had the additional significance of introducing television services not regulated under a public service remit for the first time. In many ways then, the most significant aspect of the emergence of satellite and cable in the UK was the broader political context that threatened public service broadcasting, rather than the actual competition for viewers that these new services presented. Similarly, while the new cable channels in the USA did threaten the network oligopoly, it is arguably the emergence of large media conglomerates that brought the networks and cable channels under the same corporation that has had the most impact on the television industry. Therefore, although we can usefully distinguish a broadcast, cable/satellite and digital era in each context, they are not necessarily temporally the same. In the USA, the cable/satellite era begins in the 1980s, but needs to be understood within the context of a history of cable extending back to the 1940s. In the UK, the cable/satellite era only begins in the late 1980s, but the impact of the political shifts that brought about this technological change need to be traced back over the 1980s.

Not only, therefore, are these periodizations nationally specific, they also need to be understood as fluid analytical constructions rather than fixed temporal schema. Indeed, one of the difficulties in writing about the present is being unable to step back and gain a critical perspective on the changes that are taking place around us. This makes it far harder to pinpoint key moments of change when it is impossible to know the full significance or impact of that change. Central then to the approach taken within this book is the argument that, to understand the present, we need to take a historical approach in order to trace the significance of the changes that have taken place to television. While this book focuses primarily on the period from the 1980s to 2010, when broadcasting as a dominant model for television came under threat, there is the need for further historical work that traces the historical precedents for the changes witnessed in television over the past 30 years and challenges the dominant assumptions about the broadcast era of television. It is hoped that this book will be a spur to such work.

Branding and television

These differences in the development of television have shaped the structure of this book. Parts I and II focus on the changes in the US and UK television industries in order to examine why branding emerges as an industrial strategy over the cable/satellite and digital eras. Chapter 1 traces the development of branding over the cable/satellite era in the USA, exploring the emergence of channel branding within the cable industry in the early 1980s and tracing its adoption by the US networks over the 1980s and 1990s. Chapter 2 then focuses more specifically on the digital era (from the late-1990s) and the particular problems and issues that this has raised about the use of branding within the US television industry. Part II then shifts focus from the USA to the UK. Chapter 3 focuses on the more commercial companies within

British broadcasting and examines their adoption of branding from the 1980s to the 2000s. Chapter 4 then looks more specifically at the challenges faced by the UK's public service broadcasters within a hostile political climate and with the introduction of non-public service commercial television for the first time. This chapter will address the specific debates raised by the use of branding within a public service context and ask whether the adoption of branding is indicative of the marketization of public service broadcasting in the UK. The first two parts of this book offer a detailed account of the development of US and UK television from the 1980s to 2010 and the (often varied and complex) ways in which branding was adopted by broadcasters within each industry over this period.

However, in order to examine brands as new media objects, it is necessary to look beyond branding as a feature of the industries that produce television to examine it as a feature of the texts of television themselves, which is the aim of Part III of this book. While textual studies of television have tended to focus on the programme, Chapter 5 examines channel and service brands by analysing the interstitial spaces between programmes (both on air and online) to explore how they function to manage the relationships between producers, viewers and the different texts and platforms that now encompass television as a medium. By contrast, Chapter 6 focuses on programme brands, arguing that branding theory can help us to analyse the extended texts of television that now co-exist across a range of media. Branding emerges as a strategy for the US and UK television industries over a period of significant change, when the very nature of television as a broadcast medium comes under threat. The final chapter returns to some of the issues raised here about applying branding to television in order to develop a theorization of television branding.

Methodologically, this book combines analysis of primary sources such as industry, trade and press documents, audio-visual materials and interviews, with critical interrogation of secondary historical and theoretical texts drawn from the fields of television and film studies, media, management, cultural studies and sociology. Some interviews with industry personnel have been undertaken to gain insight into the processes of brand creation, but the research focuses on primary sources such as annual reports, trade magazines, print and multimedia texts, as these are the means through which brand strategies are constructed, conveyed and explained publicly and they provide the best evidence of *how* television industries have used branding. In doing so, this book aims to further our understanding of the changes wrought by the adoption of cable, satellite and digital technologies and to offer a critical theorization of the uses of branding by television broadcasters. Just as branding emerges as a tool for the television industries to manage the new landscape of the digital era, this book argues that examining the uses of branding within television can help us to understand the ways in which the television industries and the nature of television itself as a medium have changed over the past 30 years.

Notes

1 See Celia Lury (2004: 18–28) for a history of branding from the mid-nineteenth century when, she argues, 'branding becomes a visible force in the organisation of production in industrialised countries' (2004: 18–19).

2 While this book focuses on the adoption of branding by television broadcasters, brand strategies extend to other aspects of the television industry, such as production companies and stars. There is certainly the need for further work that considers how branding functions more widely across the television industry and how these brands interact with the corporate, channel/service and programme brands of broadcasters examined here.

3 See Chapter 5 for a more detailed discussion of the history of channel idents and station IDs.

4 One difference between the USA and the UK is that the public service remits of the UK broadcasters did contribute to the construction of more distinct identities. For example, ITV has been commonly associated with populist programming (largely because it was funded by advertising and despite the fact that it was regulated by the same public service remit as the BBC), whereas the BBC has at times been seen as both avuncular and staid (occasioning the feminized moniker 'Auntie').

5 The attempts by the networks to construct a corporate identity as trustees of the airwaves could, ironically, be seen as a form of corporate branding in itself. Indeed, Chapter 4 will complicate the negative association of branding with marketization through an examination of branding by the UK public service broadcasters, Channel 4 and the BBC.

6 In its negotiations around the sale of rights to its programming in the 1940s and 1950s the BBC was adopting practices akin to brand management, such as attempting to control the uses and meanings attributed to its programming in order to protect its corporate image (Johnson 2009). Avi Santo has examined the licensing and merchandising of the television series, *Batman* (ABC, 1965–67) and *The Green Hornet* (ABC, 1966), which were managed as cross-media brands (Santo 2010). Paul Grainge argues that Disney's development of television series for ABC in the 1950s could also be understood as an early example of brand marketing in the television industry (2008: 44).

7 This is not to argue that television was simply a medium of broadcasting in this period. Indeed, one of the interesting consequences of the changes that have taken place to television over the past 30 years is that the new ideas emerging about television have provided television historians with new models with which to challenge our assumptions about television's past. My own work on the trade in rights at the BBC in the 1940s and 1950s stemmed largely from work on the increasing significance of rights in the contemporary television industry and the need to question how new these practices actually were (see Johnson 2009).

8 See for example, Graeme Turner and Jinna Tay (2009) and Lynn Spigel and Jan Olsson (2004).

Part I

BRANDING AND THE US TELEVISION INDUSTRY

1

DEREGULATION, DIFFERENTIATION AND NICHE TARGETING

The emergence of branding in the cable/satellite era

On 1 April 1987 the famous Hollywood sign in Los Angeles, California was transformed into the logo for the first new television network in over 30 years. The giant letters for the Fox network were accompanied by the characteristic searchlights associated with its sister company, the Hollywood studio 20th Century Fox (Anon. 1987: 88). Footage of the transformation was transmitted in the bumpers between programmes during the first evenings that Fox was on air (Kallan 1987: 48). In staging this spectacle Fox was not only generating valuable publicity for its new network, it was also highlighting the network's association with the glitz, glamour and history of Hollywood. More than just a publicity stunt then, the transformation of the Hollywood sign contributed to the construction of a brand identity for the Fox network that drew on the existing values and attributes of 20th Century Fox, in just one example of the ways in which the US television industry began to use branding over the 1980s.

This chapter will explore the reasons why the US television industry adopted branding over the 1980s and 1990s. It will examine the key changes that emerged over the cable/satellite era: not just the increased commercial success of cable television itself, but also the broader deregulatory policies of the 1980s, which had ramifications for the wider US media industries.[1] It will analyse how and why branding emerged within the particular industrial and economic context of cable television, looking at the examples of MTV and HBO, and the issues that arose when the national free-to-air networks attempted to adopt branding themselves in the 1980s and 1990s. In doing so, it will begin to draw out some of the characteristics of television branding and argue that it needs to be understood as much more than simply the increased use of marketing and publicity. Therefore, while the transformation of the Hollywood sign into the Fox logo is indicative of a shift towards branding, it is just one small part of a far larger picture of how and why branding was adopted in the US television industry.

Deregulation and cable television

Since 1955 US network television had been dominated by three broadcasters: NBC, CBS and ABC. The wavelength scarcity of analogue television, combined with regulation dating back to the 1950s, had protected this oligopoly and effectively prevented significant competition in television broadcasting. In the 1980s this was all to change. President Reagan's neo-liberal Republican government aimed to deregulate the telecommunications industry. Mark Fowler, appointed chairman of the Federal Communications Commission (FCC) in 1981 (to 1987), was keen to increase competition, and the deregulatory philosophy that he advocated would extend well beyond the length of his appointment and change the face of the US television industry. The biggest impact of the deregulatory approach to telecommunications that began in the 1980s was the breaking of the network oligopoly. The first threat to the networks came from cable services. Cable television originally emerged primarily as a retransmission service in the 1940s and 1950s for homes that could not receive television broadcasts through a roof-top antenna, and so developed initially more as a local community, rather than as a national, service. It was only in the 1970s and 1980s that cable began to develop as a programming service, facilitated significantly by developments in satellite technology that allowed local cable stations to be linked together as national (or global) services (see Mullen 2008).[2] So cable television began to emerge as a significant industry within a broader deregulatory climate.

As a subscription service, cable has largely been treated as an industry best served by the market (Banet-Weiser *et al.* 2007: 5–6). Although the FCC has at times regulated the franchise arrangements and price structures (see Mullen 2008), on the whole cable television has not been tied to the same extent as the national networks by public interest and ownership requirements. Hence, cable offered the opportunity for established media companies that would be barred from owning national networks to enter broadcasting. For example, the Hearst Corporation, a major magazine and newspaper publisher, launched the cable channels Lifetime and A&E in 1984 (Banet-Weiser *et al.* 2007: 130)[3] and Time Inc., another large magazine publisher, launched Home Box Office in 1972.

Even with the developments in satellite technology, these cable channels could not hope to compete with the reach of the free-to-air national networks. As a consequence, they focused on offering differentiated programme services to specialized niche audiences. This was important, as cable was funded by a combination of advertising and subscription, and so cable operators and networks had to persuade audiences that it was worth paying the extra subscription for their services and advertisers that they could offer valuable audience segments to justify the lower ratings that they gained than network television. As we shall go on to see, the characteristics of cable television as an industry made it particularly suited to the use of branding as a strategy.

'I want my MTV': launching a channel brand

A clear example of a cable network that functioned from its inception as a brand is MTV. MTV was launched on 1 August 1981 by Warner Amex Satellite Entertainment (WASE), a joint venture between American Express and Warner Communications (Tungate 2004). In 1983, Viacom formed a joint venture with WASE and Warner Communications and went on to buy a majority share in MTV Networks in 1985, which included the channels MTV, Nickelodeon, VH1 and Nick at Nite, purchasing the remaining interests the following year (Viacom 2008–9). MTV was characteristic of most cable ventures of the late 1970s and early 1980s in combining two key features that made branding particularly valuable: product differentiation and niche targeting. In terms of product differentiation, MTV was offering a service and a form of content not provided anywhere else on television – music videos transmitted in a form similar to music radio with VJs (video deejays) and playlists. In terms of niche targeting, MTV was specifically aimed at an up-market, youth audience of 15–34-year-olds, a demographic that did not include high viewers of network television and that was attractive to many of the companies that advertised on television. MTV's business strategy, therefore, was concerned with delivering to advertisers an attractive audience that the networks (who still dominated the market share at this time) could not provide. MTV thus accorded with the standard economic model of television broadcasting as a 'dual-product' market, with the first product being the programme service that is sold to audiences and the second being access to audiences that is sold to advertisers (Doyle 2002: 60). However, there was a third element to the economics of MTV. As a cable channel, MTV was also a product for cable operators.[4] In order to be successful MTV needed to persuade its audiences to pay the extra subscription to access its programmes, to persuade cable operators to carry its channel so as to be able to reach its audience and to persuade advertisers to buy airtime on its channel. From its launch, MTV used branding in order to achieve these aims.

To understand how MTV used branding in this context we need to think in a little more detail about what we are talking about when we use the term, 'brand'. As discussed in the Introduction, both Celia Lury and Adam Arvidsson argue that the brand is more than simply a design or logo added onto the surface of a product. Rather, they both claim that the brand functions as a meeting point between consumer and producer, what Lury (2004) refers to as an 'interface' and Arvidsson (2006: 8) terms a 'frame of action'. In both theorizations the brand as interface/frame manages the interactions between consumers, products and producers. Lury argues that the interface of the brand is not located in one place or time: 'Rather, like the interface of the Internet, it is distributed across a number of surfaces (of, for example, products and packaging), screens (television, computers, cinemas) or sites (retail outlets, advertising hoardings, and so on)' (2004: 50). In relation to the television channel, the brand is communicated to the viewer through programme production and acquisition, scheduling, on-screen advertising and promotion (including station IDs), off-screen advertising and promotion and ancillary products related to the channel and/or its programming. However, in order to offer a coherent frame of action, these different elements need to be unified and made visible to the viewer.

When MTV launched, the first image transmitted was doctored footage from the Apollo 11 moon landing. The sequence began with a close-up of the Apollo 11 rocket as a voice-over counted down to take-off, with the MTV logo overlaid in the bottom left-hand corner of the screen until the rocket took off. A rapidly edited montage then depicted Neil Armstrong jumping out of Apollo 11 onto the surface of the moon and planting a flag displaying the MTV logo as a voice-over proclaimed, 'Ladies and gentlemen. Rock and roll!' and a rock score faded up. The sequence ended with a close-up of the MTV logo with multiple colours and patterns fading and wiping across its surface, before cutting to the video for the Buggles track, *Video Killed the Radio Star*. From its very opening, therefore, MTV used design to communicate its identity to its audience. It took an irreverent swipe at the history and culture of the 'adult' generation. In doing so, it ironically equated the launch of MTV with man's first landing on the moon and marked out (literally by placing a flag) the space of MTV as other-worldy and distinctly different to network television. The MTV logo itself was created by a small company called Manhattan Design for only US$1,000 and was deliberately designed with its graffiti 'TV' to look primitive and cartoon-like, in contrast to the slick logos of larger corporations (Tungate 2004). This hip, irreverent attitude was carried over into the choice of the first song, which literalizes MTV's aim – to make music video, rather than radio, the destination for young viewers' consumption of music.

While the MTV logo communicated the identity and personality of MTV, this was reinforced through the opening promo and programme scheduling. This integration of content (the music videos) and promotional material (such as logos, idents and trailers) was reinforced through MTV's broadcast flow.[5] In addition to the seamless move from the opening promo to the MTV logo and into the first song (without any continuity announcement or other break between content and promotional material), the style and theme of the song and the promotional material are consistent, giving the whole channel a clear overall identity. For example, after the Buggles' song there is another promo that situates MTV as part of an evolution in human entertainment, literally combining the 'power of sight' and the 'power of sound'. This promo takes the theme of *Video Killed the Radio Star* and expands upon it, suggesting that MTV is part of a naturally evolving progression from the gramophone and radio to television and cable. This blurring of content (the music videos) and promotion was facilitated by the fact that MTV's programming was essentially a form of promotion for the records themselves.

McDowell and Batten (2005) argue that all television branding strategies have two facets, one that is audience-based and one that is advertiser-based. However, when it first launched, MTV also needed to be able to persuade cable operators to carry it as a channel if it was to reach a large enough audience to be attractive to advertisers. MTV could not just depend on constructing its brand on screen when it was only available to a small number of viewers in a restricted geographical area. To overcome this, MTV developed an innovative promotional campaign that it ran on free-to-air networks which was designed to mobilize viewers as advocates on behalf of the channel. The adverts included key pop stars of the time (from David Bowie to Mick Jagger, to Cyndi Lauper, to The Police) shouting directly out to the viewer, 'America … Call your cable company and say "I want my MTV!"'. The campaign's noisy, brash style complemented the irreverence of the channel's brand identity and reinforced the idea of MTV as a completely new form of television. But, more importantly, it attempted to instil in the viewer a sense of ownership and loyalty towards the channel. The advert proclaimed that MTV belonged to the youth of America and drew on the suggestion that US television was failing to provide them with *their* culture.

In view of this, when MTV launched, programming, scheduling, on-screen promotion and off-screen advertising all combined to present a coherent image, or brand personalization, of the channel. This brand image not only communicated a set of values to the viewer, but also explicitly acted as a frame of action, inciting the viewer to call their cable operator and demand *their* MTV. MTV fostered this sense of ownership and belonging in its viewers through the development of events, such as the MTV Video Music Awards that launched in 1984, where viewers voted for each award, and competitions, where the prizes were often personal meetings with key pop stars of the period. The intention of these different facets of MTV's brand was to position MTV as a destination for its target audience and a central part of their everyday lives. This was important, not only to attract viewers to the channel, but also to attract advertisers. Before the channel launched, researchers interviewed 600 14–34-year-olds and studied the lifestyle of this demographic in order to ascertain 'how the network should "feel"'(Robinson 1984: S6). While some mainstream advertisers were anxious about the negative impact of associating their products with the sex, drugs and rock and roll of MTV's output, MTV's sales literature emphasized that it could deliver that 'Elusive [audience of] … young upscale males and females' (cited in Billard 1983: 51). MTV's ability to attract advertiser revenue depended on being able to persuade advertisers that it 'got' this audience and could place their products seamlessly into an environment that spoke to them.[6] Paul

Temporal argues that advertisers believe that MTV knows its audience: 'Young people connect with and feel part of MTV, to the point that they are identified as the "MTV Generation" or "MTV Nation"' (2008: 26).

Temporal's comments point to the way in which the interface of the brand is not simply constructed through the creative activities of brand managers, marketers, designers and executives, but also through other forms of communication that are more or less under the control of the broadcaster, such as employees, press and viewer activity. For MTV, the brand functions as an interface not just between MTV and its viewers and advertisers, but also between MTV and its employees. John Thornton Caldwell demonstrates how employees increasingly have to brand themselves in relation to potential employers in order to gain work and how corporations use trade stories and production gossip as a form of marketing (2008: 58–59). If we look at interviews with MTV personnel in trade magazines, we can see how the MTV brand functions as an interface for the ways in which the corporation's employees talk about their work. For example, in an article in the trade magazine *Brandweek* Brian Graden (President of Entertainment at MTV and VH1) asserted the importance of research into the youth audience in the development of the MTV brand while simultaneously arguing that the brand imbues the very DNA of MTV staff: 'We're very engrossed in research here and what our audience likes and how they view the world. … Then, at a point, you walk into the other world and forget about it because it's in your DNA and you do your work' (cited in Ebenkamp 2003). This balance between insisting that the brand is based on solid research and that its values are also embodied by its staff is reiterated by Brent Hansen (President of Creative and Editor-in-Chief at MTV Networks International 2003–6) in discussing the age gap between MTV's employees and its audience in an article in *Brandchannel.* He states, 'We don't want a bunch of people my age who are programming channels. … We want people who are actively participating in those worlds. If you don't have that relevant point of view, you end up being more like a broadcaster, than like a niche channel' (cited in Rusch 2004). Similarly, an article in *Advertising Age* on MTV's digital strategy is keen to assert that the network's head of digital media, Jason Hirschhorn, not only has the right qualifications for the job, but also 'gets' the brand. He is described as a 'self-professed fan of everything from Oprah to Arctic Monkeys – "you can't pigeon-hole me," he says' (cited in Klaassen 2006b). Later in the same article, Trevor Kaufman, CEO of interactive firm Schematic, describes Hirschhorn as part of a generation of executives who 'live the digital-media lifestyle – Jason goes home and plays video games. And they're saying "here are all the places I like to spend my time; why isn't MTV there and how can we get it there?"' (ibid.). These articles profess that the best executives embody the values of their employer's brand in their work and personal lives. And the brand here is not simply positioned as the corporation's, but also as the viewer's, so that the emphasis is on asserting not only that the executive gets the audience, just like the MTV brand does, but also on proclaiming that there is no boundary between the executive, the brand and the audience – they all embody the same values and experiences. Branding becomes, then, a frame through which industry discourse about its own working practices and values is articulated. It imbues all elements of production – not just product development, launch and promotion, but also the labour of workers and the ways in which they talk about that labour. By the same token, industry talk, as Caldwell (2008) argues, becomes a form of promotion framed by the interface of the brand.

Deregulation and the new 'network': Fox

The rise of cable had a significant impact on the national networks. Between 1980 and 1990 the level of US homes subscribing to cable rose from 19.9 per cent to 65.4 per cent (Lotz 2007a: 53). At the same time the national networks saw their share decline from over 90 per cent in the 1960s and 1970s to around 60 per cent by the mid-1980s (Caldwell 1995: 11). However, the threat to the networks did not just come from cable, but also from Fox, the first network to adopt the branding strategies pioneered in cable.[7] Fox was the first new network for 30 years and was launched by Rupert Murdoch's News Corporation in 1986, significantly aided by the gradual relaxation of the rules pertaining to media ownership. Murdoch based Fox on the Metromedia group of independent stations that he purchased in 1985 and also utilized both the name and the infrastructure of the Hollywood studio, 20th Century Fox, purchased in the same year. Many saw it as inauspicious to attempt to launch a new network when the old incumbents were struggling for the first time in 30 years. Yet, Fox was different from the three extant networks right from the beginning.

Over the first half of the 1980s the number of independent US television stations rose from 160 to 275 (Farber 1987: 32), fuelled in part by the FCC's abolition of anti-trafficking rules in station sales and the common perception that broadcasting was a licence to print money (Kompare 2005: 132). These 'indies' provided an additional market for syndicated programming, but also a site for non-network first-run programming, such as *Wheel of Fortune* (1983–), which performed particularly well. At the same time network advertising rates had increased by 261 per cent to support increased programme costs (Farber 1987: 32). The aim of Fox was to use the Metromedia group (the largest group of independent stations) as the basis for a new national network that would woo disgruntled advertisers from the big three networks. Fox aimed to do this through a strategy of niche targeting and counter-programming. Rather than attempting to appeal to the broad mass audiences of the national networks, Fox adopted the niche targeting strategy of cable television by appealing to a young urban demographic. As Betsy Tobin describes:

> Fox sought the disaffiliated network viewer: those who prefer network viewing to any other type but were not being served by the big three. By pinpointing network weaknesses – lack of diversity, copycat rivalry, knee-jerk cancellation policies – and identifying demographic gaps, Fox built its own desired profile: young males aged 18–49 and disaffiliated viewers. It developed a strategy of counter-programming, movies and children's programmes, and building a network of local station affiliates clustered according to demographic profiles. Perhaps more importantly, it made programmes that were sufficiently different to attract viewers.
>
> (Tobin 1990: 16)

From the very beginning, then, Fox aimed to be distinctive from the established networks. It launched with programming on Saturday and Sunday nights, traditionally weak nights for its core demographic of 18–49-year-olds on network television.[8] After its Saturday line-up struggled in its first season it shifted to a more male-oriented line-up (including the reality television shows *C.O.P.S.* (1989–) and *Totally Hidden Video* (1989–92)) and saw its audience share increase by 12 points (Tobin 1990: 17). This audience was significant not just because the networks struggled to appeal to it, but also because research showed that these viewers were more likely to buy the kinds of products advertised on television. As the mass audiences of the national networks began to decline, advertisers could no longer assume that advertising on the networks would bring them the extensive reach offered in the 1960s and 1970s. At the same time, more accurate audience measurement enabled networks and advertisers to identify which demographic segments of the audience were watching.[9] Fox actively promoted the importance of the demographic make-up of an audience to advertisers and journalists in order to convince advertisers that it was more valuable to target the right audience for their product. They created a videotape about their core 'Generation X' demographic which they gave to advertisers in order to sell the significance and value of this target market (Kimmel 2004: 117).

The attempt to differentiate itself from the national networks also emerged in the promotional activities surrounding Fox. Initially the network was going to be named the 'Fox Broadcasting Company' (FBC) copying the acronyms of the big three networks, NBC, CBS and ABC. However, Chiat\Day, the advertising house that Fox hired to oversee the initial launch and promotion of the network, argued that this name down-played one of the network's biggest assets – the 20th Century Fox brand. Chiat\Day advised the network to take advantage of the audience's knowledge of the Fox brand and to use the iconic searchlights from 20th Century Fox as its logo. The

Fox network can thus be understood as a brand extension, utilizing the audience's long-standing association with 20th Century Fox as a producer of content for both television and cinema. Significantly, this also further contributed to the differentiation of the Fox network from the big three, as anti-monopoly regulations had prevented Hollywood studios from owning broadcast networks.

As we saw at the start of this chapter, this association was cemented in a publicity stunt timed to coincide with the launch of the network's first full evenings of television, in which the famous Hollywood sign was temporarily transformed into the Fox logo. Indeed, Fox spent more than US$13 million in advertising and promoting its new network. In order to encourage audiences to try out the new network Fox placed spot advertisements on rock radio stations, in youth-orientated magazines and on cable networks such as MTV (Davies 1997b: S32). These were sites targeted at Fox's key demographic, as well as being ones that shared the brand image that Fox was attempting to construct. Fox's then Head of Advertising and Promotion, Sandy Gunshaw, explains that they 'didn't try to sell the individual shows; we tried to put an umbrella over them' (cited in Davies 1997b: S32). In essence then, the approach taken by Gunshaw was to construct a brand identity for the network rather than simply concentrating on promoting specific programmes. One early example involved a doctored photograph of Jim and Tammy Faye Bakker. The Bakkers established the Christian cable channel the PTL Television Network in 1977, becoming America's most high-profile evangelists, but succumbing to scandal in 1987 when Jim Bakker was forced to resign amid allegations of fraud, embezzlement and sexual misconduct (Heard 1986: 50–51 and Schmidt 1987: 8). Fox produced posters with images of the Bakkers accompanied by the tagline 'Now that they are gone, we are the funniest thing on television'. The campaign epitomized Fox's brand image of being 'distinctive, different, alternative, bold, and brazen … well crafted and clever' (Sherwood 1997: S12).

In the early 1990s, the emphasis on constructing a clear brand identity for Fox was extended to the network's affiliated stations. In the USA it was common practice for local stations to be designated by call signs made up of four letters and a location, such as WBTV-TV in Charlotte, North Carolina. Each of Fox's affiliated stations, therefore, had its own station call signs and logos which had often been in use for a long period of time. In the 1991–92 season Fox began a campaign to persuade its affiliates to change their call sign to Fox, followed by the number that the station transmitted on, and to use the Fox name in all aspects of their promotion. For Fox, the aim was to 'cement a permanent image of the network in the public mind' (Kimmel 2004: 112). WNYW-TV, Channel 5, was the first affiliate to change its name (to Fox5) (Davies 1997b: S32). While many of the local stations were sceptical about this 'Foxification' of their identities, most followed suit after those that tried it found the results to be impressive (Kimmel 2004: 113).[10]

In 1994 NBC followed suit, with all its owned and operated local stations adopting NBC followed by the channel number as their call sign and utilizing a consistent logo (Caldwell 2008: 248–49).

Fox also used its programming to construct its brand identity. Its initial Sunday night line-up started on 5 April 1987 with *Married ... With Children* (1987–97, a sitcom trailed as 'not the Cosbys') and *The Tracey Ullman Show* (1987–90, a talk and sketch series showcasing the British pop star), while *21 Jump Street* (1987–91, an action-adventure about a teenage undercover cop, starring Johnny Depp), *Mr President* (1987–88, a dramatic comedy) and *Duet* (1987–89, a romantic comedy) joined the line-up on 3 May 1987. Press response indicated that Fox's initial line-up was seen as more risky and racy than those of the big three networks, with a clearer focus on younger and more upscale viewers. This programming attitude was perhaps exemplified by Fox's first global hit, *The Simpsons* (1990–), which premiered on 14 January 1990, reinvigorated the adult animation genre and caused controversy in its depiction of American family life (see Gray 2005).

However, arguably Fox's purchase of the rights to the National Football League (NFL) National Football Conference (NFC) franchise on 17 December 1993 was more significant in the network's ability to compete directly with the big three.[11] Fox bought the rights to NFC from the NFL for US$1.58 billion, stripping CBS of football for the first time in 38 years. To many, this seemed like a strange move by the new network, which did not have a news or sports division. However, News Corporation (which owned Fox) had successfully used sports rights to build its British satellite service, BSkyB, and understood that sport could act as publicity to raise Fox's profile and bring a new and loyal audience base (see Chapter 3). The NFC franchise (and the other sporting events that the network subsequently bought the rights to, such as baseball and hockey) appealed directly to Fox's target audience of young males, but also increased the network's reputation amongst advertisers and independent channels, and Fox subsequently saw a rise in its number of affiliates, many of whom jumped from CBS to Fox (Caldwell 2008: 249; Holt 2003: 19).[12] However, Fox also incorporated its sports coverage into its broader brand identity using the logo: 'Same game, new attitude'. It covered sports as entertainment and innovated with technology, including placing microphones in the stands and around the pitch (such as in bats and on the bases in its baseball coverage). This approach to sport contributed to the network's brand identity as being innovative, risky and cutting edge (see Davies 1997a: S16, S36).

The adoption by Fox, as the first new network for 30 years, of branding strategies initially used by cable epitomized the shifts that were taking place in the US television landscape over the 1980s and 1990s. Rather than attempting to emulate the mass broadcasting strategies of the big three networks, Fox adopted elements of the niche targeting of cable. However, unlike a cable network, Fox was free to air and aimed to compete with the national networks by appealing to an audience segment that was both unsatisfied with network programming and attractive to advertisers. As with the cable channels that launched in the 1970s and 1980s, Fox turned to branding for a number of reasons. First, as we saw with MTV, brands support product differentiation. From the beginning, Fox was constructed as an alternative to the big three and the network used promotion, advertising and programming to construct an identity that was clearly differentiated from the established networks. Second, brands function to manage the relationships between consumers, producers and products. Again, Fox had a clear target audience that it intended to attract and constructed an identity for the network overall that was designed to appeal directly to that audience demographic. This was not only to attract audiences to the network, but also to create loyalty and a sense of belonging between the network and its audience. As Jonathan Davies states:

> The concept of creating an image for the network as a whole – something no broadcaster had done up to that point – is reflected in audience behaviour that Fox executives love to point out. The network has such a strong brand identity that, according to researchers, viewers will say, 'Let's watch Fox', even when they don't know what's on.
>
> (Davies 1997b: S32)

Fox used branding to appeal to, and construct a loyal relationship with, a defined demographic through the construction of a clear brand identity for the network that imbued all aspects of the network's activities, from promotion and marketing to programme production and the activities of affiliates. Fox also utilized its position within the larger News Corporation conglomerate by drawing on the existing brand value of 20th Century Fox and adopting strategies such as purchasing sports rights that had been used successfully by BSkyB in the UK. As Walter McDowell and Alan Batten argue, 'Fox became the first broadcast network to stand for something in the minds of its audiences. Its youthful, risky, irreverent style of program content set the stage for the industry's move to brand marketing' (2005: 4).

The big three networks turn to branding

By the mid-1990s the three long-standing national networks (NBC, CBS and ABC) were starting to adopt similar brand strategies. Audience ratings had fallen so significantly that they could no longer attract the same mass audiences as before. So they also began to adopt some of the niche strategies of cable channels and netlets like Fox. In the mid-1990s all the big three networks embarked on rebranding campaigns. As we saw above, NBC adopted Fox's strategy of renaming its local stations to carry the NBC name. It also persuaded programme producers to carry the NBC logo within their programmes (rather than simply placing them within the junctions between programmes) in order to tie programming directly to the network (Caldwell 2008: 249). Both of these changes were part of a larger rebranding of the network that took place over the 1994–95 season and that was publicly announced in NBC's *Today Show* (1952–) in an item that previewed the new corporate identity for the network. Caldwell discusses the way in which NBC's promotion of this rebranding campaign evidenced a shift in the 'aesthetic ways that the major networks did business' (2008: 250). Promoted as a media event in its own right, the campaign positioned NBC as cutting edge, innovative, hip and 'bad'. As Caldwell argues, 'In essence, NBC had finally stopped ignoring its cable competitors and now earnestly emulated Viacom/MTV's house style – an approach that featured its ever-mutating brand logo as a persistent part of each day's programming' (Caldwell 2008: 251).[13]

NBC's rebranding campaign also extended to its programming and in particular its Thursday night line-up. Thursday nights are particularly important for network television, typically producing half of network revenues, and had long been an important night for NBC as the slot in which it screened signature shows such as *Hill Street Blues* (1981–87), *Cheers* (1982–93), *The Cosby Show* (1984–92) and *Seinfeld* (1990–98) (San Martin 2003: 32). In the 1980s NBC branded its Thursday evenings as 'the best night of television on television' (see Thompson 1997). In 1994 NBC launched new Thursday night sitcom *Friends* (1994–2004) to run alongside its hit series *Seinfeld*. This new acquisition evidenced a shift from programmes that placed actors from under-represented groups into shows with universal themes of family and friendship (such as *The Cosby Show*, with its African-American family, and *Golden Girls* (1985–92), with its older female cast) to a line-up more specifically targeted at an upmarket, urban and youthful demographic. Hence, the family sitcom of *The Cosby Show* was replaced by the pseudo-family of white, middle-class twenty-somethings in *Friends*. The new Thursday night line-up of sitcoms *Mad About You* (1992–99), *Friends*, *Seinfeld* and *Madman of the People* (1994–95) was promoted with a campaign that used the slogan 'Must See TV' (see for example, *TV Guide*, 29 September 1994, pp.196–97). Nancy San Martin (2003) argues that you can read this block of programming (particularly when *Madmen of the People* was replaced by *ER* (1994–2005) in 1995) as a single entity with shared characteristics and a normalizing narrative drive. However, this line-up also complemented the network's new edgier image. As Amanda Lotz argues of this period in NBC's history:

> During these years NBC more openly branded itself as the network of 'upscale,' college-educated, eighteen- to forty-nine-year-old viewers. Serving as president of entertainment from 1991–98, Warren Littlefield was particularly responsible for the brand of entertainment

> that came to be known as 'must-see TV.' The network's demographic specificity is most apparent in the various series scheduled in the Thursday sitcom block during the second cycle. With varying success, the network repeatedly told stories about young, affluent, white urbanites who lived in a world curiously devoid of people different from themselves.
>
> (Lotz 2007b: 270–71)

As with Fox then, NBC's adoption of branding was tied to the move towards focusing more specifically on demographics. Ironically for NBC in terms of its 'Must See TV' line-up this led to a distinct loss of diversity compared to its 1980s' Thursday night programming. Similarly, although Fox had courted the African-American audience early on, it soon abandoned this in order to focus more specifically on the advertisers' favoured urban, upscale, 18–49 demographic (Zook 1999).

NBC's adoption of branding in order to target the valued 18–49 urban, educated demographic was soon emulated by the other networks, perhaps most famously with ABC's 'yellow' campaign launched in 1997. Indeed, this demographic became so important that in 1996 Alan Sternfeld, senior vice president of programme planning and scheduling at ABC, stated that, 'The economic reality has led programmers to the head-scratching world of all-18–49-all-the-time … Advertisers are not paying for many viewers beyond that' (Stanley 1996). Thus, as Caldwell (2008: 27–29) argues, these rebranding campaigns can be understood as both appealing to specific audience groups and convincing affiliates and advertisers that the network has the right kind of identity to appeal to the audiences that they want to attract. As with NBC, ABC's campaign constructed a new look for the network that was promoted on and off screen. ABC visually rebranded itself using the colour yellow in all on- and off-air marketing, including idents and posters with slogans mocking the critical devaluation of television, such as 'Books are overrated' and 'Don't worry, you've got billions of brain cells' (see Caldwell 2008: 248), that are resonant of the edgy and 'bad' aesthetic aimed for by both Fox and NBC. The campaign was modified for the 1998–99 season after making little difference to the network's ailing profits (ABC's share of the up-front market was projected to be down by US$1.5–1.6 million dollars in the summer of 1998; see Elliott 1998). The changes included warmer and less ironic slogans with more inclusive phrases, such as 'We love TV' and 'You're breathing. We're broadcasting. Let's get together' (Elliott 1998). There were also a higher number of series-specific taglines that tied the campaign to its programming, such as print ads for *NYPD Blue* (1993–2005), which continued the ironic tone of the campaign with the tagline 'They can. You can't. That's cool' (Ross 1997), and the campaign was extended throughout the design of the interstitials to make it a key component of watching the channel (Sharkey 1998). The change in ABC's yellow campaign can also be tied to the purchase of the company by Disney in 1996, with the softening of the taglines better reflecting the extant family-focused brand identity of the Disney Corporation.

However, the ABC yellow campaign was controversial when it launched, with a number of commentators claiming that such branding was inappropriate for the major US networks. *Advertising Age* claimed that, while channel branding was relatively easy for niche cable channels, it was a far less relevant strategy for the networks:

> ABC, CBS and NBC (excluding Fox for the moment) are multi-tiered, multi-daypart programming operations, mixing shows for homebodies in the morning and daytime hours, segueing into late-afternoon news shows and, then, into the all-important primetime fare. That variety makes the Big 3 the Big 3, and very difficult to 'brand' image-wise. Efforts by the major broadcast networks to do so have only sporadically met with any success. NBC was able to build an image campaign around its Thursday primetime comedy lineup, branding it 'Must See TV.' But the departure of *Seinfeld* has pretty much turned that effort on its ear. Fox, meanwhile, branded itself in its early days as a primetime programming force for young urban adults. But once Fox became a full-fledged member of the Big 4, with a full programming slate including Sunday afternoon football, it lost that narrow focus. In the end, an overall brand isn't as important as individual shows. Develop quality programming and promote it effectively, and there will be no need to turn *yellow* with envy over a clever brand image.
>
> (Anon. 1998)

There are two assumptions made in this argument: that branding only works for highly targeted and differentiated niche cable channels; and that viewers watch programmes not channels. Thus, even at the height of the 'branding boom' in the US television industry (see McDowell and Batten 2005: 7–8), there was scepticism within the trade press about the value of channel branding for the major networks.

'It's not TV. It's HBO': branding quality

By contrast, it has been argued that branding is particularly valuable within the first-order commodity relations that characterize subscription and pay-per-view services, where viewers pay directly for programmes that are not funded by the sale of airtime for advertising (Rogers *et al.* 2002). As we have seen, a primary function of the interface of the brand is to manage the relationship between the consumer and the producer by creating and conveying 'a close "fit" between the consumer's own physical and psychological needs and the brand's functional attributes and symbolic values' (Hankinson and Cowking 1993: 10). While this is of value to the second-order commodity relations of basic cable and free-to-air network television, when a viewer is paying a premium directly for a service (as in first-order commodity relations), then establishing and maintaining this fit becomes central. For Rogers, Epstein and Reeves, the premium subscription cable channel HBO is exemplary of the increasing significance of first-order commodity relations in the digital era. HBO was launched by Time Inc. in 1972 as a cable service mainly screening sports events and theatrical films. In 1975 HBO became the first subscription cable network to be offered via satellite, screening the 'thriller in Manila' fight between Muhammad Ali and Joe Frazier that cemented the channel's reputation as the home of televised boxing. In 1977 HBO won a battle with the FCC that enabled it to transmit movies before they were screened by the networks and this became a key aspect of its brand identity. However, other premium cable movie channels emerged over the late 1970s, such as Showtime, which launched in 1976, offering competition to HBO. In 1980, Time Inc. launched Cinemax as a movie-only channel in order to allow HBO to develop as more of a mixed-programme channel offering movies, premium sports, imported dramas and documentaries not found on the networks and original programming. In 1985, following the 1984 Cable Act, HBO became the first cable network to scramble its signals regularly in order to prevent viewers accessing its programmes without paying its subscription rates, solidifying its position as a premium pay-per-view service.

Over the 1980s HBO's strategy focused upon increasing its production of original programming (see Rogers *et al.* 2002 and Metz 2004), particularly under HBO Chairman and CEO Michael Fuchs (1984–95). As more cable movie channels emerged and home video offered an alternative means of viewing movies on television HBO attempted to use original programming as a form of product differentiation from other movie channels, but also from the national networks. As a subscription channel, HBO was not subject to the same restrictions concerning representations of sex, violence and bad language as the national networks, which enabled HBO to develop more edgy and controversial content. This was targeted at a demographic of affluent, educated 18–34-year-old males whom the national networks struggled to attract. When Jeffrey L. Bewkes took over as CEO in 1995 he extended this strategy by producing programmes that not only contained explicit sex, violence and bad language, but that also had an aura of prestige and quality (Rogers *et al.* 2002: 51). The most commented upon aspect of HBO's shift towards constructing its brand as the home of quality television was its development of prestige original dramas that took 'the threads of what have been different about HBO's previously original programmes – sexuality, graphic violence, profanity – and put them in a context where they all work together to become a unique and distinctive product' (Rogers *et al.* 2002: 53). Series such as *The Sopranos* (1999–2007), *Six Feet Under* (2001–5), *Oz* (1997–2003) and *Sex and the City* (1998–2004) all tackled adult themes, such as sex, violence, morality and death in an explicit manner that would be difficult to achieve within the FCC guidelines for the national networks. Yet, in each case, such representations were not simply additional titillation for the viewer, but rather interwoven into the dramatic fabric of each series in order to allow the drama to explore its themes in a rich, textured and believable manner.[14]

HBO also developed this aura of quality around its other programming. Over the 1980s HBO had begun to co-invest in Hollywood movie production and to produce its own films. As well as garnering Emmys and critical acclaim for its original television series, 11 of the 15 movies nominated for Emmys between 1999 and 2002 came from HBO and HBO won the Emmy for Best Movie nine times between 1992 and 2002 (Haley 2002: 10A). HBO also added prestige to its televising of sports events with a portfolio of authored sports magazine programmes and documentaries that Metz claims 'represent the only critical examination of sports in American life on American television' (2004: 1113). Furthermore, in the early 2000s HBO attempted to establish itself as 'the industry standard in documentaries' (Metz 2004: 1113) and the home for new documentary talent (Haley 2002: 14A), doubling its production of original documentaries. As a result, HBO's brand of 'quality' was extended across the range of programmes that it screened and produced.

HBO communicated this shift through the development of a branding strategy coordinated around the tagline, 'It's not TV. It's HBO'. This now-famous line was developed by the agency BBDO and aimed to persuade viewers that HBO programmes were worth the price of their costly premium subscription.[15] The tag-line drew on the channel's reputation for screening first-runs of movies on television – content that was not 'TV' – as well as its attempt to signal its difference from the national networks, and was accompanied by an on- and off-screen image campaign. This included an Emmy-award-winning promo in which anthropologist Jane Goodall was depicted pondering the strange behaviour of the chimps that she was observing in the jungle, which were acting out scenes from famous films, such as *The Godfather* (1972) and *Forrest Gump* (1994). The promo ended with Goodall leaving her work to tune into *Braveheart* (1995) on HBO as the camera cut back to reveal a pack of chimps watching with her through the window of her jungle hut and the caption 'Jane Goodall, HBO viewer since 1978' faded up. The promo asserts the distinction of HBO in two ways. First, it implies that famous and learned personalities such as Jane Goodall are subscribers to HBO. Second, it suggests that even chimps could be elevated and educated by watching HBO films. Over and above this, it invites identification from cinephiles – those who are able to identify which films the chimps are re-enacting over the course of the advert. Indeed, there is an example of this campaign on YouTube, where a viewer has left a comment that simply lists the films cited by the chimps.[16]

In 1999, as the channel's reputation for original quality programming began to develop, HBO shifted its promotional strategy. As Eric Kessler, HBO's executive vice president for marketing, explained in 2001:

> We did the image advertising [such as the Goodall promo] for three years, as much as six or eight commercials. ... We stopped doing that about two years ago because the programming so clearly represented what we were about. When shows like *The Sopranos* and *Sex and the City* became pop-culture phenomena, became cultural icons, we realized the programming itself clearly presented what the line was about, so all we needed to do was show a promo for *The Sopranos* and end with, 'It's Not Just TV, It's HBO' [sic]. So we're really just applying the line to all our program advertising. ... It has become so ingrained in the marketplace and people are so well aware of it that it's something we will certainly continue to use. ... It's a line that we think perfectly articulates the position of the network.
>
> (cited in Henrickson 2001: 20)

This quotation from Kessler is particularly revealing about the way in which HBO's brand as the home of quality television developed. Initially, the network called on an ad agency to develop the tagline and produce promotional material that communicated its values and meanings to the audience. While the chimp promos do make reference to HBO programming in terms of the films quoted, the emphasis is on promoting the *experience* of watching movies on HBO and attaching an aura of distinction to that in order to encourage subscribers. By 2001, HBO's original programming had come to stand in for the brand, so that *The Sopranos* itself embodied the slogan 'It's not TV. It's HBO'.

The tying of HBO's original programming to its brand identity was reinforced through the coverage that HBO received in the press over the late 1990s and early 2000s. Much of the rhetoric of the critical reception towards HBO's programming in this period explicitly saw the channel itself as central to the success of its programmes in four ways. First, because the channel produces fewer programmes than the national networks, it can afford to spend more on production budgets. Second, HBO is seen as a risk taker, prepared to take a chance on programmes that other networks would flee from. Third, HBO is seen to give its writers and directors a free rein to develop their material without commercial interference. Fourth, the channel is freed from having to pander to the demands of the advertiser or worry too extensively about ratings, allowing it to develop content directly for its audience (see for example, Berger 1997 and Peterson 2002). As with the case of MTV, above, such media criticism constructs a brand identity for the network that speaks not just to the viewer but also to the industry. David Finnigan cites the publicity surrounding Tom Hanks's 1998 mini-series, *From the Earth to the Moon*, as showcasing HBO 'as a place where creative people could go and do solid, decidedly different work, with far fewer compromises than the typical TV or studio atmosphere' (2001). Chris Albrecht claims that, before the positive critical response to its original programming of the late 1990s, 'we never had people coming to us and say "We want to work on HBO."', but that, since, writers, directors and stars specifically want to work with HBO (cited in Finnigan 2001). At the same time, the association of big name stars, writers and directors with HBO reinforces the broader brand image with consumers and suggests that this is a channel associated with truly original, creative, programming, unconstrained by commercial pressures.[17]

Such publicity has the additional benefit of being free and, surprisingly, despite a number of high profile ad campaigns for its original programmes (such as an extensive poster campaign across New York for the second season of *The Sopranos*), HBO's total media spend decreased over the period in which its brand identity as the home of original programming took off, falling from US$109.6 million in 1997 before the launch of *Sex and the City* to $65.2 million at the time of the second season of *The Sopranos* in 2000 (Finnigan 2001). Thus, over the second half of the 1990s HBO developed a brand identity as the home of quality television in the USA that drew on a wide range of its programming but was centred on the shift towards producing adult, edgy, authored and high-budget original drama series. While the brand identity was initially constructed through the promotional efforts of HBO itself, and then increasingly depended on these signature shows to stand in for the network, it also significantly depended upon critical acclaim within the media more broadly to support its claim to be the home for creative talent.

Avi Santo (2008) argues that the differences between HBO and the free-to-air networks have perhaps been overstated. For example, HBO used the Sunday night schedules to place its new drama series, aping Fox's strategy of targeting a night that has traditionally been seen as a weak point in the schedules of the national networks. By 2000, HBO had enough original series to run for the entire year on Sunday nights. Repeats were then scheduled at regular points through the week to enable alternate points at which viewers could access their programmes of choice. HBO used scheduling in this way to tie a range of programmes to its own brand identity. As Haley argues, 'HBO promoted an appointment with an evening, rather than a particular programme' (2002: 8A), a strategy that Santo claims was borrowed from network television campaigns, such as NBC's 'Must See Thursday'.

However, the different economics of network and subscription television do alter their use of branding. Central for HBO was that it did not have to depend on advertiser funding. Rather its aim was to create a programming mix that would be valuable enough for audiences to be prepared to pay the additional subscription for its service. While both HBO and NBC used branding to promote the difference of their programming slates, NBC (and the other free-to-air networks) also needed programmes that generated significant ratings to attract advertisers. It is this funding based on individual programme ratings that is arguably behind the criticism by the trade press of network branding strategies. After all, it is only in the cable television market that the channel emerges as a product itself, whether for sale to cable operators (as in the example of MTV) or for sale directly to viewers (as in the example of HBO). It is unsurprising, therefore, that channel branding should be seen as most valuable and appropriate in those markets where the channel itself functions most overtly as a product.

However, since the mid-2000s the future of HBO's channel brand identity has come under question in the face of the ending of a number of its signature shows, the increasing presence of similar, edgy, adult, quality content on other premium and free-to-air networks and the syndication of HBO's programming by basic cable and national networks. Each of these areas indicates the difficulty for television channel brand identities in managing the relationship between the channel brand and the programming that it airs. Indeed, much of HBO's content carries brand associations outside the channel – whether that of a Hollywood star, studio or director, or that of a major sports personality, team or league. While HBO's own brand identity can benefit from being associated with such brands, at the same time, it cannot risk becoming too dependent on external content that could be poached by a competitor. Therefore, HBO's move towards original programming could be seen as an attempt to construct a brand identity over which it has more control.

However, when Chris Albrecht became CEO and chairman of HBO in 2002, he focused specifically on moving HBO into theatrical film, home video, syndication and other non-television outlets. Such non-subscription revenue was important to HBO's financial future as the growth in subscribers had slowed over the previous few years. Writing in 2004, Higgins and Romano argued that HBO 'is now dependent on businesses like DVD sales and theatrical movies for 20% of its revenues' (2004: 6). Chris Albrecht argued in 2002 that HBO was looking towards syndication for its potential to be both 'revenue and awareness producing' (cited in Haley 2002: 18A). As Kathy Haley argues, the extension of HBO's programming beyond its cable channels is valuable 'not only to boost revenue, but to expose the HBO brand to non-subscribers' (2002: 4A). However, although the extension of the HBO brand beyond the subscription network might help to generate new subscribers, it also has the potential to undermine HBO's brand identity itself.

Thus, the economic demands on HBO as a media business that combines production, distribution and exhibition can run counter to the demands of

HBO's channel brand (see Kelso 2008). For example, in October 1990, HBO Independent Productions (HBOIP) was set up to develop original series for broadcast and cable channels in order to exploit the reputation within the industry that HBO had built up for successfully launching new comedic talent (Santo 2008: 22–23). HBOIP has produced hit programming for Fox, CBS and ABC (Santo 2008: 23 and Peterson 2002), potentially contributing to the broader dilution of HBO's brand as the home of quality US television. As Avi Santo (2008: 20) argues, there is a central contradiction for HBO between affirming the exclusivity of the aura of quality around its brand and the need to generate greater numbers of subscribers and to create revenue from syndication and merchandising. The danger for HBO is that the more that it makes its programmes available beyond the bounds of its pay-channels, the more it undermines the branding of those channels as the exclusive site of quality television. Since its production of *Dream On* (1990–96), HBO has regularly simultaneously shot both edgy and 'clean' versions of its programming in order to facilitate syndication (*Dream On* was syndicated on Fox, Santo 2008: 23). When an HBO programme is syndicated elsewhere, the brand values of the programme and its association with HBO's own brand of exclusive quality can be co-opted by the syndicating channel. For example, A&E's executive vice president justified its purchase of the rights to *The Sopranos* from HBO for US$2.5 million an episode by claiming that, '*The Sopranos* speaks so eloquently to what A&E is all about. … That show will be the most eloquent expression of what our brand stands for' (cited in Anon. 2006b).

Furthermore, as I have argued elsewhere (Johnson 2007), not only can programmes contribute to the brand equity of more than one corporation, they can also function as brands in their own right. For example, *The Sopranos* consists not only of the original television series, but also of DVD box sets with a range of additional material, a website, online games, ancillary merchandise such as clothing and household items, food and books. Constructing *The Sopranos* as a brand that frames consumers' interactions with these different products supports the strategy of generating as much revenue as possible from one media product.[18] As we shall examine in more detail in Chapter 2, the increase in media conglomeration and the rise of new digital technologies over the past 15 years have made the development of programme brands an increasingly important aspect of the US television industry. As the major conglomerates that now own the cable and national networks in the USA depend upon the exploitation of their content across multiple revenue streams in order to generate profits, programmes themselves are increasingly constructed as brands extended across a number of different products.

Conclusions

Branding was initially adopted as a central strategy in the US television industry by cable networks to support product differentiation and niche targeting. Cable networks such as MTV were developed and promoted with specific brand values communicated to viewers through programming and promotion in order to position the network as a central part of the viewers' lives and identities. Here, branding functioned as a frame of action or interface to manage not just the interactions between viewers, the channel and its producers, but also the relationships of the network with its advertisers, cable operators and employees. When the Fox network launched in 1986 it adopted many of the strategies of cable networks such as MTV, similarly using branding to differentiate itself from the established networks and to communicate its identity to and manage its relationships with viewers, advertisers and affiliates.

By the mid-1990s the big three networks were following suit, as part of a broader shift within the industry to target an advertiser-friendly, young, upmarket and urban demographic. Yet, the industry trade press was sceptical of the value of branding for the national networks. Central here is the argument that, while channel branding might be suitable for niche cable channels, for the national networks offering a range of different forms of programming, success depends on the quality of the programme mix, rather than the construction of a differentiated brand identity. This argument is somewhat complicated by the example of HBO, which demonstrated how a channel could construct an identity that extended across a range of different forms of programming (from original drama, to sports, to documentary). However, the economics of HBO are quite different to those of the national networks, suggesting that it is in the context of the cable television industry, where channels emerge as products in themselves, that channel branding is most valuable.

Yet, even in the context of cable television, the relationship between a channel's brand identity and the programming that it airs is complex. HBO's attempts to increase revenue from its programming in the face of declining revenue from channel subscriptions threatened the values upon which its channel brand identity had been established and point to a potential conflict between channel and programme brand identities in the US television industry. To understand this conflict we need to examine the rapid changes that take place over the late-1990s and 2000s as the US television industry moved from the cable to the digital era. These have a significant impact on the industry's use of branding and will be examined in the next chapter.

Notes

1 See Introduction for a discussion of periodization in US television history.

2 In the 1980s fibre optics also increased the number of cable channels that could be carried. Cable television increased rapidly over the 1980s, from around 12 cable networks in 1980 to around 60 by 1992 (Mullen 2008).

3 The Hearst Corporation has developed into a diversified media company with interests in magazine and newspaper publishing, cable networks, television and radio broadcasting, television production, internet businesses and real estate (see Hearst Corporation 2009).

4 According to Jessica Josephson, MTV in the USA received 60 per cent of its revenue from advertising, 35 per cent from subscriber fees and 5 per cent from ancillary sales in 1990 (1990: 20). Chapters 2 and 6 will examine the economic significance of ancillary sales to the US television industry.

5 See Klanten, Meyer, Jofré and Lovell (2005) for examples of a range of different MTV graphics, promos and idents produced for its wide range of global channels and websites.

6 MTV also innovated with product placement and co-branded partnerships with key youth brands (see Temporal 2008).

7 Officially called the Fox Broadcasting Company (FBC), it is more commonly referred to as the Fox network, although strictly speaking it does not broadcast enough hours to fulfil the FCC's definition of a network and so is sometimes referred to as a netlet.

8 Fox originally launched on 1 October 1986 with *The Late Show starring Joan Rivers* (1986–87), but it was not until 5 April 1987 that it offered prime-time programming, starting with Saturday and Sunday evenings (see Farber 1987: 31–33). It was not until June 1993 that Fox offered programming seven nights a week (Kimmel 2004: 80).

9 Ardvisson argues that new data from the 1980s allowed targeting of specific consumers by advertisers (2006: 63).

10 It was common for the stations to combine the Fox name and logo with their own call sign. For example, see the logo for WTXF-TV-29 Philadelphia in News Corporation (2010).

11 The first broadcast of an NFL game on Fox was on 12 August 1994.

12 On 23 May 1994 Fox Inc acquired a 20 per cent share in New World Communications Group with a US$500 million investment. This resulted in the largest ever realignment of network affiliation, with 10 VHF stations owned by New World changing affiliation from CBS/NBC/ABC to Fox (Anon. 1997b).

13 Chapter 5 will examine the use of on-air branding by the national networks in the mid-1990s in more detail and will offer a more complex picture of the extent to which the US networks adopted channel branding in this period.

14 There is a significant amount of academic writing on HBO's original drama series. See, for example, Creeber (2004), Jacobs (2005), Nelson (2007) and the essays collected in Leverette, Ott and Buckley (2008).

15 See Johnson (2007) for more discussion of the ideology behind this advertising slogan.

16 Available HTTP:<http://www.youtube.com/watch?v=H2RrPOCTYQI> (accessed 5 December 2010).

17 It is perhaps worth stressing that this is the rhetoric surrounding HBO, rather than a reflection of the actual workings of the network. After all, HBO is a profit-oriented organization that does undertake overtly commercial practices around its quality programming, such as tie-ins with advertisers and product placement deals. Indeed Santo (2008) argues that HBO is not as different from network television as its marketing rhetoric might suggest. The important point here is that, as academics, we should study the rhetoric, rather than buy into it.

18 Programme brands will be explored in more depth in Chapter 6.

2

FROM CHANNEL BRANDS TO SERVICE BRANDS?

US television enters the digital era

Historically, US television has been what Rogers *et al.* (2002) would term a second-order commodity. That is, viewers did not pay for television directly. Rather, television came into their homes free to air through a small number of channels that organized what could be viewed and when. Of course, television wasn't actually free. Viewers paid indirectly by buying the products advertised on television. Economically, therefore, television was conceptualized as a dual-product market, selling programmes to audiences and audiences to advertisers (see Doyle 2002: 60). Historically, both of these products were aggregated around the television channel as the means through which programmes were delivered to and organized for consumption and the site through which airtime was sold to advertisers.

As we saw in Chapter 1, however, the US television industry changed dramatically over the 1980s and 1990s and this altered the nature of the US television market and, with it, the significance of the television channel. Cable introduced the television channel itself as a product in the television industry that could be sold to cable operators or directly to viewers through subscriptions. These cable channels tended to be more highly differentiated and targeted than the national networks that had dominated the television industry since the 1950s. And it was these cable networks that first adopted branding as a central strategy in order to construct channel brand identities that could be clearly communicated to viewers and to other stakeholders, such as cable operators and advertisers. McMurria (2003: 72) argues that the television channel has become a commodity in three ways: as a licensed property sold to cable systems; as a collector of audiences for sale to advertisers; and as a channel sold directly to viewers via subscription. Rogers *et al.* (2002) argue that the last of these is the most significant in that it signals the shift with the arrival of cable, satellite and, more recently, digital technologies from the second-order commodity relations of the broadcast era to first-order commodity relations in which viewers pay directly for the television that they watch. Basic cable combines first- and second-order commodity relations, as viewers pay a subscription for a cable service of a package of channels that are also funded by advertising. First-order commodity relations are more apparent for premium cable channels, such as HBO, where the viewer pays a monthly subscription specifically for HBO channels, or for pay-per-view and on-demand services, such as the sports events that can be viewed for a one-off payment through services such as DirecTV. Yet, to define these networks as solely first- or second-order commodity relations is to downplay the complexity of the means through which contemporary television operates economically. As we saw in Chapter 1, increasingly HBO depends not only on revenue from subscription, but also on revenue from ancillary sales (particularly DVD) and syndication.

In addition, the changes since the 1990s as television entered the digital era have further complicated the economics of the television industry. Digital television and new media technologies have multiplied the number of available channels and introduced new ways of delivering, organizing and paying for television programmes. One consequence of these changes is that the economics of television are no longer aggregated around the channel, as new sites of distribution and consumption have become increasingly important in the television marketplace.[1] While the channel was, once, the only (and, even after the arrival of the video cassette recorder (VCR), still the primary) means of consuming television, by the new millennium the centrality of the channel was being challenged by the arrival of new technologies, such as DVD, VOD (video on demand), the internet and the personal media player.

As the television landscape has changed, the role of the channel brand has come under pressure. This chapter will examine the changing ways in which branding has been used by the US television industry over the digital era and the changing relationships that have emerged between channel, programme and new service brands. It will examine the development of a new digital capitalism dominated by large media conglomerates with businesses that extend across the wide range of digital technologies. As the television channel becomes decentred as the primary means through which television programmes are watched, this chapter asks whether this has undermined the role of the channel brand in the US television industry, and if so, what has emerged in its place?

The rise of media conglomerates and digital technologies

Over the 1990s the landscape of US television was being radically altered by two interrelated developments: the rise of media conglomeration and the emergence of new media technologies that affected television viewing, such as the DVD player, computer consoles and the home computer. Conglomeration was in fact a consequence of the deregulatory policies of the 1980s, which gradually relaxed the rules concerning ownership of the media. In the mid-1980s all three networks were purchased by larger corporations: NBC by General Electric, CBS by Laurence Tisch and ABC by Capital Cities. However, what differed by the mid-1990s was that it became possible for corporations with significant media holdings to purchase broadcast networks, leading to the emergence of large media conglomerates with interests in publishing, cable, broadcasting, syndication, film production, radio and often music and new media. As we saw in Chapter 1, News Corporation was the forerunner here, with its purchase of 20th Century Fox and establishment of the Fox Broadcasting Company in the mid-1980s to add to its international slate of newspapers and direct broadcast satellite television (see Chapter 3 for more on News Corporation's European satellite businesses).

However, the shift towards conglomeration was significantly hastened by the 1996 Telecommunications Act. David Hesmondhalgh argues that the Act 'represents the culmination of the trend towards marketisation in US policy' (2002: 130). The Act continued the process of deregulation in broadcasting and cable by increasing broadcast station ownership caps (so that one company could now own television stations reaching up to 35 per cent of the US population) and extended deregulation to the telecommunications industry by allowing local telephone companies to enter into the long-distance market and suspending cross-media ownership rules between telephone and cable, and television and radio (see Hesmondhalgh 2002: 129–30 and Hilmes 2003: 66). Meanwhile the emerging computer industry was treated by government as if it was separable from telecommunications and was allowed to develop free from regulation to fulfil corporate needs (Schiller 1999: 6–7). However, the emergence of the internet over the 1980s and 1990s challenged the separation of computing from telecommunications and other media services. The internet refers to a 'decentralized set of networks' connected to a central backbone that enables the interlinking of computers and the exchange of data (Schiller 1999: 10–11). Dan Schiller argues that the internet provided the 'production base and the control structure of an emerging digital capitalism' (1999: 37). Central to this was the emergence of large transnational global corporations, initiated principally in the USA over the 1990s, but soon spreading to other developed economies in Europe and the Far East. Thus, in the mid-1990s there was a rise in cross-border mergers, production and marketing, leading to the emergence of global conglomerates that depend on sophisticated network systems (Schiller 1999: 39–40).

In the media industries, there was a wave of mergers and acquisitions as companies sought to take advantage of the ability to move into previously restricted industries, which resulted in conglomerates with businesses across a range of media industries, but also with operations across the globe. Hence, although the 1980s and 1990s was a period of increased fragmentation for the US television industry with the emergence of new cable and national networks, it was also a period of increased concentration of ownership.

National Amusements, the major cinema exhibitor, purchased a majority stake in the syndication company Viacom in 1987, which owned a major share in MTV Networks. After Viacom's purchase of Paramount Pictures in 1994, combining the largest syndication business with a major Hollywood studio, it went on to launch a new national network, UPN, in 1995. Viacom merged with CBS in 2000 and, although the two companies separated in 2005, they are both still owned by parent company National Amusements.[2] The magazine publisher Time Inc., which had merged with Warner Communications in 1989, moved into network television in 1995 when it launched a new US national network, The WB, and purchased Turner Broadcasting in 1996.[3] In 2000 AOL and Time Warner merged to create a vast media conglomerate. Today, US broadcasting (both cable and network) is dominated by five conglomerates: News Corporation, Time Warner, National Amusements, NBC Universal and Disney. As Table 2.1 indicates, these conglomerates have businesses across a wide range of media (those listed are just a small selection of the businesses owned by each corporation).

The new media conglomerates that emerged over the 1990s are, therefore, huge and complex businesses that operate both nationally and internationally. Within these global media conglomerates, television is positioned as just one part of a much larger entertainment business, which changes the nature of television as a business. The television channel becomes a product brand that can be extended into new markets. Most of the *global* television brands have been cable and satellite channels that had already been conceptualized as products for sale to cable operators (see Chapter 1) and were able to take advantage of the technological possibilities of covering large geographical areas provided by satellite. Cable networks, such as MTV and HBO, have built on their brand reputation in the USA and extended this into new overseas markets, with MTV developing 100 channels across the globe reaching a billion viewers (Temporal 2008: 112). The four main national networks ABC, CBS, Fox and NBC have also been extended into new markets, such as ABC Family (a cable network launched in 2002 following the sale of Fox Family Channel to Disney), CNBC (a global business news network) and CBS College Sports Network (a cable network covering college and US Service Academy football).

While a strong brand can militate against the financial risks of developing new service or product lines, particularly when entering a new market, there is also some benefit in a conglomerate distinguishing separate brand identities for its products and services. This is particularly the case for brands that have established strong reputations within one market. Rogers *et al.* give the example of AOL/Time Warner, arguing that 'In the case of the AOL/Time Warner merger, then, it is in the best interest of the parent company to maintain the brand identity of CNN and keep it distinct from HBO's brand, though both networks are now on the same team' (2002: 56). Indeed Jaramillo argues that Time Warner deliberately attempted

Table 2.1 A selection of the businesses of the conglomerates that now own the major US networks, as of January 2011

	News Corporation:	*Time Warner:*	***National Amusements:***		*NBC Universal:*	*The Walt Disney Company:*
			Viacom:	*CBS Corporation:*		
Cable:	Fox Movie Channel, Fox News Channel, FX, National Geographic Channel	CNN, TNT (both part of Turner Broadcasting Systems), Cinemax, HBO	MTV Networks, BET Networks	Showtime	Bravo, MSNBC, Syfy	A&E, Lifetime, ESPN
Production and Distribution:	20th Century Fox, Fox Searchlight Pictures, Fox Television Studios, Blue Sky Studios	Warner Bros Entertainment	Paramount Pictures, MTV Films	CBS Television Studios, CBS Home Entertainment	NBC Entertainment, Universal Media Studios, Universal Pictures	Touchstone Pictures, Pixar, Walt Disney Studios
Television Networks:	Fox Broadcasting Company (Fox network), Fox Sports	The CW (joint venture with CBS Corporation)		CBS, The CW (with Warner Bros Entertainment)	NBC	ABC
Direct Broadcast Satellite:	BSkyB, FoxTel					
Publishing:	Harper Collins, News International, *The Wall Street Journal*	Time Inc.		Simon & Schuster		Disney Consumer Products
Online:	Myspace, Hulu	NASCAR.com, CNN.com	Atom Entertainment	CBS Interactive	Hulu, iVillage	disneystore.com, Disney Interactive Media Group
Parks and Resorts:					Universal Studios Hollywood, Universal Orlando Resort	Disneyland Resort, Tokyo Disney Resort

to create the appearance of competition between its different channels (she gives the examples of HBO and Cinemax in the 1980s and HBO and TNT in the 1990s) in order to encourage subscribers to take both channels (2002: 70). Murray (2005) argues that, by focusing consumer attention on the subsidiary brands, rather than the conglomerate brand (HBO rather than Time Warner), media conglomerates attempt to allay public hostility towards media concentration. This is apparent if we examine the websites for some of the major corporations within the contemporary US television landscape. For example, while The Walt Disney Company's corporate site gives details of its different businesses, its public-facing sites for Disney and for ABC have distinct visual identities, with only a small logo in the bottom left-hand corner indicating the relationship between ABC and The Walt Disney Company. Time Warner also has a corporate site that offers information about its different businesses, but again its public-facing sites are clearly distinguished. Despite some similarity in design between the corporate Time Warner site and HBO's site, there is little to indicate that there is any relationship between the two companies, while other subsidiaries such as The Warner Bros and CNN have completely distinctive websites with no indication of any association with Time Warner or with each other.[4]

The emergence of global media conglomerates is also tied to the development of digital technologies. As Boddy (2004: 80) argues, the term, digital television, is ambiguous, encompassing the enhanced picture quality of high definition television, the viewer interactivity of new two-way digital technologies and the expansion of television channels with the removal of wavelength scarcity. Indeed, digital technology has profoundly altered television both for the industry and for the viewer. First, digital transmission vastly increases the number of channels, allowing broadcasters to offer three or four channels where previously only one analogue channel would have been possible (Lotz 2007a: 54). It also increases the sites where one can access television, so that it is now possible to view television on the internet and on one's mobile phone or portable media player.

Second, digital alters the nature of television viewing. The possibility of watching television on a home/work computer or on a mobile phone moves television out of the domestic environment. But, perhaps more significantly, digital technology transforms television from a push to a pull medium. Traditionally, television viewing was controlled by the scheduling of television channels, so that content was 'pushed' to viewers by broadcasters. The emergence of the VCR in the 1980s began to place more control in the hands of the audience, allowing the viewer to time-shift and to buy and watch pre-recorded programmes. This has been further expanded with the development of DVD and DVR (digital video recorder)/VOD technology. The DVD in particular has had a big impact on the television industry, because it enables full seasons of series to be sold as one unit in a far more convenient and less bulky package than on VHS (video home system)

(Kompare 2006). However, digital video recorders and video-on-demand technologies have a more profound impact on television viewing. These technologies allow viewers to sidestep the schedules and 'pull' the programmes that they want to watch. Programmes can be selected in advance from electronic programme guides and whole series can be programmed to record. Viewers can also stop, pause and rewind programmes during transmission, placing far greater control in the hands of the audience. Meanwhile, viewers can now increasingly access programmes on the internet, often bypassing the networks altogether and downloading programmes from peer-to-peer file-sharing sites.

Third, new digital technologies alter the uses for the television set itself. As with the DVD and DVR, the antecedents for this stem from the 1980s and the rise of home computer consoles such as the Sony Playstation. By 2005, 39 per cent of US homes had a home video-game system (Lotz 2007a: 55). Furthermore, digital technology enabled the computer game console to merge with other media technologies such as the DVD and Blu-Ray player, as in the case of the Playstation 3, and it is now possible to use one's television as a monitor for a computer, where one can access online news, television, radio and books, go shopping, chat, make and receive phone calls and make new friends. Digital technology has thus increasingly blurred the boundaries between different media forms. As James Murdoch stated in his 2009 MacTaggart lecture at the Edinburgh Television Festival:

> What were once separate forms of communication, or separate media, are now increasingly interconnected and exchangeable. So we no longer have a TV market, a newspaper market, a publishing market. We have, indisputably, an all-media market.
>
> (Murdoch 2009)

The consolidation of the 1990s was particularly desirable in the increasingly converged world of digital, where the boundaries between different forms of media, such as publishing, television, cable, computing and telephony, were increasingly blurred. Furthermore the Telecommunications Act of 1996 placed the development of digital television within the hands of the existing major US broadcasters. The intention of the Act was that the extant broadcasters would develop high-definition services in exchange for free access to the UHF (ultra-high frequency) spectrum. Yet the Act failed to provide any significant restrictions on how this spectrum was to be used. The position of the incumbent broadcasters was further strengthened by the extension of the broadcast licences and new terms which made licence renewal far easier (see Hilmes 2003: 66 and Hesmondhalgh 2002: 129). Indeed, Michele Hilmes (ibid.) argues that, while the Act is deregulatory in tone, in fact it functioned primarily to protect the privileged position of the existing media conglomerates and hence should be understood more as protectionism than deregulation. Similarly, Douglas Gomery argues that, while broadcasters feared the impact of digital, by 2005 the four major broadcast networks – ABC, CBS, NBC and Fox – continued to thrive, managing 'to reap disproportionate advertising price increases relative to other media, not to mention outgrowing the overall growth in the industry' (2006: 27).

In this emerging digital era there are new financial possibilities for the television industry. The first of these is the syndication market, which Caldwell argues became the most important aspect of the television industry over the 1990s (2008: 260). With the expansion of channels that began with cable in the 1980s and was escalated by digital over the second half of the 1990s, the need for content, and the number of outlets through which content could be sold, increased. At the same time the gradual relaxation of the Financial Interest and Syndication (fin-syn) Rules (which prevented the networks from owning stakes in programming) and their eventual removal as part of the 1996 Telecommunications Act made syndication particularly important for the networks. The fin-syn rules (and the Prime Time Access Rule passed in 1970 that restricted the number of hours that the networks could broadcast in prime time) had been premised on the scarcity of programme outlets at a time when the big three networks dominated broadcasting. The rise of cable and satellite channels over the 1980s changed this, leading to arguments that there was no longer the need for regulation to curb the power of the networks (Kompare 2005: 150 and Lotz 2007a: 86). The FCC began eroding the fin-syn rules in 1991 and they were completely eliminated by 1995, at the same time that the media conglomeration noted above brought together broadcasters, distributors, studios and so on.

With conglomeration, syndication buyers and sellers are often now part of the same company. The removal of the fin-syn rules alongside the consolidation of the mid-1990s effectively removed the boundaries between producer, studio, network and station. Derek Kompare argues that this altered the nature of the television programme from content primarily designed to sell mass audiences to advertisers, to 'long-term projects, ripe for continuous recirculation and re-packaging' (2005: 157). From the late 1990s repurposing became a standard mode of distribution for the networks. Programmes are licensed to air multiple times on different platforms (nationally and globally), thus extending the potential profits that can be made from one programme (Lotz 2007a: 124). The networks also used repurposing to support their channels, for example, by licensing a hit network show to run on a new cable channel owned by the same corporation in order to increase the audience's knowledge of the channel brand.

The impact of these changes on the US television industry is complex and still uncertain. While (as we saw above) the television channel has emerged as a product that can be extended and sold globally, at the same time the centrality of the television channel as the site for accessing content is being undermined by the emergence of new platforms for the distribution of programming, and the programme itself has become an increasingly important commodity. Todreas (1999) argues that digital television threatens to undermine the fundamental ways in which the television industry operates by breaking the distribution bottleneck that characterized the broadcast and cable eras of television and providing alternatives to advertiser funding. While cable and satellite broke the three-network oligopoly, over the 1980s the limited number of cable operators and networks retained an effective bottleneck at the point of distribution in the television industry. It was only with the emergence of digital that the distribution bottleneck was truly broken, both in terms of the huge increase in the number of sites through which television programming could be distributed and in terms of the new forms of distribution (such as peer-to-peer sites) that threatened to take control of distribution away from broadcasters.

Todreas argues that, as viewers are faced with an increasing choice for points of access to television programming and distributors face greater competition, the bottleneck will shift from distribution to content. In the new digital era, content creators can make their programmes available without the need for the networks by setting up their own websites. However, with the vast expansion of the sites through which viewers can access content comes the need for mechanisms that help viewers find the content that they want to see: 'how will users find the content that they are interested in consuming? Users need some sort of filtering mechanism. Choice in media products becomes overwhelming for two reasons: limited time and limited patience' (Todreas 1999: 166). Todreas argues that, although the internet and digital on-demand television services offer the opportunity for viewers to 'pull' content, there will still be significant demand for mechanisms that 'push' content to viewers, on the ground that, as media use is largely leisure time, viewers do not want to work too hard or too long to find content that they want to watch. Research demonstrates that consumers tend to consistently choose between around seven brands, regularly visit only a handful of websites bookmarked on their web browser and typically concentrate television viewing on 5–8 channels, despite the vast increase in channels over the past 20 years (Todreas 1999: 180). A key question for the digital era, then, is what will emerge as the best way to organize and package content? Todreas argues that:

> There will be two winners in the Digital Era, and both will be in the content business. Content creators will be in increasing demand as firms down the supply chain seek to differentiate their commodity-like products. A handful of digital brands will emerge as the principal means to organize content for the information weary consumer. The firms that have an opportunity to create the best digital brands are television networks.
>
> (Todreas 1999: 99)

Digital brands will become the new bottleneck in the digital era, because 'Well-liked brands can give consumers trust and confidence in products' (1999: 173). Within the television industry it is the networks (rather than the production companies or the cable service operators) that have established strong brand identities, and Todreas argues that these brands are ideally situated to act as 'that trusted place where users can go to get a particular type of entertainment or information' (1999: 178).

Todreas was writing in 1999 when the impact of digital technology was still relatively unknown. Since then, the national networks have extended their channel brands onto new media platforms in order to retain their value as the site for accessing television programmes. Domestic access to the internet in the USA rose significantly in the second half of the 1990s, with 50 per cent of US homes having internet access by 2001, a statistic that was higher in those households, with college students and high incomes, so favoured by the networks (Ross 2008: 38). Following the rapid success of YouTube after its launch in April 2005, the networks began to see the internet as a site for the distribution of programmes. In October 2005 iPod and ABC announced a deal that would allow users to download selected ABC programmes immediately after transmission on the iTunes site (Lotz 2007a: 135). In 2007 ABC launched its 'start here' campaign, which positioned the network as a multiplatform experience that could be enjoyed 'anytime, anywhere' (Green 2007). On-screen idents used graphics of iPods, mobile phones, computer monitors and television screens showing extracts from key ABC programmes, such as *Ugly Betty* (2006–10) and *Desperate Housewives* (2004–). The promos invited viewers to 'start with us' on a journey across these new platforms for experiencing television, positioning the network as the ultimate navigation device for television viewing in the digital era (this is discussed in more detail in Chapter 5). This exemplifies Todreas's vision of the network as a brand that could be extended onto the digital landscape to help viewers find the content that they want to watch. In 2011, all the networks have dedicated websites that offer information about programmes, clips, episodes – and even full series to watch online, forums for discussion, games and other multimedia content – extending the brand identity of the network onto the web.

However, although the major US broadcasters have extended their channel brands onto the web, no single strategy has yet appeared for the distribution of television content online. For example, in response to the rise of websites such as YouTube and Yahoo! that stream audio-visual content, Viacom purchased a number of different distribution sites such as Gametrailers, Neopets, iFilm and Xfire, and made deals with all the major mobile companies in the USA to provide audio-visual content with the intention of placing MTV programming 'everywhere the MTV viewer might want to be' (Klaassen 2006b). Alongside this, Viacom developed a suite of websites that corresponded to the content and brand personalities of its on-air channels, such as a site devoted to *The Daily Show* (Comedy Central, 1996–), a pop music site, VH1Eyecandy.com, linked to its channel VH1, and a site tied to and actually featured on its Nickelodeon show *iCarly* (2007–), all of which offer audio-visual content. Jonathan Hemingway claims that, by the end of 2007, MTV Networks had more than 300 websites globally (2007: 3). Viacom therefore combined extending its existing channel and programme brands onto the web with a strategy of developing new brands that adapted its cable television strategy. Kaufman argues that MTV's digital strategy builds on 'what they've done well in cable – taking a particular kind of relatively inexpensive content and providing the wrapper that makes that content cool or compelling to a certain type of audience'. Furthermore, Viacom's online strategy can be used to support its television channels. For example, Viacom purchased Atom Films in 2006 (<http://www.atom.com>) to function in part as an incubator for new MTV cable content. What emerges, then, are a range of sites through which content owned by MTV and Viacom can be accessed, some of which is specifically branded as MTV content and some of which is associated with new niche online brands, such as Atom.

By contrast, HBO has focused on developing an on-demand service for its cable channel subscribers and has approached distribution across new media platforms such as the computer and mobile phone in much the same way as it views other syndication deals. For example, HBO places promotional clips for its programming on YouTube as part of a broader deal by Time Warner to distribute content from its media holdings (Anon. 2009). The YouTube deal enables HBO to gain revenue from short-form content by sharing the profits from advertiser sales with YouTube, while also promoting its programming and its brand to non-subscribers.[5] In 2007, HBO used the social networking site MySpace to preview an episode of its series *Flight of the Conchords* (2007–9) rather than launching a microsite specifically for the series (Morrissey 2007). This enabled HBO to promote its content on a website that its target audience already frequented, even if viewers were directed to HBO's official site to view the episode.

These online strategies point to a key difference between the broadcast and cable eras, when the channel was the dominant means of accessing television, and the digital era, in which the channel sits alongside other means of organizing and delivering programming, whether on the television (such as the rise of on-demand services and electronic programme guides) or on the internet and mobile phone (through streaming and downloading of long- and short-form content). All these new means of delivering and organizing content have more in common with the database than the traditional flow of the television channel. A database is a way of organizing data in such a way that it can be easily located and retrieved. While the channel organized television programmes into the temporal flow of a linear schedule, the database is a non-linear means of organizing content in order to facilitate its retrieval.

The database depends on the user inputting a request for data/content, offering more control to the user than the television channel.

However, not all databases are the same. Hubert L. Dreyfus (2001: 8) argues that traditional databases are organized along the lines of classification schemes designed by experts and tied to a specific form of practice and the needs of intended users. The organization of the electronic programme guide into genres would be an example of such a classificatory scheme tied to the assumption that genre is a key way by which viewers might want to search for and retrieve content. Dreyfus goes on to argue that, by contrast, the organizing principle of the internet as a database is 'the interconnectedness of all elements. There are no hierarchies; everything is linked to everything else on a single level. … With a hyperlinked database the user is encouraged to traverse a vast network of information, all of which is equally accessible and none of which is privileged' (2001: 10). Viacom/MTV's strategy of placing its content in a wide range of different sites online would seem to be targeted towards this conception of the internet as a hyperlinked database where content should be spread into multiple sites in order to be wherever potential viewers might be. Similarly, HBO's use of social networking sites to promote its content also recognizes the centrality of the hyperlink to the way in which content is organized on the internet, so that the aim is to provide a link to HBO content where the viewer is most likely to find it.

However, Allison Cavanagh argues that the notion of the internet as an open network where all points connect back to each other is false. Rather, she argues that, 'The shape of the web, at least, then, is highly fragmented overall but exhibits clustering around centres of gravity formed by the pull of brands and portals' (2007: 53). The internet is dominated by a number of large commercial sites and portals, such as Google and Yahoo!, that provide the primary points of access to online content. The strategy of placing content from HBO on popular sites such as YouTube and iTunes is one way by which the television industry has attempted to position itself within such 'centres of gravity'. The other alternative is for television corporations to attempt to launch new sites that might come to operate as centralized portals on the web. A good example of this is ABC, who launched ABC.com with the intention of ensuring that its online content could only be viewed in an ABC-branded environment (Becker 2007: 3). In 2007 ABC modified this strategy by making its branded video player available on AOL Video (it had already made some content available through iTunes). Anne Sweeney (co-chair of Disney Media Networks and president of Disney-ABC Television Group) argued that the video player itself now provided a branded environment for viewing ABC content that the network could control (both in terms of quality and user experience, and in terms of advertising sales). Making it available through AOL Video, however, increased the audience that might encounter ABC content online. In this way, ABC identified AOL as a 'centre of gravity' that it could exploit in developing its online video business.

Relationship branding: channels, programmes and services

However, as we saw in Chapter 1, brands don't just function as forms of product differentiation; they also function as an interface to manage the interactions with products and services. In the increasingly competitive context of the cable era, channel branding helped networks like MTV form loyal relationships with viewers who were invited to identify with the values of the network. In the digital era, the competition for viewers has increased. The value of brands in the digital era, therefore, is not just to be where the viewer is, but also to be where the viewer wants to be. John Thornton Caldwell argues that the move of the television networks onto the internet was not simply an attempt to colonize this new platform for television distribution. It also built on an emerging orthodoxy within marketing more broadly that, in the information age, price and product are no longer enough.

> The current mediascape no longer follows the once-trusted laws of or 'rationality' of Fordist-era industry, where appropriate pricing and (sometimes) heavy-handed advertising simply persuaded mass-market buyers to use a product by changing their minds. Now, instead, a number of brand buildings enjoin corporations in the 'information age' of niche economics to shift from an older emphasis on product and pricing to carefully targeted emotional, therapeutic, and 'relationship' branding strategies.
>
> (Caldwell 2008: 245)

The interactivity of the web is ideally situated to 'relationship branding', because the internet offers the possibility of two-way communication and social networking. All the US national networks attempt to utilize these features in their websites. For example, the front page of NBC.com advertises its 'community' section by highlighting the contributions of specific users. These community forums tie the social activities of viewers to the corporate space of NBC's website in an attempt to embed NBC within the everyday lives of viewers. CBS.com refers to its forums as 'social viewing rooms' where users are invited to 'Hop right into one of the rooms below, invite your friends and start socializing!' (accessed 4 September 2009).

In the contemporary media industry, corporate social responsibility initiatives have emerged as central to supporting the relationship branding of corporations. As Paul Temporal argues, 'Research has shown that, in many organizations, there is a direct correlation between community-building initiatives, including the creation of relationships with customers through customized service, and a positive influence on profits' (2008: 50). He goes on to advocate that corporations should monitor opinion polls to identify the key concerns of its target audience in order to gain, 'the valuable data required for public relations or community-building initiatives, which may result in meaningful long-term associations with customers when they act as advocates for consumer interests' (2008: 51). Corporate social responsibility campaigns are based on the belief that corporations need to do more than simply provide a service or product that consumers wish to buy. They must also embody the ideals and values of the consumer in order to form meaningful emotional relationships between the consumer and the product/corporation.

Ouellette and Hay argue that the merging of charitable acts and commercial profitability in corporate social responsibility campaigns can be situated within a broader shift in US democracy towards a model of citizenship based on private enterprise and 'empowerment through self-help' (2008: 34–36). They give the example of ABC's 'A Better Community' campaign. The aim of this campaign was to encourage ABC viewers to volunteer in environmental and community projects within their local area. The campaign included adverts in which stars associated with the network urged viewers to become involved in their communities. Viewers were directed to ABC's 'A Better Community' website where they could find help and ideas about how to get involved with volunteering. The campaign utilized ABC's flagship charity-based reality television programme *Extreme Makeover: Home Edition* (2003–), which epitomized the ideology of the corporate citizen by presenting ABC as a benevolent force that identified and saved needy viewers by transforming their homes, and consequently their lives. At the end of each programme the viewer was encouraged to follow suit by going to the 'A Better Community' website to find out how they could get involved in their own community (see Ouellette and Hay 2008). The campaign thus not only created an identity for ABC as a caring corporate citizen, but also attempted to construct a relationship between viewers and the network that extended beyond the act of watching television by mediating their volunteering activities.

Deregulation over the 1980s and 1990s had largely removed the requirement for television networks to act in the public interest. However, Ouellette (2008) argues that while the 'A Better Community' campaign ostensibly aimed to encourage and facilitate community action, it can be better understood as a network branding strategy that attempted to manage anxieties about civil society and the role of the corporation. The activities promoted on the 'A Better Community' website and the people supported in *Extreme Makeover: Home Edition* were carefully selected in order to protect ABC's brand identity (Ouellette and Hay 2008: 50–51). So, participants in *Extreme Makeover: Home Edition* must be home owners and are carefully vetted in order to weed out 'undeserving' applicants (such as those with criminal records) and to pick those that reflect the ideals of ABC, such as people who have given to their own communities. The campaign also supports ABC's corporate aims in a number of ways. The website encourages purchase of

Extreme Makeover: Home Edition on DVD by offering to give one dollar to charity for every copy sold (Ouellette and Hay 2008: 56). It also promotes ABC's corporate partners, such as Sears and Ford, who both sponsor *Extreme Makeover: Home Edition* and place their products extensively in the show, and ABC's own parent company Disney. Indeed, although branding is used by media conglomerates to distinguish their different services, it can also be used to connect them when this supports the brand identities of the different corporations. In this example, the 'A Better Community' campaign ties in directly with Disney's focus on families and children. Disney was even the corporate sponsor of the 2005 meeting of the National Conference on Volunteering and Service (Ouellette and Hay 2008: 41).

Furthermore, as Ouellette (2008) points out, the 'A Better Community' campaign also functioned to attempt to strengthen the ties between the network and its affiliates. With the increased competition from cable and the rise in the number of national networks, relationships between the networks and their affiliates became increasingly strained. In Chapter 1 we saw how Fox used its purchase of NFL games to poach affiliates from CBS. From the mid-1990s there was not only more competition for audiences, there was also potentially more competition between networks for affiliates. Furthermore, the emergence of the internet offered a point of distribution for the networks that bypassed the affiliates altogether, placing further pressure on relationships with the networks. The 'A Better Community' campaign enlisted affiliates to the campaign in order to tie them to the broader brand identity being constructed by ABC and to strengthen the relationship between the affiliates and the network.

ABC is not the only US broadcaster to construct an identity for itself as a benevolent corporate citizen. NBC, A&E and MTV have all used corporate social responsibility campaigns (see Ouellette and Hay 2008 and Temporal 2008). For example, MTV has a long history of promoting voting and social awareness amongst young people, and has a dedicated community website dealing with issues such as discrimination, violence, religion, human rights and drugs.[6] These campaigns create events that provide the networks with programmes that tend to rate highly and support the construction of a positive corporate image that obscures the commercial imperatives driving the business. As the example of ABC's 'A Better Community' demonstrates, such branding campaigns also function to support and manage the networks of relations that make up contemporary media production, whether in the relationships between a business, its parent company, its affiliates and its sponsors, or in the relationships between a viewer, the programmes they watch, the websites they use, the DVDs they buy and the social activities that they get involved with. In doing so, ABC is attempting to encourage and manage social activity around its programmes that is utilized for corporate and financial gain.

The use of relationship branding is a central aspect of ways in which the networks have extended their programmes onto the web. Take the example of NBC's show *The Office* (2005–), adapted from the successful UK series of the same name.[7] For NBC, *The Office* is not simply a *television* series aired on its network and repurposed in syndication and overseas sales.[8] The series has its own microsite on the NBC website. This website is styled to look like an office notice board, with files and notes offering different forms of information. On the website you can find out when the next new episode will be transmitted and see a sneak preview of it, as well as watch clips of old episodes. There are adverts for season 5 on DVD and Blu-ray, as well as for *The Office* merchandise (such as *The Office Clue Game*, which is a tie-in with the board game Clue, known as Cluedo in the UK), available to purchase from the NBC Store. The site also offers fictional blogs by characters from the show, as well as fictional Twitter conversations between characters from the show. The site also includes numerous invitations to participate. Viewers can send in pictures of 'things in jello' (in reference to an episode in which one character put a stapler in jello/jelly), they can contribute made-up words to the 'Addictionary' and they can comment on videos related to the show. The site also offers links to *The Office* sites on Facebook and Twitter, shows you how to access *The Office* website on your mobile phone, provides wallpaper and widgets related to the show that you can use to customize your computer and a link to NBC Direct, which allows you to view selected full-length NBC programmes on your PC in standard and high definition.[9]

There are a number of facets to NBC's extension of *The Office*. First, the website uses *The Office* to promote a number of its other services, such as NBC Direct. In an era of media conglomeration, successful programmes can be used to develop and promote new services. For example, the Japanese electronics manufacturer Sony moved into content production after it acquired the Hollywood studio Columbia Pictures in 1989. It subsequently used specific television programmes to promote new technological developments, such as pioneering 'mobisodes' to promote its new generation of mobile phones. Second, *The Office* has been extended onto products beyond the initial programme that allow for additional profits for the network, either through direct sales (such as DVDs) or through licensing (such as *The Office Clue Game*). This points to the shifts in the financing of television that have taken place over the digital era, in which television is funded by a far greater range of means than just the sale of advertising. This stems in part from the threat to advertiser funding that emerged in the digital era, when advertisers could no longer rely on the vast reach of the national networks, and new digital technologies made it easier for audiences to avoid the adverts altogether. Consequently, new relationships have emerged between advertisers and networks/studios, such as product placement and sponsorship deals (see Lotz 2007a: 153–72). As Arvidsson argues, although the transformation of the media environment in the 1990s diminished the reach and the effectiveness of traditional advertising, it also offered new opportunities for advertisers and producers/distributors alike. Consequently, media products were increasingly conceived of as brands:

> When a particular media product (or 'content') can be promoted across different media channels and sold in different formats, what is marketed is not so much films or books, as 'content brands' that can travel between and provide a context for the consumption of a number of goods or media products.
>
> (Arvidsson 2006: 75)

The Office, then, is no longer simply a television programme, but a content brand that encompasses a range of products and services. Significantly, though, Arvidsson argues that content branding is not just a way of linking together different products. Over and above this, Arvidsson argues that brands provide 'a context for consumer action' (2006: 76). If we return to the website for *The Office*, we can see that the site actively invites participation on the part of the viewer and uses social networking sites such as Facebook in an attempt to embed the series within the everyday lives of its viewers. Arvidsson sees such strategies as part of a wider consequence of 'the integration of media culture into life in general and the proliferation of new informational tools' (2006: 75). In the digital landscape where viewers can avoid advertising and are more wary of traditional hard-sell techniques, advertisers have to find alternative ways of engaging consumers with their products: shifting from advertising to brand management. Branding emerges as the new advertising tool because it operates at the level of the social, functioning as a mediator between product and consumer.

> Brands provide a propertied micro-context of consumption, it suggests ways in which a product or service can be experienced, related to or 'felt'. While product placements, themed environments, sponsorship, event marketing and branded communities are important, there is also a recognition that this identity is only *realized* insofar as consumers are involved in its co-creation.
>
> (Arvidsson 2006: 82)

The use value of a brand, therefore, lies in what people do with the brand. And, consequently, branding is as much about managing the activities of consumers (to ensure that the social world that is constructed by consumers around the brand fits with that desired by producers) as it is about constructing a brand image. Branding, then, takes its financial value from the activities and uses that consumers put the brands to in their everyday lives. While, as Arvidsson argues, branding can help advertisers to engage with audiences experientially, it is also being used by the television industry to form relationships between their core products and services and viewers.

Thus, in the example of the website for *The Office* (as in ABC's 'A Better Community' campaign), the invitations for participation are attempts to encourage viewers to engage in activities that support the brand values that are being created around the series. These activities can range from copying events within the programme itself, to generating talk and gossip around the series. However, they also include actions that tie the series to the network brand, such as encouraging viewers to visit the NBC store or to sign up to NBC Direct to watch NBC programmes online.

'An evil plot to destroy the world – enjoy': Hulu as service brand

Gillian Doyle accords with Todreas in arguing that:

> the digital environment favours strong and recognizable brands. … Without recognizable brands and worthwhile levels of consumer awareness, potential newcomers to the online universe may well find that the high initial costs involved in establishing an online presence (typically involving extensive campaigns on conventional media) represent an effective deterrent to market entry. Large and established media content providers with strong brands and access to valuable back catalogues of images, text and sound have several advantages when it comes to exploitation of the additional scale economies made possible by digitization.
>
> (Doyle 2002: 145)

While their established brands and content libraries have certainly facilitated the move of corporations such as MTV, HBO and ABC onto the web, the range of different strategies that have been used suggest some uncertainty about which kind of brands are most valuable. On the one hand, as digitization makes it increasingly easy to duplicate, repackage, and reformat content, the programme brand would seem to be more valuable than the channel brand. It is notable that both of the examples above of relationship branding were oriented around key programmes brands, even though they were framed by channel brands. On the other hand, the nature of the internet as a vast database would imply that some kind of organizational structure is needed to help viewers find the programme brands that they want to watch. Considering that some of the most successful online brands for delivering audio-visual content have been service brands, such as YouTube and iTunes, it is perhaps no surprise that one of the most recent strategies adopted by the US television industry to distribute its content online has been a service brand: Hulu.

Hulu is a joint venture between NBC Universal and News Corporation that was launched in March 2008 (ABC-Disney has since joined). While

NBC, ABC and Fox (owned by News Corporation) all have their own network-branded sites offering audio-visual content, Hulu represented the first focused attempt by the US television networks to use the internet as a platform for distributing long-form television. The site offers clips, movies, whole episodes and even whole series of selected programmes from the back catalogue of each broadcaster, as well as content from 150 content providers, including all the major US television production companies except CBS (which is developing a rival service, TV.com) (O'Leary 2009). Hulu's home page is dominated by a large central box which displays a still, title and brief description of a selection of shows (accessed 28 January 2011). Above this is Hulu's logo and a menu of buttons, such as 'TV', 'movies', 'browse', 'most popular', 'recently added' and 'spotlight'. Below this, it lists 'recent episodes', 'popular clips', 'featured content', 'my videos', 'popular shows', 'popular movies', 'more to explore' and 'Hulu recommends'. As such, the design of Hulu's site is that of a database. The headings used in the database suggest that the primary means of selecting programming is popularity, rather than genre, transmission date, or writer/director. What is particularly striking, given that Hulu was developed by two corporations that own US networks, is that channel branding is entirely absent from this front page and there is nothing to indicate the relationship between Hulu, NBC, Fox and Disney. If you click on the 'TV' tab at the top of the home page you are taken to a page where you can browse through television titles, and only then do you come to a menu that allows you to browse by network. All of this would suggest that Hulu does not expect its viewers to use channel branding as a primary way of finding the content that they want to view on the site.[10]

The use of a large banner with images from selected programmes on Hulu's home page does, however, indicate the value of programme brands to Hulu's own identity. Yet, this is quite different to the use of programme brands in the construction of channel brand identities that we saw in Chapter 1. Rather than drawing on a specific form of content and tying this to the identity of the brand, as in MTV's music television and HBO's quality original drama, Hulu chooses to emphasize the *range* of programming available. In addition, its focus on popularity as its primary categorization suggests an identity defined by its users, rather than imposed by Hulu itself. Ultimately, Hulu's brand is based on selling a service. To be sure, that service depends on the quality and range of programming that it offers, but it is more clearly defined by the *experience* that Hulu offers to its viewers. Thus, Hulu could be said to have the characteristics of a service brand.

Leonard L. Berry (2000) argues that, with product brands, the source of the customer's experience will be a particular product, rather than the company that produced the product. To borrow Berry's example, people experience the Cheerios brand, rather than the brand of its producer, General Mills. By contrast, Berry claims that, with service brands, 'the source of the experience is the locus of brand formation' (2000: 130). Service performance plays a particularly important role in the development of brand meaning, and the service company is viewed as the provider of the experience offered by the service brand. Hulu accords with this definition of service brands in that it is positioned as the provider of the experience of viewing television on the web. This is articulated in the adverts for Hulu first screened during the 2009 Super Bowl, in which Alex Baldwin is revealed to be part of an alien invasion force that has developed Hulu as an evil plot to rot our brains and make them edible by alien infiltrators. While the advert depicts a lair underneath the Hollywood sign, with banks of television screens with some recognizable shows, such as *Family Guy* (Fox, 1999–) and *Saturday Night Live* (NBC, 1975–), the focus is on selling Hulu as providing an enhanced experience of television viewing, one that is promoted as better than broadcasting (albeit, ironically, better at melting human brains).

The construction of Hulu as a service brand providing a particular experience is continued within the site itself, which includes discussion boards and 'Hulu labs' in which viewers can get involved in trials for new services such as Hulu desktop and publisher tools that facilitate the embedding of Hulu content into other websites. Hulu also allows viewers a certain amount of control over the viewing experience, offering them the opportunity to watch content with adverts distributed throughout, or with all the advertising upfront, as well as allowing viewers to create their own clips that can then be embedded in social networking sites such as Facebook (Kelly 2009). While both Hulu and the traditional television channel are offering viewers the experience of watching television, for the television channel that experience is primarily defined (and differentiated) by the nature of the content on offer and how it is organized on air (see Chapter 6). By contrast, what Hulu offers is *an experience defined by what you can do with television*. For some viewers, this might simply be the experience of being able to choose what to watch and when. For others, it might be the option of being able to comment on or share what they have watched.

However, unlike the service brands examined by Berry, such as Enterprise Rent-A-Car, viewers do not pay directly for Hulu, as Hulu is funded by advertising. In many ways then, as a product, Hulu is closer to traditional free-to-air network television than a premium channel brand such as HBO, which is funded by subscription. For the real product that is being sold on Hulu is the audience (or at least the audience's attention) and, because Hulu can invite viewers to subscribe to its service, it can gather detailed information about each of its viewers. This potentially enables Hulu to offer more-targeted marketing for advertisers. O'Leary describes one such initiative:

> In the past couple of months, Hulu, working with behavioural targeting company Audience Science, has launched additional initiatives like 'retargeting,' which uses cookies to monitor a user's browsing

> history. A consumer who visits P&G's pg.com, for example, will see P&G advertising when they watch Hulu content. Hulu's ad-selector option also allows viewers to choose the kind of ad they want to see: An automotive marketer might offer the choice between watching a spot for a sports car, a minivan or a sedan. 'It's great for the user. They can control their ad experience,' says Colaco [Hulu's senior vice president of advertising]. 'We learn a lot about the user, about their life stage and experiences and who we can target. Over time, we can create a profile for that person and get a whole set of interests for that user.'
>
> (O'Leary 2009)

Hulu has also experimented with strategies that allow viewers to interact with adverts, with Nielson research suggesting that Hulu viewers have greater recall of the products advertised on the site than on traditional television (ibid.). Although Hulu is unable to offer the kind of reach of broadcast television advertising, this provides advertisers with the possibility of targeting their products directly at the right consumer. Hulu is not just providing its viewers with a new way of experiencing television; it is also providing advertisers with new ways of engaging with their target audience. In doing so, Hulu is not only monetizing the experience of watching television (as with advertiser-funded broadcast television), but additionally monetizing the other kinds of activities and experiences associated with television viewing, such as discussing and sharing content. By March 2010 Hulu was offering 10,000 hours of content and had 13.6 million unique users in the USA (Fry 2010). Hulu's brand identity (for both advertisers and users) is based on positioning itself as a portal through which to engage in the extended experiences of television viewing that are enabled by the internet. While many of these activities may have existed before the internet, the digital era makes these activities more accessible and more visible.

Conclusions

With the emergence of the digital era, the place of the television channel has been decentred within the television industry as new ways of delivering and organizing content have emerged. While some see this as the death knell of the television channel (see Ytreberg 2002), the rise of global media conglomerates has seen the development of the television channel as a global media brand that can be adapted and extended into new markets. Within the domestic US market, the networks have also experimented with extending their channel brands onto the web. In the digital era, then, the networks are attempting to reconstruct themselves as brands that are loyal and trusted guides through the cluttered media environment. But, more than this, today the networks are attempting to position themselves as central parts of our social communities. They are well placed to do this because television has always been part of everyday life and the social fabric of our lives – talk about television is not new, whether in the press or around the water cooler. The networks are attempting to co-opt this social aspect of television viewing and to position themselves as central facilitators of this in an attempt to position their network brands as 'frames of action' (to paraphrase Arvidsson 2006: 8) for consumer use of the wide range of converged media. So, the networks are attempting to be more than just filters for accessing television content but, rather, brands whose financial profitability is based on their ability to control and exploit the activities of viewers/consumers.

Yet, at the same time, the television networks are now just one small part of large media conglomerates and, within this new industrial structure, the programme brand emerges as a valuable commodity that can be exploited across a wide range of products and points of distribution in order to generate revenue across a number of different businesses. This could undermine channel brands which tend to be defined (as we saw in Chapter 1) to a large degree by their programme brands. At the same time, with the increasing presence of audio-visual content on the internet, new service brands that emphasize experiences over content are emerging as alternative ways of delivering and organizing television viewing for audiences. Hulu incorporates a range of different activities into the experience of watching television. While these activities can take place outside of Hulu (and were part of the experience of watching television before the internet), Hulu brings them all under one branded experience. While all brands, as social objects, function as interfaces in our engagement with those brands more broadly, Hulu attempts to bring more of this engagement within one site and to monetize this experience (what we do with television) more directly. By branding an experience, Hulu is less dependent on programme mix and so avoids some of the problems of the relationship between channel and programme brands seen in Chapter 1. While it is too early to know whether this will be economically successful, it does point to the ways in which corporations are using brands increasingly to control and monetize our everyday experiences of watching television.

Notes

1 Although television has always made money from ancillary and syndication markets, these markets have become larger and more central to the US television industry over the past 25 years, as we will examine in more depth in Chapter 6.

2 Ironically, Viacom had been formed in 1971 out of CBS's syndication arm after CBS was forced to divest itself of its syndication operations following the introduction of new FCC rules that prevented the networks from owning vested interests in the programmes that they did not produce and from engaging in domestic syndication (Kompare 2005: 146).

3 As with Fox, the two networks that launched in 1995 both used names that drew on their associations with established Hollywood studios: The WB and its association with Warner Bros, and UPN (United Paramount Network) and its association with Paramount

Pictures. Both The WB and UPN began broadcasting over a limited number of evenings in prime time. In 2006 Warner Bros and CBS Corporation (which owned UPN) merged The WB and UPN into a new network, The CW.

4 These sites were accessed in the UK where, in some instances, such as Disney's non-corporate site, it is only possible to access the UK version of the site (<http://www.disney.co.uk>).

5 HBO also made its programmes available for download through iTunes.

6 For an example of MTV's corporate social responsibility see MTV (2010).

7 The UK version of *The Office* (BBC, 2001–3) had previously aired in the US on BBC America and won Golden Globes in January 2004 for best comedy series and best comedy actor (for Ricky Gervais as David Brent) (Rosser 2004: 2–3). See Jeffrey Griffin (2008) for a discussion of the adaptation of the series in the US.

8 As part of the deal between NBC and the BBC for the rights to *The Office*, the BBC retained a first-look deal for the transmission of the US version in the UK and screened it on its digital channel BBC Three in 2005.

9 As shall be discussed in more detail in Chapter 6, NBC also produced a short-form web spin-off of *The Office* in 2006 called *The Accountants*, which became embroiled in the writers' strike in 2007–8 after the network classified it as promotion, leaving its writers ineligible for compensation or residuals.

10 This does not mean that Hulu's users are not aware of channel brands. The discussion forums on Hulu.com/discussions do sometimes include references to the channel on which a programme was originally broadcast, despite the lack of channel branding on the site.

Part II

BRANDING AND THE UK TELEVISION INDUSTRY

3

COMPETITION, FRAGMENTATION AND COMMODIFICATION

The emergence of branding in the UK television industry

> Five years ago, I was working for the BBC on an on-air promotion, and at that time, 'brand' was a dirty word. Marketing was rather a nasty thing that lesser mortals, in less lucky occupations, became engaged with.
>
> (Robin Wight, chairman of marketing agency WCRS, cited in Douglas 1997)

As in the USA, over the 1990s the British television industry adopted branding as a key strategy, despite the very different landscape of public service broadcasting in the UK. In many ways this is not surprising as the changes facing each industry were similar. UK television policy from the 1980s was, likewise, largely deregulatory and heavily influenced by governments with neo-liberal and market-oriented philosophies. As in the USA, the 1980s and 1990s ushered in an increase in the numbers of television channels and broadcasters with the emergence of cable, satellite and digital television services. While, in the USA, this broke the dominance of the three-network oligopoly, in the UK it broke the dominance of the duopoly that had existed between the BBC and ITV from 1955 to 1982. The UK broadcasters have similarly had to adjust to the emergence of new forms of distribution for television, such as the internet, as well as an increasingly globalized and competitive media landscape. However, in the UK the use of branding, with its associations with marketing for commercial gain, was seen as particularly contentious within the context of public service broadcasting, as the quotation above suggests. While Chapter 4 will ask whether branding undermines public service broadcasting, focusing specifically on Channel 4 and the BBC, in this chapter we will examine the more commercial players in British broadcasting, including Sky Television, Channel 5, ITV and UKTV.[1] Within the context of increased competition, deregulation and the emergence of new digital media, what was the role of branding for these commercially funded broadcasters operating in the mixed market of a commercial and public service television industry?

The rise of non-public service television: Sky and the 1990 Broadcasting Act

When television emerged as a full service within the UK in 1936 it did so within the tradition of public service broadcasting that was already established for radio. Like radio, television was seen as a public utility and a powerful medium that needed to be safeguarded from the influences of both government and commerce. Like radio, television was seen as dependent on the scarce public resource of the limited airwaves that needed to be carefully used and put to good social and cultural purpose. Like radio, it was not possible to charge for television at the point of reception and so new 'sound and vision' licences were introduced for those who owned television and radio receivers. And, like radio, television was expected to inform, educate and entertain its audience (see Scannell 1990 and Tracey 1998). Although commercial television was introduced to the UK in 1955, the new commercial channel, ITV, functioned under an almost identical public service remit to the BBC (see Johnson and Turnock 2005). In fact, despite changes in regulation and in the interpretation of public service broadcasting over the decades, British television remained resolutely a public service medium until the 1980s.[2]

Yet, by 1990, the British television landscape had been transformed, with the emergence of the first non-public service television channels available on cable and satellite and new legislation that introduced free-market principles to the public service broadcasters. And it was within this context that branding began to be adopted within the British television industry. The new technologies that became more widely available over the 1980s – satellite, the computer and fibre optic cable – threatened two of the founding reasons for the introduction of broadcasting as a public service in the UK: the scarcity of the airwaves and the problems of charging for broadcasting at the point of reception. All three technologies offered a future teeming with television channels providing pay-per-view programmes and services that could be charged for according to use. Once television ceased to be a scarce resource, then the need to manage or protect the use of television as a public service became more open to challenge. As Tom O'Malley argues (2009: 4), these technological changes, combined with the election of Margaret Thatcher's Conservative government in 1979 with its strong free-market agenda, led to a shift away from television being perceived as essentially or primarily a public service. The Conservative Party believed that cable and satellite television should be developed with private, rather than public, funds and, famously, Thatcher was keen to see advertising replace the licence fee as the means of funding the BBC (Tracey 1998: 109).

The principal regulatory attack on public service broadcasting came from the Peacock Report of 1986 and the following 1990 Broadcasting Act. Thatcher's Conservative government set up the Peacock Committee to examine the funding of the BBC, and it was widely expected to recommend the introduction of advertising to the BBC. While its report bucked this particular expectation, it did propose that British broadcasting 'should move towards a sophisticated market system based on consumer sovereignty' (Peacock 1986: 132, para. 592).[3] This was a significant shift from previous broadcasting policy, which had conceptualized the audience as citizen, rather than consumer. The report also argued that, in the future, public service provision should be reduced to those programmes not provided for by the market, reconceptualizing public service broadcasting as certain programme types, rather than as an overall system or approach to broadcasting. Although many of the specific recommendations made by the Peacock Report failed to materialize, Goodwin (1998), O'Malley (2009) and Collins (2009) all agree that the report's greatest impact was to move British policy, 'from public service itself as the underlying principle of broadcasting to a notion that broadcasting should be organized as a marketplace for independent voices' (Goodwin 1998: 92).

At the same time, the Conservative government was overseeing the development of cable and satellite television. Initially, government policy balanced a market-led approach to these new technologies with concern about their impact on the quality and reputation of British public service broadcasting (see Tracey 1998). While cable and satellite television were to be developed as private industries, there was concern about the effect of foreign cable and satellite television in terms of the impact of low-cost satellite 'super-stations' from Europe or the opening up of UK cable and satellite franchises to foreign (particularly US) companies (see Goodwin 1998). Ultimately, however, free-market principles overrode these concerns. Direct broadcast satellite (DBS) television developed in the hands of commercial companies, with the UK franchise, BSB, being awarded to a consortium whose members included Reed International, Granada and Pearson (Anon. 1990).[4]

However, before BSB could launch, it faced competition from Sky Television, a DBS service operating from the Astra satellite (controlled by the Société Europeénne des Satellites, based in Luxembourg, which fell outside UK regulation) and owned by Rupert Murdoch's media conglomerate News Corporation. Sky Television launched in the UK in February 1989, 15 months ahead of BSB and, following technical problems and rising costs, BSB and Sky merged in November 1990 to create BSkyB (commonly referred to as 'Sky'), with News Corporation owning a controlling share (Bose 1996). Controversially, the merger contravened BSB's contract and left British satellite television in the hands of a large foreign conglomerate. Despite early political fears of exactly such an eventuality, the government did not intervene, possibly because Murdoch (who owned a number of important newspapers in the UK) was a powerful political ally for the Conservative government (Goodwin 1998: 52). Furthermore, not only did BSkyB have a monopoly on satellite television in the UK, but it was also able to dominate cable television. BSkyB took advantage of the slow development of cable television in the UK by offering a package of channels to cable providers that were struggling to develop new services.[5] The UK government also failed to prevent overseas involvement in cable television, with the sector receiving a significant boost in the late-1980s as US investment in the industry increased (see Tracey 1998 and Goodwin 1998).

At the same time, the 1990 Broadcasting Act had a significant impact on the extant public service broadcasters. Controversially, the ITV franchises were to be auctioned, rather than allocated primarily on public service principles, although a 'quality threshold' was introduced that all potential franchisees had to pass (see Johnson and Turnock 2005). While Channel 4 (which had launched in 1982 as the third public service broadcaster with a particular remit to serve minority audiences) had been protected from the market by a funding system in which ITV provided a baseline of funding in exchange for selling advertising on the channel, this was also to change, as Channel 4 was to sell its own advertising for the first time. The Act also replaced the IBA (Independent Broadcasting Authority – the regulator of commercial public service broadcasting) and the Cable Authority (the regulator for cable television) with the ITC (the Independent Television Commission), a new light-touch regulator to oversee all television services provided from within the UK (other than those provided by the BBC).[6] Furthermore, media ownership rules were relaxed (these relaxations were further extended in the 1996 Broadcasting Act) allowing foreign investment into UK television and enabling the consolidation of the regional ITV franchises over the first half of the 2000s. Finally, all public service broadcasters would have to commission at least 25 per cent of their programming from independent producers for the first time.[7]

By the early 1990s, therefore, the British television industry had been significantly transformed. The incumbent public service broadcasters faced competition from emerging commercial satellite and cable services dominated by the global media conglomerate News Corporation. This, alongside legislation requiring Channel 4 to sell its own advertising, increased competition for advertising revenue for commercial broadcasters. The political commitment to free-market ideologies began to shift the focus of regulation from maintaining and protecting a public service ethos to supporting competition, and from conceptualizing the audience as a citizen to addressing the audience as a consumer. It also opened up television production to increased competition by forcing the BBC and ITV to commission a significant amount of their programming from independent producers, introducing market conditions into programme production.

Branding emerged within this industrial context in a number of ways. In launching DBS in the UK for the first time, both Sky and BSB spent heavily on marketing. Sky had a significant advantage in the shape of the British newspapers owned by News Corporation, which promoted the service and derided the competition (the *Sun* newspaper referred to BSB as 'toff's telly' (Bose 1996)). As in the USA, revenue for cable and satellite services was generated from a combination of subscription and advertising sales. In addition, as service providers, Sky and BSB gained additional revenue from fees paid to carry other channels. Initially, therefore, Sky and BSB had to focus on generating sufficient subscriptions to be attractive to advertisers and other channels. While BSB felt that its unique selling point was the superior quality of its new D-MAC technology, as the *Economist* pointed out in 1990, this was 'invisible to most of its customers [and] ... the difference between D-MAC and PAL was (and is) almost invisible on all but the newest television and video-cassette recorders. Viewers wanted a choice between programmes, not technologies' (Anon. 1990). By contrast, Sky focused on promoting choice and targeting the C1–C2 demographic that was less well served by existing public service broadcasting. Research in 1990 showed that the core market for DBS was large families, with Sky Movies, a channel clearly distinguished from the existing terrestrial channels, the most popular channel (Clemens 1990: 46).

In the early 1990s after the merger between Sky and BSB, BSkyB focused on developing other channels that offered something different from existing terrestrial television. Unlike the existing UK terrestrial channels that adhered to the long-standing public service tradition of providing a mixed programme schedule (in terms of genre and audience address), BSkyB offered a package of branded niche channels. Alongside Sky Movies, BSkyB launched Sky News, Europe's first dedicated news channel, providing a rolling news service that allowed viewers to choose when to watch. Its package also included Sky One, an entertainment channel that exploited News Corporation's ownership of the Fox Network by acquiring the rights to screen *The Simpsons* in the UK. However, key to BSkyB's success in the early 1990s was its acquisition in May 1992 of the exclusive rights to broadcast Premier League Football in the UK for its new Sky Sports channel, which had launched in 1991. Significant sporting events, such as football in the UK, attract fans prepared to pay the additional revenue to view matches and advertisers keen to buy airtime within programmes that attract the elusive male audience that can be hard to find elsewhere on television (see Anon. 1995). In addition, Sky developed innovative ways of presenting sports, such as offering a live on-screen score-line to keep fans up to date with developments in matches as they happened. By June 1993 BSkyB subscriptions were up by 45 per cent (Bose 1996). BSkyB effectively introduced narrowcasting to the UK with a package of channels targeted at specific audience groups. The channels and the service characterized a key aspect of Sky's corporate brand identity: choice (Sky 2009), a brand identity that exemplified the neo-liberal emphasis on consumer sovereignty even while BSkyB's effective monopoly on satellite television went against the free-market ideal of open competition.

In the trade press in the early to mid-1990s branding was clearly associated with satellite and cable television services and channels, such as BSkyB and Sky Sports. Writing in *Cable and Satellite Europe* in 1995, Paul Barker argued that it was 'heresy' for British public service broadcasters to talk of television channels as brands. The branding of television channels was seen as appropriate only for the commercial niche cable and satellite channels operating across Europe, where branding was necessary to stand out from the competition and an effective way of targeting a specific audience demographic (Barker 1995: 24). However, just two years later there was a complete shift in the broadcasting trade press, with numerous articles proclaiming the importance of marketing and branding to the future success of *all* television.[8] In a report on a European Broadcasting Union workshop held in November 1996 regarding the problems facing European public service broadcasters, Edgerley claims that 'The marketing of programming and the channel as a whole has become a necessity' (1997: 51). Meanwhile, Dignam (writing in *Media Week*) argued that terrestrial broadcasters were beginning to follow BSkyB's lead in using marketing, on-air promos and branding, claiming that 'stations themselves have to project a brand personality and value that gives them a point of difference' (1997: 8). Both the BBC and ITV appointed heads of marketing from outside broadcasting (ITV appointed Procter and Gamble's European cosmetics chief and the BBC appointed Jane Frost from Lever Bros and Shell) (Dignam 1997: 8–9). At the same time, branding was central to the launch of Britain's first new public service channel since 1982, Channel 5, which has been described as 'the first terrestrial channel [in the UK] to see itself first and foremost as a brand' (Anon. 1997a: 1).

Launching Channel 5 as a brand

Channel 5 was established as a terrestrial commercial channel with limited public service obligations. The development of a new commercially funded free-to-air channel was shaped by pressure from advertisers who wanted an alternative mass channel to ITV on which to promote their products and specifically a channel that would target a younger and more upmarket audience, which was seen to be inadequately served by the existing terrestrial channels (Fanthome 2003: 120). As such, from its inception Channel 5 combined an appeal to mass audiences with a specific focus on young, upscale viewers. While it had been traditional for public service broadcasting to focus as much on giving audiences what they need as what they want (see Tracey 1998 and Scannell 1990 for a history of public service broadcasting in the UK), from its inception Channel 5 approached television as a market and its audience as consumers, and branding was central to this. This approach was quite different to the launch of the last public service channel, Channel 4, in 1982.

Channel 4 was established with a specific public service remit to serve audiences not catered for by the main terrestrial channels, to innovate in its programming and to commission programmes from the independent sector. Although Channel 4 famously developed a distinctive ident (see Chapter 5), this was quite different to the branding strategy adopted by Channel 5. Channel 4's identity was determined by public policy (laid out in the 1980 Broadcasting Act) and aimed to fill a gap in public service provision perceived by policy and programme makers. As John Ellis (2000: 152–53) argues, under its first Chief Executive, Jeremy Isaacs (1982–87), Channel 4 adopted an offer-led approach to commissioning. Commissioning editors were given the freedom to define policy in their areas of programming. Rather than basing commissioning on audience research into the 'wants' of the audience, commissioners and producers were free to develop ideas on the basis of what they felt public service broadcasting, and the audience, 'needed'.

By contrast, Channel 5's identity was based on market research. Before launching the channel, David Brook (Channel 5's Director of Marketing and Communication) commissioned research focusing on its target audience of 25–40-year-olds asking what viewers might want from a new channel and what identities they attributed to the existing terrestrial channels (Fanthome 2003: 120–21).[9] Brook used this research to establish a brand identity for Channel 5 as 'modern mainstream', which 'became a catchphrase for Channel 5 as a whole' (Fanthome 2003: 121) and was even trademarked by the new channel in order to protect what it saw as a key market position for the future of British television (Anon. 1997a: 2). Channel 5's commitment to branding was further apparent in the decision to commission the brand identity company Wolff-Olins to design its brand image, rather than a television graphics company as was industry practice at that time. Wolff-Olins developed an image based on the old television signal test card, but updated with five vibrant colours and the number 5 in a circle in the central stripe. This brand image was used in advance of the launch of the new channel (on the leaflets sent to potential viewers about the need to retune their VCRs and satellite/cable decoders in order to avoid interference with Channel 5 and on all pre-launch promotion) and in on- and off-air publicity once the channel had launched. From its inception, Channel 5 was developed as a product based on market research and branded to appeal to its target audience.

There are a number of similarities between Channel 5's launch as a brand and the branding of US television channels in the 1980s and 1990s discussed in Chapter 1. As with the Fox network, and later the other national networks, Channel 5 combined an appeal to a mass audience with the specific targeting of a young up-market audience attractive to advertisers. As with MTV, Channel 5 based its identity on research into its target audience and used this research to determine its brand identity. As with the ABC yellow re-branding, Channel 5's brand image was designed to be instantly recognizable. Indeed, Channel 5's pre-launch campaign, which combined its 'stripes' brand image with the tagline 'Give Me 5', even echoed MTV's 'I Want My MTV' campaign from the early 1980s (see Chapter 1). As with

MTV, Channel 5 drew on established stars to support this promotional campaign. In particular, it signed a deal with the Spice Girls to promote the channel.

The Spice Girls had shot to fame in the summer of 1996 and become part of an optimistic spirit of 'Cool Britannia' associated with the international success of British art and pop music ('Brit pop'). The Spice Girls were a manufactured band with a clear brand identity, adopting the tagline 'Girl Power'. They used design and styling to construct five identities (Posh, Ginger, Sporty, Baby and Scary) that were easily identifiable, exemplified their personalities and appealed to a broad young audience. By the end of 1996 the Spice Girls were endorsing products for major consumer brands, such as Pepsi and Sony Playstation, and in January 1997 the Spice Girls had managed the difficult task of breaking the US market. By securing the Spice Girls to promote Channel 5, Brook was attempting to associate the new channel with the ideals of strength, fun, vibrancy and youthfulness epitomized by the band. The Spice Girls fitted perfectly with the concept of 'modern mainstream' as a modern, young band with big mainstream pop appeal. Channel 5 was also able to use the Spice Girls to appeal specifically to the young fans of the band, as well as to appeal to advertisers by suggesting that Channel 5 would offer the same audience appeal as the Spice Girls. In using the Spice Girls, Channel 5 tied its own brand identity with that of the band. Channel 5's preview promotional film, which ran on the channel's frequency before its launch, began with the Spice Girls, each dressed in one of the five colours of Channel 5's brand image, shouting, 'Channel 5, Easter Sunday, 6pm'. The band also appeared on posters, radio and at a launch for the channel in Hyde Park, as well as opening the channel's first broadcast with a reworked version of Manfred Mann's '5-4-3-2-1' retitled 'The Power of Five'. The song linked Channel 5 and the Spice Girls as the band overtly endorsed the channel, singing, 'Take it from us, it's girl power. Take it from us, it's the power of five'. The use of cross-branding continued in the advert break on the first night of Channel 5's launch, which included advertising for Chanel No. 5 perfume, an advert for Kelloggs that used the Channel 5 stripes brand image and one in which travel firm Thompsons welcomed the channel to the air (see Fanthome 2003).

Brook also used a high-profile poster campaign that combined the colourful stripes brand design with images of key stars and programmes. These were accompanied by irreverent comments that signalled Channel 5's difference from the other channels. For example, one poster included an image of Keanu Reeves with the tagline 'See him perform without breaks', drawing attention to Channel 5's policy of screening movies without a break for the news, which was common practice on ITV (see Fanthome 2003: 125–26, 152). Other posters made fun of other channels, with one featuring an image of new Asian chef Nancy Lam wielding an electric whisk as a weapon with the tagline 'Grossman. Cogitate on this.' The poster contrasted Lam with the verbose and pretentious approach to cooking epitomized by Lloyd Grossman, who presented the BBC's cookery programme *Masterchef* (1990–).[10] This poster campaign, and the Spice Girls promotions, spoke to a young audience in their own language. As Fanthome argues, it 'carried the implication that Channel 5 understood that its audience, like itself, was bored with what it perceived as the institutional output to be found elsewhere' (2003: 126). The campaign didn't just promote Channel 5's programming; it also created and communicated a branded identity for the channel that was tied to the values and attitudes of its target audience.

The pre-launch campaign was particularly successful in generating awareness and interest in the new channel, with Channel 5 claiming in March 1997 that its campaign had achieved 85 per cent recognition for the channel's brand nationally (Anon. 1997a: 1). So successful was this branding that it was decided to use it in the channel's on-air idents which were created by Californian company Silver Hammer. The presentation style that Silver Hammer developed retained the logo with the number five in a circle and the five coloured stripes, but reduced their significance, for example by using them to underline boxes in which promo films appeared. The aim was to draw on the personality already created by the branding campaign, but to enable it to be adapted, rather than fixed to a singular repetitive image.[11] In addition, Channel 5 was the first UK terrestrial broadcaster to include its ident in the corner of the screen throughout all its programming (Anon. 1997a: 4).

A key difference between Channel 5 and MTV, however, was in the relationship between the brand identity created and the programmes aired. Chapter 1 demonstrated how MTV (and later Fox and HBO) developed a branding strategy that extended across all aspects of the channel's output, so that the programming, scheduling, on-screen promotions and off-screen advertising combined to present a coherent brand personalization for the channel. By contrast, Channel 5's programming failed to live up to the identity conveyed by its brand image. Dawn Airey (Channel 5's Director of Programmes) struggled with a low programme budget and the channel's Chairman, Greg Dyke, claimed that the channel suffered from 'marketing ideas not reality' (cited in Fanthome 2003: 130).[12] Although Channel 5 was the first UK television channel to be developed as a brand, there was still a significant separation of branding from programme production. The Channel 5 brand failed to act as a frame or interface between consumers/viewers, the channel and its producers, because a central aspect of the way in which a channel communicated its identity to its consumers (its programming) was at odds with the personality communicated in the promotion of the channel.

Essentially, although Brook developed a brand personality for Channel 5, branding was used principally as a promotional tool, rather than as an overall approach to the work of the channel. In fact, while Channel 5 went to the trouble of trademarking the term 'modern mainstream', it is more commonly associated with another phrase attributed to the channel by its Director of Programmes, Dawn Airey, in 1999. In the years following its launch Channel 5 continued to struggle with its programme budget and in 1998 introduced a late-night segment of risqué and often explicit programming. The ITC criticized Channel 5's late-night sexually explicit content, and a report from the Broadcasting Standards Commission claimed that viewers were concerned about sex on television. Responding to these criticisms in an article in the *Guardian* newspaper, Airey claimed:

> We are a bit rude, there's no two ways about it. Bosoms, balls and brutality are occasionally part of our programming mix. To be blunt, *Channel 5 is films, fucking and football*, but we are more than that. We do not go out to deliberately shock our viewers, because if you shock your viewers you alienate them and you may as well go home. However, we're not afraid to be raw and raunchy.
>
> (Dawn Airey, cited Gibson 1999, my italics).

The phrase 'films, fucking and football' was subsequently picked up by the media and has replaced the largely forgotten phrase of 'modern mainstream' as an unintentional branded identity for the channel. It is ironic that, while Channel 5 launched with the aim of attracting a young upscale audience, it ended up being associated with the kind of programming (particularly football and films) more likely to appeal to Sky's target audiences of C1s and C2s.

ITV's 'From The Heart' campaign

If Channel 5 struggled to develop a coherent brand identity that extended across the promotion and programming of the channel, this was even more complex for its main competitor, ITV. ITV was established in 1955 as a federation of regional companies funded by advertising, but with a specific remit that included serving their local communities. While a small number of regional franchises came to dominate the provision of networked prime-time programming (see Johnson and Turnock 2005), the regional structure of ITV remained intact into the 1990s. These regional franchises often had very clear channel identities communicated through recognizable idents, often with a particular regional flavour.[13] However, relaxation of media ownership rules in the 1990s enabled consolidation in response to the increasing pressures on the individual ITV franchises from commercial competition. Meanwhile, the replacement of the IBA with the ITC following the 1990 Broadcasting Act transformed the structure of ITV. Previously, the IBA had acted as both a broadcaster and regulator for ITV, with the individual franchises acting as suppliers of programmes that the IBA transmitted. This gave the IBA the power to preview programmes and approve schedules prior to transmission. By contrast, the ITC was established purely as a regulator. National Transcommunications Ltd (NTL) was set up to take over the transmission services of the IBA (and then privatized). Meanwhile, the ITV Network Centre was established with the responsibility to commission and schedule programmes to be shown across the ITV network (see Johnson and Turnock 2005: 28).

By 1997 the ITV franchises were largely distributed amongst three corporations: Granada, Carlton and United News and Media (UNM). In the same year, John Hardie from Proctor and Gamble was appointed as ITV's first marketing and commercial director in the face of a declining audience share. A key problem facing Hardie was that the overall identity of ITV as a network was seen to be in conflict with the individual identities of the regional franchises. For example, Jim Hytner, marketing director at BSkyB argued:

> You can't have the [regional franchises] Carlton or LWT brand stronger than ITV. We'll probably still see them promoting themselves but that shouldn't happen. Everything should fall under the umbrella brand and all the regional marketing resources must report in to the marketing director.
>
> (cited in Crawford 1997)

Hardie centralized the promotional activities of the network so that all on- and off-air marketing for its programming was consistent across the output of all the regional franchises (Marsh 1998). As well as developing consistent promotion for its programming, ITV also launched a campaign designed to convey an overall brand identity for the network. The 'From the Heart' campaign included a short promotional film shown across the network drawing on key ITV networked programmes, such as *Heartbeat* (1992–2010), *Inspector Morse* (1987–2000) and *Coronation Street* (1960–), with a voice-over that emphasized the 'new passion' and 'new blood' of the 'new ITV'. The promotional campaign drew attention to the range of genres offered by the channel – from drama, to sport, to quiz shows – as well as positioning the channel as coming from 'the heart of the nation'. It began and ended with a new ITV logo accompanied by a small heart ident. The network's aim was that the idents of the individual franchises would eventually be replaced by this ITV logo, much as Fox attempted to persuade its affiliates to rebrand themselves with the Fox name and logo in the USA in the 1990s (see Chapter 1). However, it was not until the second half of 1999 that ITV managed to persuade the franchises to carry the new ITV ident and tagline because of fears that this would dilute their own regional channel identities. Even then, the ITV logo was used alongside the logos of the individual franchises, and the franchises in Scotland and Northern Ireland refused to carry the ITV logo at all (Bentley 1999).

The rationale for ITV's attempt to construct a singular identity across the franchise was twofold. First, the network believed that, in order to compete effectively with the new commercial companies, it needed to have a more coherent and clear identity with which its viewers could identify. This stemmed in part from pressure from the advertising industry, which had seen ITV's audience share diminish at the same time as advertising rates had increased. ITV's key competition for advertising revenue came from cable and satellite stations (as well as imminent competition from digital, as we shall see below), which were able to deliver targeted, but small, audiences for advertisers. A key advantage that ITV had over advertiser-funded cable and satellite services to advertisers was its potential reach to a wider, if less differentiated, audience. However, this reach was only possible across ITV's networked programmes, making ITV's unique selling point to advertisers its reach as a national network.[14] As branding became more accepted in the UK television industry, the ITV national network appeared to be lacking a clear brand identity, even though many of its regional franchises actually had very clear and long-standing brand identities that were targeted to their specific regional audience segments. It is perhaps ironic that, while elsewhere the industry was increasingly turning to niche targeting, the ITV network was effectively attempting to undermine the relationships that some of its long-standing regional franchises had with their audiences. Andrew Bowden (2002) argues that a corporate identity for the ITV network was not necessary, as viewers were able to carry the dual association of their regional franchise with the network overall, and the regional franchises often had strong brand identities based on loyal relationships with their target viewers. It is possible, then, that the 'From the Heart' campaign was driven more by the corporate needs of the increasingly consolidated ITV network to construct an identity, particularly in its relationship with advertisers, than by a desire to connect more clearly with viewers. Second, ITV was about to launch a new channel, ITV2, to be provided by the digital terrestrial services that were emerging in the UK during 1998. As we shall go on to see, the new digital channels launched by the public service broadcasters over the late 1990s were primarily approached and understood as brand extensions that could draw on the value and audience loyalty of the original public service brand. It was therefore important for ITV to improve the value of its overall ITV brand in order to support its ambitions to generate new brand extensions.

Television goes digital

Despite some of the anxieties and inconsistencies in the adoption of branding by the British television industry, the emergence of digital television in the late 1990s consolidated the role of branding as a central strategy in the changing media landscape. It was the Conservative government's Broadcasting Bill and the subsequent 1996 Broadcasting Act that drove the development of digital terrestrial television in the UK. The government charged the ITC with the job of allocating the six available multiplexes on the newly proposed digital terrestrial broadcasting system (DTB), with slots guaranteed for BBC One and Two, ITV, Channel 4, S4C (Welsh-language service in Wales) and Channel 5.[15] The BBC bid for the first multiplex, with ITV and Channel 4 sharing the second, and Channel 5 and S4C taking space on the third (Sparks 2007: 37). ITC invited bids for the rest of the third multiplex and the final three available multiplexes. The main bidders for these final multiplexes were Digital Television Network (DTN), headed by the US cable company Cabletel, and British Digital Broadcasting (BDB) a partnership between BSkyB and the two ITV companies, Carlton and Granada.[16] Sparks argues that this combined bid demonstrated that the major British broadcasters preferred to move forward in this venture with BSkyB as a partner, rather than a competitor (2007: 39). However, the European competition authorities deemed BSkyB's involvement as anti-competitive and the company was forced to withdraw and act only as a programme provider to BDB (Sparks 2007: 40).

Meanwhile, BSkyB was looking to develop a digital satellite service, which it launched in 1998. Initial customer take-up was good, and from the summer of 1999 BSkyB offered consumers its digital set-top box for free in order to further enhance subscriptions, which, as Goodwin argues, were becoming the fastest growing form of new revenue within the British television industry in the 1990s (1998: 157). Meanwhile, BDB branded its new digital terrestrial service as ONdigital, but now faced direct competition from BSkyB's digital satellite service, which was able to build on its established analogue satellite business. As Sparks argues, 'Unable to compete with satellite on channel quantity, ONdigital desperately needed some compensating distinction – but it was hard to detect' (2007: 45). Faced with direct competition with an established pay-television provider, ONdigital struggled to generate sufficient subscribers and, in 2001, decided to rebrand the service ITV Digital, making use of the established ITV brand name in order to attract customers. However, following continued financial problems, exacerbated by a misjudged deal with the Nationwide League for football coverage, ITV Digital went into administration in March 2002.[17] The BBC stepped into the digital terrestrial arena through a joint venture with Crown Castle and BSkyB to launch Freeview, a free but more limited digital terrestrial service. In convincing the government that three competing commercial subscription digital platforms (digital satellite, digital cable and digital terrestrial) were not commercially viable, the BBC also secured a central position for the corporation in the digital landscape as provider of free programming that would make it much harder for future governments to remove the licence fee (Sparks 2007: 80–81).

As in the USA, the development of digital television opened up the possibility of a far greater number of television channels, and all the existing broadcasters launched new digital channels. Branding played a significant part here. As we shall see in more detail in the next chapter, all of the terrestrial broadcasters used the arrival of digital terrestrial to develop new channels based on their existing channel brands. ITV launched ITV2 in 1998, ITV3 in 2004 and ITV4 in 2005. Channel 4 launched FilmFour in 1998, E4 in 2001 and More4 in 2005. Meanwhile, the BBC launched BBC News 24 in 1997, BBC Choice in 1998 (relaunched as BBC Three in February 2003), BBC Knowledge in 1999 (relaunched as BBC Four in March 2002) and CBeebies and CBBC in 2002.[18] Channel 5 (rebranded as Five in 2002) launched Five USA (originally Five US) and Fiver (originally Five Life) in 2006. While all these digital channels depended significantly on exploiting the brand name of the terrestrial broadcaster, branding was also used to distinguish the new commercial ventures of the public service broadcasters from their public service brands. From the late 1980s all the public service broadcasters had begun to expand into various commercial ventures, from Granada's and Carlton's failed attempts to enter the commercial satellite and digital terrestrial arenas, to the increased focus of Channel 4 and the BBC on expanding their commercial enterprises (see Chapter 4). In April 1992 the BBC joined with Thames Television (which had lost its ITV London franchise) to create UK Gold, a satellite channel drawing on the archives of both companies (Tracey 1998). The BBC then went on to extend its development of commercial channels in 1997 through a joint venture between BBC Worldwide (the BBC's commercial arm) and Flextech, called UKTV. The UKTV channels illustrate the value of branding for the public service broadcasters as a way of distinguishing such commercial ventures from their public service activities.

UKTV

Before launching its BBC-branded digital channels, BBC Worldwide entered into a joint commercial venture with Flextech, UKTV, to build on its success with UK Gold and develop a slate of new channels to be carried on cable and satellite services (and on digital after it launched in 1998).[19] Flextech's biggest shareholder was TCI, which part-owned cable operator Telewest, one of the first cable operators to carry the new UKTV stations (Sage 1997). For the BBC, the venture provided a guaranteed site through which to financially exploit its extensive back catalogue of programmes, with UKTV having a first-look deal on all BBC Worldwide programmes. The BBC's content was particularly valuable to the deal because of the lower budgets for cable and satellite television production.[20] While, in 1997, the typical budget for a terrestrial drama was £500,000 per hour, UKTV's average budget was only £10,000 per hour for original programmes (and these only made up 15 per cent of its schedules). The centrality of BBC content not only made sense financially, but also in terms of attracting audiences to the new channels. As Pippa Considine wrote of the venture, 'The output of UKTV also reflects its backers' strategy of sticking with building on the strengths of BBC brands, including reformatted and extended versions of established shows such as *Top Gear GTI*' (1997: 16).

However, the place of the BBC brand in UKTV is complex. On the one hand, the venture relied heavily on the audience's knowledge of and interest in the BBC programmes that the channels aired. On the other hand, BBC Worldwide and Flextech did not use the BBC's corporate brand for the new channels, but developed a new brand identity that united the channels around the moniker 'UKTV'. The absence of the BBC's corporate brand identity here functioned to clearly separate out this joint commercial venture from the BBC's public services, such as its terrestrial channels and the digital channels that it was developing at around the same time. However, the strong association of key programme brands, such as *Top Gear* (BBC, 1978–), with the BBC allowed the UKTV channels to draw on the brand equity of the BBC's corporate brand through the use of its programming. Indeed, as Julie Light (2004: 98) points out, a number of the channel names emphasized UKTV's association with BBC programming, such as factual channel UK Horizon (drawing on the BBC's long-running topical science programme, *Horizon* (1964–)) and arts channel UK Arena (drawing on the BBC's arts strand, *Arena* (1975–)).

Indeed, UKTV's entire strategy in developing channels was based around programming. The company identified key programme genres targeted at specific audiences and branded each channel accordingly. It launched three channels (in addition to UK Gold, which showed classic comedies) in November 1997: UK Horizon, UK Arena and UK Style (leisure and lifestyle programmes).[21] Each channel name emphasized the generic basis of the programming and united the channels through an association with Britishness. A further key benefit of this strategy was that UKTV effectively acted as an 'umbrella brand' (Keeling, cited in Revoir 2002: 17), offering UKTV the value of a branded presence on the electronic programme guides that became increasingly central to the navigation of television following the emergence of digital in 1998, as well as providing the possibility for cross-promotion and complementary scheduling.

By 2003, UKTV had a slate of seven channels, having added UK Food, UK History and UK Bright Ideas, with plans to add more channels in the coming years. In 2001 it teamed up with Sony's broadband service, Go Interact TV, to offer enhanced television services, such as DIY tips on UK Style and quizzes and trivia on UK Gold (Anon. 2001: 9). In 2006, UKTV signed a two-year deal with the Microsoft portal, MSN UK, to offer short clips from its shows for download. Each clip would be branded with the relevant UKTV channel logo and offer a click-through to the UKTV channel website. As Amber Coley (UKTV's commercial manager) argued of the deal, 'This partnership is a cost-effective way to introduce UKTV's compelling broadcast and online content to a much wider audience' (cited in Thompson 2006: 5). By 2006, UKTV was the UK's second largest non-terrestrial broadcaster (after BSkyB) and its collective audience share in digital homes over Christmas 2005 exceeded that for Channel 5 (Snoddy 2006: 14).

However, by 2006, UKTV was dealing with a broadcasting environment that was rapidly changing due to the emergence of television on the internet and the move towards digital switch-over. In September 2005 Tessa Jowell (Secretary of State for Culture, Media and Sport) announced the government's plans for a phased switch-over to digital, beginning in 2008 and ending in 2012 (Sparks 2007: 111).[22] In the same year, the launch of YouTube demonstrated the possibility of the internet as a site for the distribution of audio-visual content online, more homes had digital television than did not, the majority of UK homes had access to the internet and the number of mobile phones exceeded the total population of the UK (BBC 2005: 5). At the same time, Freeview (launched in October 2002) had proved hugely successful in driving the take-up of digital television, and all the terrestrial broadcasters, including the BBC, had launched a slate of channels available across all the digital platforms. Such activities threatened UKTV's position in the non-terrestrial marketplace. In 2006 Dick Emery (UKTV's Chief Executive) complained that ITV and Channel 4's digital channels unfairly benefitted from their national sales teams and cross-promotional possibilities on their terrestrial channels (Snoddy 2006: 14). As the BBC extracted more value from its archive through repeats on its own digital channels, BBC Three and BBC Four, the value of UKTV's archive deal with BBC Worldwide was being diminished. Effectively, the BBC had become both a competitor and a partner with UKTV.

UKTV's response to these threats was to rebrand its slate of channels in order to more clearly articulate its relationship with its audience. It began by rebranding UKTV G2 as 'Dave' for its launch on Freeview on 19 October 2007 (replacing UKTV Bright Ideas). The rebrand aimed to target the channel more directly at a core audience of upmarket 16–44-year-old men. As Julia Jordan (Executive Director of UKTV) explained, this was important not only to make the channel stand out and appeal to this niche demographic, but also to attract advertisers who would better understand the personality of the channel (2007). This rebranding campaign turned UKTV G2 from a numerically identified channel that existed as part of the umbrella of UKTV channels to a personality whose name embodied the idealized perception of its audience. Red Bee's rebranding campaign for Dave created a tagline for the channel as 'the home of witty banter' that explained the kind of personality that the channel was attempting to convey and reconstructed the channel as a destination. Indeed, the channel idents and advertising campaign for Dave were based around the idea of a not-too-aspirational gentlemen's club, with patterned wallpaper, oil paintings and stuffed animals, creating the sense of the channel as an environment that the viewers could inhabit (Mawer 2009). This personality chimed with the core BBC programmes offered by the channel, such as the motoring show *Top Gear*, the sitcom *Men Behaving Badly* (BBC, 1992–99), and the quiz show *QI* (BBC, 2007–). At the same time, the channel increased its spending on original programming in order to further stand-out in the market. As *Campaign* claimed of the rebrand:

> Dave has grown from the 29th to the tenth-largest channel in multichannel homes and is more than three times bigger in share and volume terms than UKTV G2. And Dave has delivered a 1.2 per cent share compared to UKTV G2's 0.4 per cent (Barb [Broadcasters' Audience Research Board], June to July). Importantly, in a difficult market, Dave has grown from being the fifth-most profitable channel in the UKTV portfolio to the second, contributing an extra £25 million in ad revenue following the relaunch. Spontaneous awareness of the channel has increased from 2 per cent for UKTV G2 to 32 per cent for Dave and during its first six months on air, Dave attracted more than eight million new viewers to the UKTV network. ... The tone and weight of Dave's marketing (launch advertising featured a strange world of images such as oil paintings and stuffed giraffes designed to deliver '*Peter's Friends* meets *The Royal Tenenbaums*' feel) created a distinct culture for the brand in an overcrowded market and has helped to maintain an industry buzz around the channel, more than a year on from its launch.
>
> (Anon. 2008)

Following this success with Dave, UKTV commissioned Red Bee to rebrand the rest of its slate of ten channels, which have also been given personalities, such as turning UKTV People into Blighty, UKTV Drama into Alibi (shifting from a general drama channel into a specific crime drama channel) and UKTV History into Yesterday. Charlie Mawer, Executive Creative Director of Red Bee Media, claims that these rebrands have enabled the channels to engage in cross-promotional deals with other commercial brands, citing the partnership between Blighty and the clothes retailer Ted Baker, who created Blighty window displays (Mawer 2009). Essentially UKTV shifted from a brand strategy that emphasized its network of channels to one that focused on communicating the distinctive personality of niche channel brands with core targeted audience groups: from an umbrella brand to a set of personality brands.

The branding strategy adopted by UKTV is in stark contrast to that adopted by the terrestrial broadcasters, who have used their corporate brand identities and numerical attributes when developing new digital channels. This extended to the branding of their online on-demand services, such as

Channel 4's 4oD, the BBC's iPlayer and ITV's ITVPlayer. As we shall go on to see in more detail in the next chapter, the corporate brand was central to the movement of public service broadcasters into digital television, not only because it helped draw audiences to these new services, but also because it reinforced the public service value behind their digital initiatives. This is particularly the case with the BBC. Its new Charter published in October 2006 laid out six 'public purposes' for the BBC, including 'taking a leading role in the switchover to digital television' (BBC 2006: 3). These public purposes were key criteria against which the BBC's performance would be evaluated and provided a framework and justification for the BBC's use of licence fee revenue to develop new services, such as its digital channels, its websites and the on-demand catch-up service offered through the iPlayer. As such, the Charter made these services a central part of the BBC's public service remit and, therefore, a central part of its corporate brand. By contrast, the BBC's involvement in the UKTV channels was part of the commercial activities of its subsidiary BBC Worldwide, which functions 'to maximize profits on behalf of the BBC by creating, acquiring, developing and exploiting media content and media brands. … and return profits to the BBC to be reinvested in programmes and services to help keep the UK licence fee as low as possible' (BBC Worldwide 2010), even if these commercial ventures are in competition with the BBC's digital channels, as is the case with the UKTV channels. While the BBC Annual Report and Accounts for 2003–4 stressed that 'BBC Worldwide will only engage in activities that fit the BBC's values' (BBC 2004: 68), it is also important that these commercial ventures are clearly distinguished within the UK from the BBC's services that embody its public service values, and the use (or not) of the BBC brand contributes to this distinction.[23]

Conclusions

The reasons for the shift to branding in the UK are similar to those in the USA, with deregulation, the emergence of cable, satellite and digital services, and the impact of the internet all creating a more competitive commercial environment. As in the USA, in the UK this has led to an increase in channels, such as Dave, targeted at and branded to appeal to valuable niche demographics. As in the USA, strong brand identities have also assisted the major broadcasters in expanding into new services that are offered across a wider range of platforms in an attempt to militate against increased competition. In addition, in the UK we have also seen the increasing importance of the repurposing of content and the value of strong programme brands that can also add value to different channel brands, such as in the BBC's exploitation of its archive in developing the UKTV channels. In each case, branding has been used by the broadcasters examined in this chapter for competitive commercial advantage.

In contrast to the traditional public service position, these branding strategies have depended on a conceptualization of the audience as consumer, rather than citizen. Channel 5's brand identity was determined by market research that identified a gap in the market and targeted the channel to the perceived wants of its intended audience. The fact that Channel 5's carefully constructed brand identity has been largely forgotten in the wake of a comment by one of the broadcaster's executives that better reflected the actual identity of the channel's service exemplifies the limits of brand management. It also points to the way in which branding functions as an interface that shapes, but cannot totally control, the consumer's engagement with the brand. ITV's attempts to develop an umbrella brand identity that eclipsed the individual identities of its regional franchises was driven by the commercial demands of its advertisers and its plans to extend its channel brand into digital, over the needs of its differentiated audience or its public service remit to serve that audience. UKTV was developed as an umbrella brand drawing together a range of generically differentiated channels in order to help each new channel stand out in the marketplace. However, in the face of increased competition from the development of digital television and new media, UKTV shifted towards rebranding its channels as personality brands, defined in relation to the values and identities of their target demographics, rather than by the genre of their programming. This strategy was also valuable as it created an identity for the channels that was not so dependent on programming at a time when the repurposing of programmes was becoming more common (as we saw in the USA).

All of these examples would suggest that the emergence of branding within the UK television industry is tied to the increased marketization and commercialization of British broadcasting. Yet, there are also hints in this history at a more complex picture. Over the past 25 years, the UK's public service broadcasters have had to engage in more and more commercial practices in order to remain financially viable, such as the BBC's co-development of the UKTV channels. At the same time, however, these public service broadcasters, and particularly the BBC, have been charged with supporting the take-up of digital and have developed new digital services and initiatives that potentially conflict with their commercial services in order to fulfil this public service remit. While the BBC has extended its corporate and channel brands onto new platforms in launching new digital channels and services as part of its new public purpose, it has also developed separate brand identities for its commercial services in order to distinguish them from its core public services. While it appears, therefore, that branding emerges as a response to the shift away from television as a public service towards conceptualizing television as a consumer product in a commercial marketplace, it does appear that branding has been used to support the public service, as well as the commercial, activities of the BBC. In the next chapter we will ask whether the use of branding in relation to the public service provision of the BBC and Channel 4 ultimately undermines their core public service remits, or whether branding can be used to support the values of public service broadcasting.

Notes

1 Although Channel 4 is funded by advertising, it has a stronger public service remit than ITV, which has successfully campaigned to have its public service requirements reduced over the past 15 years (see Johnson and Turnock 2005).
2 A centre-right critique of public service broadcasting existed in the UK from the 1940s, but remained marginal until the 1980s (O'Malley 2009: 8).
3 David Hesmondhalgh argues that the subsequent government decision not to introduce advertising to the BBC was for economic reasons, as commercial companies feared increased competition for advertising revenue (2002: 123).
4 The BBC did attempt to develop two DBS channels in the early 1980s, but pulled out after it failed to secure financial partnerships with technology manufacturers (see Goodwin 1998).
5 See Tracey (1998) and Hollins (1984) for the early history of cable in the UK.
6 Radio broadcasting was now to be regulated by a separate body, the Radio Authority.
7 Channel 4 was established as a publisher, rather than a producer, of programming, but ITV and the BBC had produced the majority of their programming in-house.
8 As we shall see in Chapter 4, public service broadcasters such as the BBC and Channel 4 were using branding before the mid-1990s, but it was only in the mid-1990s that the adoption of branding became more generally recognized across all of the industry as a key strategy and that branding began to form a central part of the industrial discourse about public service television.
9 Channel 5 epitomized the redefinition of public service television at this time from giving the audience what they need to being accountable to the audience and serving their wants as much as their needs.
10 *Masterchef* has since been relaunched as a more entertainment-oriented cookery contest.
11 As we shall see in Chapter 5, around this time the adaptability of on-screen presentation became an important way of tying the identity of the channel to the programmes that it aired.
12 It is worth bearing in mind that, when Fox launched, it began with just two nights of programming and then gradually expanded its hours over time. This was a luxury that was not available to Channel 5, which had to launch with a full slate of programmes.
13 This did vary from region to region. In some places the regional franchise had changed hands a number of times or did not cover an area with a clear and coherent regional identity. By contrast, other franchises had strong histories and a clear connection with their local community, such as Granada in the North-West and Anglia in the East.
14 This is not to argue that the ITV franchises did not also sell regionally targeted advertising, but that its unique selling point in relation to competition from niche cable and satellite services (particularly at a time when the regional franchises were consolidating) was its national reach to a mass audience.
15 Over the BBC's history, the official ways of rendering its channel names have been subject to change. For consistency, this book will adopt the current method of spelling its channel names (BBC One, rather than BBC1), which was adopted in 1997 as part of a larger corporate rebrand.
16 The BBC's commercial arm, BBC Worldwide, also added its support to the bid by offering its new pay UKTV channels to BDB.
17 It is perhaps ironic that ITV Digital was brought down by a deal to air football, considering the central role that sports played in the success of BSkyB's analogue satellite service. However, the Nationwide League did not contain the major football teams and so

was not enough on its own to drive up significant subscriber numbers. It also suggests that we should be wary of attributing the success of large corporations such as BSkyB to one programming decision. Indeed, Michael Sparks canvassed those involved in ITV Digital about the reasons for its failure and they identified problems with technology, inaccurate forecasts about coverage, and regulation that prevented effective commercial competition as the key problems (2007: 75–76).

18 The BBC also launched BBC Parliament in 1998 following its purchase of the Parliament Channel which had run on cable. Initially, BBC Parliament was an audio-only service, adding visuals in 2002.

19 In 1997 Flextech bought an 80 per cent share in UK Gold, having previously owned a 27 per cent share in the channel, and it was subsequently brought under the UKTV umbrella brand.

20 The BBC was not the only terrestrial broadcaster in the UK to launch satellite and cable channels in the mid-1990s. In 1996 Granada launched a boutique of services as part of GSkyB, a joint venture with BSkyB, and Carlton launched Carlton Select and the Carlton Food Network after purchasing SelecTV. Both ventures initially struggled to generate audiences, a difficulty that Andy Bird (co-managing director and executive vice-president at Turner Broadcasting Systems) claimed was because 'Granada and Carlton are not brands – they are part of ITV' (cited in Considine 1997: 17).

21 In 2001 UK Arena was rebranded as UK Drama to give it a clearer brand identity. The rebranding was accompanied by a joint campaign between Sky and UKTV that ran on television, radio and in the press (Anon. 2000: 6).

22 Switch-off of the analogue signal actually began in 2007 (see Sparks 2007).

23 We will examine the complexity of the BBC's and Channel 4's commercial activities and their relationship to public service broadcasting in more detail in Chapter 4, including the use of the BBC brand by BBC Worldwide in launching new international channels, such as BBC America.

4

THE END OF PUBLIC SERVICE BROADCASTING?

Branding Channel 4 and the BBC

In the 1980s it was public knowledge that the British Prime Minister Margaret Thatcher was keen to see advertising replace the licence fee as the means of funding the BBC. Consequently, when the Conservative government set up the Peacock Committee in the summer of 1985 to consider the future funding of the BBC, it was widely expected that the committee would recommend the introduction of advertising on the corporation's services (see Chapter 3). On 20 January 1986, while the Peacock Committee was still meeting, an episode of BBC One's prime-time chat show *Wogan*, hosted by popular presenter Terry Wogan, took the unusual step of cutting to an advert break part way through the programme.[1] The ad break consisted of a promotional film directed by Alan Parker based on the Monty Python sketch 'What have the Roman's ever done for us?' and starring John Cleese and a host of stars who all appeared for free. In the film Cleese is depicted in a pub complaining about the cost of his licence fee and exclaiming 'what have the BBC ever given us?' A slew of BBC stars then came forward listing the wide range of different kinds of quality programmes offered by the corporation, leading Cleese to admit:

> Apart from excellent drama, the natural history programmes, the sports coverage, news, current affairs, documentaries, the consumer programmes, series, films, Radio 1, Radio 2, Radio 3, Radio 4, children's television, science, comedy, alternative comedy and music, what have the BBC ever given us?

Terry Wogan then appeared on a television screen in the corner of the pub saying 'well, there's chat shows'. The film ended with the caption, 'The BBC. Is 16p a day really too much to ask?', making reference to the daily cost of the licence fee. After cutting back to *Wogan* at the end of the film, Terry Wogan went on to launch a competition for viewers to name all of the stars in the ad and complete a tie-breaker, 'The BBC is good value at 16p a day because … '. The winning tie-break announced on the *Wogan* show on

31 January 1986 was 'it's cheaper than a paper or a pint'. The BBC then adopted this concept in 1993 with a further set of promotional films that equated the daily cost of the BBC with a range of cheap household items, such as a picture hook and one prawn.

Although the Peacock Report, published in 1986, argued for retaining the licence fee, this was only to be until broadcasters were technologically able to sell their programmes directly to viewers, and the report strongly advocated moving broadcasting towards a full market as soon as possible (see Chapter 3). A year later, in 1987, the BBC launched a corporate branding strategy 'in anticipation of the increasingly competitive and complex broadcasting market' (BBC 1991: 65). In addition to a new corporate logo, coat of arms and flag, the BBC introduced logos for its different units, such as BBC Sports and BBC Education, new idents for its radio stations and a rebranding campaign for its two main terrestrial television channels, BBC One and BBC Two. The BBC also broadcast a televised 'annual report to licence-payers', entitled *See For Yourself*, every January from 1988 to 1992 that demonstrated how the corporation spent the licence fee.[2] While the BBC described these films as 'accountability programmes', as with the John Cleese film, they functioned to communicate publicly the role and value of the BBC in the midst of political pressure on the corporation and on public services more broadly. As the BBC claimed of these various corporate branding activities, 'It is important to the BBC that the public is made aware both of its name and of the range and quality of the programmes which carry that name' (BBC 1991: 65).

As examined in Chapter 3, such branding campaigns were adopted by British broadcasters in response to the deregulation of broadcasting, the emergence of commercial satellite, cable and digital services, and the impact of the internet and other new media. While branding might seem to be a natural strategy for the competitive commercial environment of US television, the adoption of branding, with its historic associations with marketing for competitive advantage and commercial gain, has been more problematic for UK public service broadcasters. As a consequence, a key question in discussions of branding and UK television has been whether the explicit adoption of branding by UK public service broadcasters is merely indicative of the commercialization of British public service television, or whether branding can support the aims of UK public service broadcasters. It is to this question that this chapter will turn more directly, focusing on the BBC and Channel 4.

The BBC's position as the licence fee funded public service broadcaster has made it particularly vulnerable to the neo-liberal political turn in broadcasting policy and regulation since the mid-1980s. Over this period the BBC's licence fee has been threatened and reduced, and the BBC has been forced to become more competitive and more commercially self-sufficient. It is within this context that it began to adopt branding as a more central strategy. As we shall see, these activities have been seen to threaten the

BBC's position in British broadcasting in two ways: either by undermining its public service provision, or by opening it up to criticisms of exploiting its privileged funding position to gain commercial advantage. Yet, as the above quotation suggests, the BBC did not see the adoption of branding purely in commercial terms, but also as a way of communicating the value of the BBC to the public.

However, the BBC is not the only public service provider in the UK, with the commercially funded broadcasters ITV, Channel 4 and Channel 5 also regulated as public services. While ITV has responded to the increased pressures of the contemporary media landscape by arguing for a reduction in its public service requirements, and Channel 5 has always had a relatively limited public service remit, Channel 4 has continued to argue for retaining its central place within the UK's public service provision, offering innovative content for audiences not served by other broadcasters. Yet, Channel 4 has also had to respond to the changes in the media landscape in order to retain its audience share and advertising revenues and, as we shall see, has also been accused of turning away from its public service values in favour of profit.

In the limited academic debate about branding in the UK there are two positions taken towards its impact on public service broadcasting, which mirror the broader arguments about public service broadcasting in the digital era. On the one hand is the argument that branding contributes to a broader decline of public service broadcasting (see Born 2004). This argument has three facets. First, branding and marketing decisions are seen to dominate programme production over public service values. Second, branding constitutes an address to the viewer as a consumer, rather than a citizen. Third, branding reduces public service values to banal taglines and reductive logos. On the other hand, branding is regarded as a necessary strategy in a more commercially oriented media landscape. For example, as Petros Iosifidis claims, when arguing that the full licence-fee should be retained for the BBC and not 'top-sliced' to pay for public service programming on other channels, such as Channel 4, 'institutional competition for PS [public service] provision risks becoming unacceptable if this implies a weaker BBC, which is Britain's most powerful global brand and most trusted source globally (most people turn to the BBC's website for reliable information)' (2008: 33). Here, the development of the BBC as a 'powerful global brand' has significant value for the UK economy, nationally and globally. This brand, based as it is on the values, history, identity and reputation of the BBC, is inextricably linked to public service broadcasting. In this chapter I want to examine in more detail the debates about whether branding is detrimental to public service broadcasting by comparing the branding activities of the licence fee funded BBC and the commercially funded Channel 4: two broadcasters that have both publically stated their commitment to retaining public service broadcasting as central to their operations.

Channel 4: branding, niche audiences and the attention economy

When Channel 4 launched in November 1982 it included distinctive on-screen idents of coloured blocks spinning through the air in a variety of sequences before forming the iconic number four. Designed by Martin Lambie-Nairn, and using computer-generated imagery not yet introduced in Europe, the logo perfectly encapsulated Channel 4's public service remit to cater for a wide range of different audiences with programmes not found on the other channels: of being something for everyone some of the time. Despite this use of a distinctive ident that articulated Channel 4's identity and that Jeremy Isaacs (Chief Executive of Channel 4, 1980–87) described as 'the envy of our peers' (1989: 41), it was not until the 1990s that branding emerged as a more central strategy for the channel, either in branding itself as a corporation or branding its channels, programmes and services. In fact, Channel 4 only turned to branding as a more systematic strategy after the 1990 Broadcasting Act. The Act changed the way that Channel 4 was funded. Up until 1993, ITV sold advertising on Channel 4, providing the channel with a fixed income. From 1993 Channel 4 would be required to sell its own advertising (although, because of a levy to ITV, it did not get to keep all the revenue from its advertising sales until 1999). Furthermore, the merger of Sky with BSB in November 1990 (see Chapter 3) signalled the emergence of satellite television as potential competition for terrestrial broadcasters and, in particular, with the increase in the number of commercially funded channels, offered competition for advertising. Channel 4's turn to branding was intricately tied to two other strategies adopted in response to these shifts and in the light of the broader deregulatory and neo-liberal political landscape outlined in Chapter 3: niche targeting and commercial expansion.[3] These strategies are outlined in Channel 4's annual reports in the early 1990s, and particularly in 1993, the year in which it began to sell its own advertising.

Channel 4 and niche targeting

In 1991 Channel 4 outlined its strategy to increase its audience share in order to prove to advertisers that the channel could deliver sufficient audiences to justify purchase of its airtime and to provide a cushion from the increasing competition anticipated from cable and satellite. However, Channel 4 was not simply interested in increasing overall share. In addition, the channel focused on two specific demographic groups that had already been identified as sections of the population that the channel was particularly good at attracting: 16–34-year-olds and ABC1s (the youth and upmarket demographics), both of whom were light viewers of ITV and of television in general (see Channel 4 1991). When Channel 4 started to sell its own advertising in 1993 it based its sales strategy on selling advertisers these key niche demographics, rather than selling based on brute ratings. This is described in Channel 4's Annual Report for 1993 as a strategy designed:

> to sell advertisers specific types of audiences (e.g. 16–34 year old men) which closely match their target purchasers, thereby utilising the channel's strength in delivering a different viewer profile from ITV. (The ITV policy has primarily been based on broad audience groups rather than specific type.)
>
> (Channel 4 1993: 28)

While this strategy of niche targeting was a commercial one designed to increase revenue for the channel, Channel 4 was at pains to assert that it was also entirely in line with its public service remit. For example, as Chairman of Channel 4 in 1991, Richard Attenborough claimed, 'Our remit attracts audiences who have great appeal to advertisers; audiences not easily identified on ITV. The remit is therefore our great commercial strength as well as our mission' (1991: 3). This is a rhetoric that is repeated over the 1990s as justification for the channel's strategy of niche targeting, claiming that Channel 4 was not changing its identity and programming or turning its back on its public service remit, but merely capitalizing on its existing appeal to the niche demographics that stemmed from its very public service remit to be different from other television channels. The problem, however, is that not all minority audiences have the same value to advertisers. For example, a survey of Asian audiences in 1991 found that, amongst this demographic, Channel 4 had the best reputation for Asian programming out of all the British television channels (Channel 4 1991: 11). Yet, this demographic did not form part of Channel 4's strategy of niche targeting, presumably because it did not have the same value to advertisers as the youth and upmarket demographics. Hence, the strategy of niche targeting valued those commercially important audiences over other significant sections of Channel 4's diverse audience.[4]

Channel 4 and commercial expansion

The second strategy adopted by Channel 4 in the early 1990s was commercial expansion. In 1993 Channel 4 created Channel 4 International as a wholly owned subsidiary to incorporate all Channel 4's commercial activities apart from the sale of airtime. Commercial expansion anticipated a threat to advertiser revenue from new commercial satellite and cable services by providing revenue from other sources. This was seen as necessary in order to enable the core terrestrial channel to remain financially viable and able to fulfil its public service remit. Over the 1990s, and particularly under Michael Jackson as Chief Executive (1997–2001), Channel 4 expanded into a number of commercial areas that were grouped under the umbrella of 4Ventures. In 2001, when 4Ventures first became fully operational, it had a turnover of £156 million (Channel 4 2001: 22) and 10 businesses operating under its umbrella. These ranged from facilities (124 Facilities), to digital channels (E4 and FilmFour), to new media ventures and programme support (4 Interactive and 4 Learning), to commercial distribution and exploitation (Channel 4 International and Consumer Products). Essentially, in the period between 1990 and 2001, Channel 4 moved from being primarily a television broadcaster/publisher (that was also involved in the British film industry) to being a corporation with commercial businesses across a range of media-related areas.

As with Channel 4's adoption of niche targeting, such commercial expansion was not without its problems for a public service broadcaster. In particular, there were concerns raised in 2001 about the relationship between Channel 4's public service terrestrial channel and the corporation's other commercial businesses, as well as about the balance of investment in the public service channel as opposed to new commercial ventures. In fact, 4Ventures was specifically set up to differentiate the corporation's commercial enterprises from its core public service channel. This restructuring clearly separated the core public service terrestrial channel from Channel 4's other commercial businesses, even when those businesses could be seen to support the corporation's public service remit (as with 4Learning, for example).

Promoting and marketing Channel 4

The third strategy adopted by Channel 4 in response to increased competition and the responsibility to sell its own advertising was tied to the shift towards niche targeting and commercial expansion: increased spending on promotion and marketing, including the adoption of a specific branding strategy. Channel 4 increased its spending on off- and on-air promotion and other forms of marketing over the 1990s in a strategy that was described as follows by the Channel 4 Annual Report for 1993:

> The responsibility for generating revenue within an increasingly competitive marketplace, has brought with it the need to market the channel: both to viewers to maximise audiences, and to advertisers and their agencies to maximise revenue. In the last two years, Channel 4 has been one of the few television channels consistently to support its programming and brand images with co-ordinated campaigns in the press, on-air and through paid-for advertising. Investment in this activity has increased significantly and research has shown both high awareness and appreciation of it amongst viewers.
>
> (Channel 4 1993: 30)

Here, the strategy of increased investment in promotion is positioned as a direct response to Channel 4's new financial position within a more competitive marketplace, and aligns perfectly with the standard economic model of commercial television as a dual market product – selling programmes to viewers and viewers to advertisers (see Doyle 2002). It is notable that the corporation here is concerned not just with advertising Channel 4's programmes, but also with supporting the channel's 'brand images'. This coordinated branding of Channel 4 overall is perhaps most apparent in the 'tapping' campaign adopted in 1993 when the channel began to sell its own advertising for the first time.

Channel 4's 'tapping' campaign

This award-winning on-air campaign was used in the interstitial breaks between programmes in 1993. In the campaign, different stars associated with Channel 4 would approach the screen and appear to tap on it from within the television set. These short segments, which ran for only a few seconds, were particularly powerful in their direct address to the viewer. Through the campaign, Channel 4 explicitly invited its audience to associate the channel with the values and qualities attributed to these stars and the programmes on which they appeared. As with Channel 5's use of the Spice Girls (see Chapter 3), the 'tapping' campaign tied the stars and programmes to the channel's own attributes and values. Furthermore, within the campaign these stars directly connected with the audience, looking them in the eye and even tapping the inside of the television screen. Not only are we invited to pay attention and watch, but the campaign playfully suggests that these stars live inside our screens within our own homes and are reaching out to make direct contact with us through Channel 4. Channel 4 thus positioned itself as our point of contact with these stars and programmes, while asserting the values of connection – Channel 4 connects with its audience and belongs to its audience; these stars are our stars. While the campaign was conceived as a series of on-air interstitials in order to brand Channel 4's terrestrial channel, Channel 4's Annual Report for 1993 used frame grabs of the campaign on its front cover, rather than the usual Channel 4 blocks logo. In doing so, the brand identity created for the terrestrial Channel 4 was positioned as inseparable from the overall corporate identity for the organization, Channel 4.

A significant issue for Channel 4 as it adopted a brand strategy for itself as a corporation and for its public service channel was how to articulate its specific identity, which derived largely from the way in which it interpreted its public service remit, into a set of brand values. In addition to public service requirements for the quality and range of programming commissioned from independent producers, Channel 4 had a specific public service remit for innovation, originality and diversity as laid out in the 1990 Broadcasting Act, which mandated that, 'Channel 4 programmes contain a suitable proportion of matter calculated to appeal to tastes and interests not generally catered for by Channel 3 [ITV], and that innovation and experiment in the form and content of those programmes are encouraged' (1990: para. 25: 1(a), (b)).

Channel 4's brand identity, therefore, needed to be malleable enough to cover the diversity of its programming and the different identities of its diverse audience. Yet, at the same time, Channel 4 was specifically targeting two commercially valuable niche demographics (16–34s and ABC1s) in order to attract advertisers to buy airtime on its channel. Examining the stars (and the programmes that they represent) that were used in the images from the tapping campaign on the cover of Channel 4's Annual Report in 1993, highlights that there is a clear preponderance of entertainment, comedy and youth-oriented programmes, rather than a reflection of the full range of programming on offer.[5] Although this is only a selection of the programmes used for the tapping campaign, it is those that Channel 4 chose to represent it as a corporation. Contributing to this is the fact that the tapping campaign lends itself to an emphasis on seriality and longevity, devaluing the single one-off programme in favour of series and strands that appeal to the young and/or upmarket demographics in the articulation of Channel 4's brand identity.

The example of the 'tapping' campaign would seem to support the argument that the adoption of branding undermines the remit of public service broadcasters. The difficulty in attempting to develop and communicate a brand personality for the channel that created loyalty by selling a set of values and attributes that viewers are invited to personally identify with, was how to address the variety of the channel's output and audience. At the same time, however, the tapping campaign supported the strategy of niche targeting, rather than determining it. In this sense, it is not necessarily branding per se that undermines Channel 4's public service remit, but rather the decision to focus on specific commercially valued audiences, which stemmed from commercial pressures brought about by changes in government policy (which forced Channel 4 to sell its own advertising and allowed satellite and cable television to develop as advertiser-funded commercial services in competition with the terrestrial public service broadcasters). Furthermore, as Channel 4 continued to expand commercially over the 1990s and 2000s, its use of branding became more complex, further problematizing an easy association of branding with a decline in public service broadcasting.

Channel 4 programmes, imports and expansion

Although Channel 4 used programmes and stars as a core part of its corporate and channel brand identity in the 1993 tapping campaign, the relationship between Channel 4 and the programmes that it airs is complicated by its status as an aggregator, rather than a producer, of content. As Channel 4 was set up to act primarily as a publisher of material produced by the independent production sector, the relationship between the programmes that it airs and its brand identity is particularly complex. Nowhere is this more evident than in its use of US imports.

Channel 4 has imported US programmes from its inception. However, as a central part of Channel 4's *raison d'être* was to boost the independent television production sector in the UK, foreign imports have historically been problematic for the channel. After the 1990 Broadcasting Act, Channel 4 was accused of turning its back on its previous innovations, focusing excessively on attracting a youth audience (as we have seen in its emphasis on the commercially valuable 16–34s) and over-relying on US imports.[6] Yet, at the same time, as Janet McCabe has argued, 'Reliance on American syndicated material has helped Channel 4 build a distinct corporate brand identity for itself' (2005: 212). A clear example of this can be found in Channel 4's acquisition and use of HBO programming at the turn of the millennium when Channel 4 attempted to construct an identity for itself as the home of HBO programming in the UK, importing the shows *The Sopranos* and *Six Feet Under*, which had secured HBO's reputation as the home of quality television drama in the USA (see Chapter 1).[7] This use of US programming in the construction of its brand identity was not without problems for Channel 4. Channel 4's terrestrial channel has to work within the restrictions placed upon it in terms of its targets for original programming, its public service remit and its scheduling guidelines. While HBO showed the gangster series *The Sopranos* (which contains explicit scenes of violence and nudity) at 8–9pm, Channel 4 showed the first season in 1999 after the 9pm watershed, between 10pm and 11pm, while subsequent seasons were scheduled even later and often at erratic times (see Johnson 2007). This was also the case for *Six Feet Under*.

One of the ways in which Channel 4 dealt with the restrictions placed on it regarding the acquisition and scheduling of imported programmes was through the use of its digital channels. As Paul Rixon (2003: 55) argues, at the point at which the ITC enforced restrictions on Channel 4 imports, Channel 4 launched a new digital channel, E4, which began transmission on 18 January 2001. E4 was not subject to the same regulations as Channel 4 as it was only available initially through subscription cable and satellite services. E4 is a classic example of brand extension, taking the core brand values of Channel 4, but developing them to provide a linked, but different, service. Channel 4 described E4 as follows:

> Offering the same, distinctive brand of cutting-edge entertainment pioneered over the last two decades by Channel 4, E4 is the next logical step in Channel 4's cross-platform strategy. It will protect and develop the Channel 4 brand in an increasingly fragmented and

> competitive landscape and reinforce Channel 4's reputation as the home of cutting-edge entertainment and the best new comic talent.
> (Channel 4 2000: 33)

From its launch in 2001, E4 used the scheduling of US imports to attract audiences. For example, while the first two seasons of *The Sopranos* had premiered in the UK on Channel 4, the third season was initially screened on E4 in 2001, five months before it would premiere on Channel 4. Similarly, E4 began transmitting the second season of *Six Feet Under* in 2002 just one week after the first season had finished its run on Channel 4, and eight months before it would be screened on Channel 4. In 2005, Channel 4 used repeats of *The Sopranos* when it launched its new digital channel More4, a channel specifically set up to offer thought-provoking adult programming. Clearly, here, US imports were being used as a driver to encourage audiences to subscribe to satellite, cable and digital services and to watch Channel 4's new digital channels. Channel 4 also developed minisites for each series on its website, which interpolated the US series into the corporation's branded space.

What emerges from this specific example is the increasing complexity of the television landscape as Channel 4 diversified into new channels and new markets. We can see in this example how one programme, *The Sopranos*, has contributed to the identity of HBO, Channel 4 (as a channel and a corporation), E4 and More4, in different ways and at different times, and the way in which the programme's association with HBO has been both valuable and problematic for its role in Channel 4's brand identity. We can also see how Channel 4's diversification into new channels allowed it to increasingly specialize and target its programmes more directly. Channel 4's expansion onto digital television accorded with its broader strategy of focusing on the 16–34 and ABC1 demographics. FilmFour, with its focus on independent cinema, appeals to an upmarket audience, E4 is clearly aimed at 16–34s, and More4 at ABC1s. With this expansion, branding can play two related roles – to offer differentiation between products or services and to offer unification of different services within one set of core values. Kevin Lygo's (Director of Television and Content, Channel 4, 2003–10) description of the difference between Channel 4, E4 and More4 exemplifies precisely this dual function of branding. He has described E4 as 'Channel 4 without the boring bits' and More4 as 'Channel 4 without the silly bits' (cited in Bashford 2005: 23). Hence, both these digital channel brand extensions have an essential 'Channel 4' quality to them, associated with innovation, experimentation, controversy and difference, yet each focuses on a particular interpretation of these qualities – E4 offering more irreverent fun and More4 offering more serious and thought-provoking adult content.

Therefore, as Channel 4 has expanded into the digital era, branding has emerged as a way of creating an identity, but one that is malleable enough to be targeted at different sections of the Channel 4 audience and to be extended and differentiated across new services and platforms. In the digital era branding, therefore, becomes more than just a strategy; it becomes an important asset for a media corporation. It is unsurprising, therefore, that in 1999 Michael Jackson claimed that, for Channel 4, 'As a broadcaster without a production base, our principal assets are our brand and our audience' (1999: 5). This is particularly important for Channel 4 because, although the corporation uses programmes and stars in order to articulate its brand values, as an aggregator of content, its family of brands is largely made up of forms of distribution. As we have seen in the earlier chapters of this book, a key feature of the digital era of television is the threat posed to the distribution bottleneck that characterized the UK and US television industries in the 1960s and 1970s. In the UK, the BBC and ITV had a duopoly on television broadcasting from 1955 to 1982, and although ITV was made up of a federation of television franchises, the sites through which television programming was distributed nationally were significantly restricted. The introduction of Channel 4 opened up independent production, which was further strengthened by the 25 per cent rule for independent production introduced by the 1990 Broadcasting Act, which loosened the hold of the BBC and ITV on programme production. However, throughout the 1980s there remained only three major sites for the distribution of television: BBC, ITV and Channel 4.

In Chapter 2 we saw how Timothy Todreas (1999) argued that cable, satellite and digital services broke the distribution bottleneck in the USA by vastly multiplying the number of sites through which television programmes could be watched. Todreas argued that, as a consequence, branding would become more important as a means of helping viewers find the content that they wanted to watch in a more crowded and fragmented media landscape. In the UK there has also been an explosion in the number of sites through which television can be viewed, with a vast increase in the number of satellite, cable and digital channels, as well as new services offering television programming online and through portable media devices. Indeed, by 2008 the UK had the greatest percentage of digital television homes in the world at 75 per cent (Christophers 2008: 241).

However, Brett Christophers argues that, despite the challenge to the old BBC/ITV duopoly, the British television industry remains distributor-dominated. He notes that, although the viewing share for all terrestrial broadcasters has slipped from 95 per cent at the start of the 1990s to 69.2 per cent in 2006, this is actually a smaller loss than one might expect. Furthermore, although the terrestrial commercial broadcasters (ITV1, Channel 4 and Channel 5) had seen their share of all home adult commercial impacts decline to 58.1 per cent, this is not matched by their loss in advertising revenue, which has declined from almost 100 per cent in the early 1990s only to 72 per cent in 2006 (2008: 245–47).[8] Furthermore, Christophers states that seven of the 10 largest multichannel-only channels ranked by viewing share were wholly or partly owned by terrestrial broadcasters (CBeebies, BBC Three, ITV2, ITV3, E4, More4 and UKTV Gold) (2008: 249).[9] For Christophers, this continued dominance of the terrestrials is particularly negative in that these old established broadcasters have been allowed to maintain their power over independent producers. While he does not consider the fact that it is the terrestrials who have a specific public service remit for original commissions (unlike the non-public service digital channels, that tend to rely mainly on repurposed or imported programming), or take into account the sites of distribution for television programmes beyond the television set itself, his insights do suggest that Todreas's arguments about the value of an established brand identity might have some weight in the UK. In particular, Christophers argues that the continued dominance of the terrestrials can be attributed to viewer inertia, superior programming and marketing budgets (to which we might add an increased spend on promotion), and the cross-scheduling and promotion possibilities offered between their different channels. All of these are enhanced and supported by the development and expansion of corporate and channel brand identities.

Furthermore, Christophers argues that, as the value of the analogue spectrum decreases (particularly in the build up to analogue switch-off in 2012), 'television is shifting from a "distribution economy" to an "attention economy"' where the power of the terrestrial broadcasters shifts from 'their ability to reach an audience (power based on distribution scarcity) to their ability to originate and maintain an audience (power driven by attention scarcity)' (2008: 248).[10] Therefore, although Channel 4 managed to retain a strong position within the television landscape in the UK, as the distribution bottleneck breaks, it is important for Channel 4 to exploit new forms of delivery in order to retain the 'attention' of its audience. This is most evident in its launch of 4oD, an online on-demand service that allows viewers in the UK and Republic of Ireland to view programmes broadcast on Channel 4, More4 and E4 in the past 30 days, as well as classic programmes from the Channel 4 archive.

As with Channel 4's digital channel brand extensions, a strong brand militates against some of the financial risks of moving into such new areas by drawing on the values and consumer relations already established by the core brand. As Channel 4 continues to expand into new media platforms, its brand has become an asset to be both exploited and protected. This is particularly important because Channel 4's key demographic groups (ABC1s and 16–34-year-olds) tend to be early adopters of new technology. Extending the Channel 4 brand into new areas protects the brand's equity by helping it to stay relevant for and connected to its core audiences. This can be seen, for example, in Channel 4's launch of 4Mobile, which offered television listings, clips from Channel 4 and E4 comedy shows, film reviews and short videos delivered to a mobile phone. 4Mobile specifically targeted a youth demographic, including offering specially produced videos about teenage health concerns to accompany its television series *Embarrassing Teenage Bodies* (2008–) in an attempt to retain Channel 4's relevance and value to this key demographic.

However, these online initiatives are used not only in an attempt to retain audiences, but also to support Channel 4's public service remit. For example, its commitment to independent production is enhanced through 4Docs, a website where aspiring documentary makers can submit their films, get advice on documentary film-making, and view documentary films. Meanwhile, its remit for educational programming is supported by 4Learning, which provides online educational resources for primary and secondary schools. This suggests that Channel 4's brand equity lies not only in its appeal to the core youth and upmarket demographics, but also in its underlying public service remit. Yet, at the same time, unlike 4oD and 4Mobile, 4Learning and 4Docs are distinctly separate sites from the core Channel 4 site. 4Learning is actually provided through Espresso Education, and so is a joint commercial venture. 4Docs is provided by the Channel 4 BRITDOC Foundation, a stand-alone non-profit foundation that developed out of Channel 4's documentary department in 2005, although powered by Channel 4 and hosted by Shooting People (a networking organization that supports independent production) with support from The Co-Operative (a family of businesses owned by its members). The complexity of relationships within and between these different Channel 4 branded online initiatives points to the increasingly complex environment within which public service broadcasters operate. As we shall go on to see with the BBC, this makes it increasingly difficult to make any simple claims about the relationship between public service and commercial, competitive practices.

The BBC: branding public services and commercial expansion

If Channel 4's strategic adoption of branding can be located in response to the 1990 Broadcasting Act, then the BBC's can be traced a little earlier to the political context of the Peacock Report published in 1986, which proposed that British broadcasting should be developed into a genuinely competitive market (see Chapter 3). As with Channel 4, the BBC saw their corporate brand as an asset that needed to be supported in the face of increased commercial competition and the marketization of broadcasting. For example, in 1987–88 the BBC produced a document entitled 'The Next Five Years' summarizing its policy objectives in the face of the fragmentation of the television industry and the threat that this presented to the future of broadcasting. Under the heading 'Brand-leader' the document stated that: 'the BBC's aim must be to remain the brand-leader, setting the standard by which quality and service to the public are judged' (cited in BBC 1988: 5). So, as early as 1988, the BBC was already positioning itself as a corporate brand. Importantly, this corporate brand was not (at this point) articulating commercial value, but rather was positioned in relation to the BBC's public service remit. The BBC corporate brand is here defined as 'quality and service to the public' and the value of its brand is asserted insofar as the BBC is able to maintain its position as the leader in achieving and determining the criteria for both these values. While positioning the BBC as 'brand-leader' comes in response to increased competition and fragmentation in broadcasting, branding is not here articulated as a commercial strategy or value, but rather embodies a set of public service values.

The BBC's understanding of itself as a brand extended into its core television channels, which were given new brand identities in 1991 as part of 'a coherent corporate branding strategy begun three years ago in anticipation of the increasingly competitive and complex broadcasting market' (BBC 1991: 65). Designed by Martin Lambie-Nairn (who had designed Channel 4's famous blocks logo), the new idents created a more coherent feel by utilizing the numbers 1 and 2. While BBC One did retain the globe, which had been its central motif since the arrival of BBC Two in the 1960s, this was accompanied by a large numerical 1 which could also be used in continuity frames and manipulated, such as when it was gift-wrapped in the idents for BBC One Christmas in 1994. BBC Two replaced the written 'TWO' with a sans serif numerical 2. Lambie-Nairn produced a range of versions of the 2 logo, such as 'paint' in which paint was thrown across the screen at the number and 'silk' in which the number was visible under a sheet of rippling silk fabric. The BBC also produced themed idents tied to seasons of programmes, such as an image of a table laid out for tea with the numerical 2 as a white teapot, which accompanied BBC Two's 'Little England' season in 1991. The aim of this rebrand was to change viewers' perceptions of the channels – particularly BBC Two, which research suggested was seen as old-fashioned.[11]

At the same time, the rise of multichannel television placed increased emphasis not only on determining and marketing the values of each channel, but also on defining the different positions of the BBC's channels, much as Channel 5 had determined its identity on the basis of an analysis of its position in relation to the other terrestrial channels (see Chapter 3). Georgina Born (2004) argues that this represented the adoption of a marketing-led approach at the BBC borrowed from the US system of branding channels as exemplified by Fox and MTV (see Chapter 1). In 1996 the BBC drew up a marketing plan that combined market research with a commitment to the BBC's public service remit. For example, a key marketing objective for BBC Television was:

> to engage the audiences then most distant from the BBC – lower socio-economic groups, young people and female viewers. Stress was also laid on 'needs mapping', an experimental research project

> designed to understand the needs of audiences, so as to serve them better.
>
> (Born 2004: 259).

The plan also unveiled 'ideal brand perceptions' for the BBC's terrestrial television channels:

> 'Our BBC1', was to be a channel of broad appeal, the nation's premier channel; it should be perceived as entertaining, engaging, trustworthy, authoritative, contemporary, warm, welcoming, elegant and so on. 'My BBC2', by contrast, should be perceived as topical and relevant, diverse, playful, modern, challenging, surprising, able to take risks, a channel of ideas. Certain values – being accessible, innovative, intelligent and stylish – were repeated as desirable features of both.
>
> (ibid.)

To coincide with this marketing plan, the BBC launched a new corporate logo and rebranded its main channels again. While BBC Two's on-air idents retained the sans serif 2, BBC One's logo was overhauled, removing the numerical one and introducing a globe-shaped hot-air balloon in red and orange, which was depicted flying over key sites in the UK. The BBC had always used on-air idents for its channels and these had always contributed to the values and identities associated with each channel. What changed in the 1990s was that these idents animated and created a personality for each channel. The BBC One hot-air balloon and the BBC Two sans serif 2 became living creatures with their own identities that could be slightly varied depending on the content being screened, and that could be tied to the strategic positioning of each channel in relation to commercial and political pressures (see Chapter 5 for a more detailed discussion of the role of idents in channel branding).

In addition to focusing increasing resources on communicating a set of brand values through rebranding its on-air channel idents, in 1997 the BBC produced a promotional video based on a cover of the Lou Reed song, 'Perfect Day', to promote the corporation overall. The film was broadcast on air as well as being released as a charity single for the BBC's annual Children in Need fundraiser. It featured an array of talent, from pop stars such as Boyzone and Gabrielle, to rock royalty such as Elton John, Tom Jones and Bono, to popular classical performers, Lesley Garrett and the Brodsky Quartet. In the film the stars sang of a 'perfect day' in a range of musical styles ending with the lyrics 'you're going to reap just what you sow', as a voice-over proclaimed, 'Whatever your musical taste, it is catered for by BBC radio and television. This is only possible thanks to the unique way the BBC is paid for by you. BBC: you make it what it is.' The film promoted the diversity and value of the BBC's musical output through the use of a wide range of musical performers. At the same time, these stars were effectively demonstrating their support for not just the ethos of the BBC's public service remit, but also the licence fee. The campaign asserted the value of the licence fee by emotionally appealing to its audience and inviting them to feel identification with and ownership of the BBC as a public service broadcaster.[12] As Paul Grainge argues of the 'Perfect Day' campaign:

> It was devised as a felt expression of what the BBC stood for as a public service broadcaster in the UK at a time when political questions about the licence fee, and the threat of its non-renewal, continued to hang in the air. In a period in which media companies were competing aggressively for audience loyalty, 'Perfect Day' was the first attempt by the BBC to make its brand literally and metaphorically sing.
>
> (2010: 4)

Georgina Born argues that:

> The most significant effect of the rising influence of marketing on the culture of the BBC was that under the impact of brand-thinking, the guiding values of the corporation and of each of its services had now to be consciously formulated and *performed* by branding, where before they had been part of the collective subconscious.
>
> (2004: 268)

Yet, this implies that it was the rise of marketing within the BBC that led to the need for the corporation's values to be 'consciously formulated and performed'. By contrast, I want to suggest that the BBC's adoption of marketing and branding stemmed from a need to respond to the *external* pressures on the corporation. The BBC needed to promote the value of the licence fee and of public service broadcasting through branding campaigns such as the 'Perfect Day' film because those values were under threat from government policy and from commercial competition.[13] I therefore want to argue that, while the BBC's adoption of branding in the 1990s can be understood as part of a broader marketization of all aspects of British broadcasting (including production, scheduling and promotion), it did not represent a retreat from public service values.

To elaborate on this, it is necessary to examine in a little more depth what is meant by marketing. Marketing developed in the commercial sector as a means to maximize sales and profits by 'identifying, anticipating and satisfying customer requirements profitably' (Chartered Institute of Marketing, cited in Proctor 2007: 1). It is this association of marketing with satisfying the desires of the customer in order to maximize profits that has been central to marketing being understood as inappropriate or even damaging in the public sector. While traditional marketers work from the assumption that 'the customer is always right', Proctor (2007: 7–8) points out that working for the public good or in the public interest, even when this might go against individual people's wants or needs, is a central aspect of the public sector, particularly in organizations (such as the BBC) that exist to provide a service legislated by government policy. However, over the 1980s and 1990s the commercial world began to redefine its understanding of the objectives of business from commercial survival and profit to creating value for stakeholders in order to retain their investment. As a consequence, marketing shifted its focus from increasing profitability to maintaining and increasing shareholder value. In the light of these changes, Proctor argues that marketing can be redefined as, 'the management process responsible for identifying, anticipating and satisfying stakeholder requirements and [that] in doing so serves to facilitate the achievement of the organisation's objectives' (2007: 2). This definition of marketing is less controversial when applied to the public sector. Here, marketing could be understood as supporting the means by which public organizations fulfil their public service objectives.

In this regard, it is useful to distinguish between marketing and marketization. The UK government introduced marketization into the public service broadcasting sector over the 1980s and 1990s through policies that subjected public service broadcasters to the competitive forces of the commercial marketplace. Not only were UK public service broadcasters now expected to compete with the commercial cable, satellite and digital broadcasters that emerged over this period, but the 1990 Broadcasting Act also introduced a 25 per cent quota on independent production, creating an external market for programme production. The BBC responded to this marketization by introducing market-driven commissioning practices and adopting marketing practices to support them (Born 2004: 306–8). Producer Choice (introduced by John Birt in 1991 and applied across the BBC in 1993) extended marketization by allocating budgets to programme makers, who were free to use internal or external resources to service their productions (BBC 1992: 21). Born argues that Producer Choice was as much a political as an economic move: a means by which the BBC demonstrated to the government (which was introducing an internal market to other public services, such as the National Health Service) that it was 'zealous for marketisation' (2004: 60).

However, marketing is not dependent on marketization. For example, Proctor argues that marketing can be used within the public sector to promote the self-interest of an organization in order to secure its continued existence, or to promote the area of responsibility of a particular public organization. It is these two forms of marketing that better describe the 'Perfect Day' film. This film aimed to promote the work and value of the BBC as a public service broadcaster, while also promoting public service broadcasting itself as a concept to the viewer, communicating the meaning and role of the licence fee and its relationship to the viewing and listening experience. Furthermore, the 'Perfect Day' film can be understood as a form of marketing that is communicating not just with the BBC's viewers, but with the other key stakeholder for the corporation – the government. For public sector organizations such as the BBC, branding communicates 'the idea that such organisations are values driven' (Proctor 2007: 141), rather than undermining those values.

For the BBC, this kind of promotional film is particularly important because of the rather unusual nature of the service provided by broadcasting. While most public sector organizations primarily provide services, rather than products, there is quite a difference between the traditional service brand and public service broadcasting. Most traditional service brands involve a face-to-face 'service encounter', such as flying with Virgin Atlantic, attending college, or consulting a doctor, and it is this service encounter that is key to the customer's experience of and attitude towards the service (see Berry 2000). By contrast, the service encounter of public service television is not face-to-face, but is made up of the viewer's experience of watching the television channels provided by a broadcaster and the programmes and people that appear on those channels. Thus, while channels and programmes might have their own brand identities, they also function as the access point through which viewers encounter the service provided by broadcasters, such as the BBC. This made it increasingly important for the BBC (and other public service broadcasters) to use broadcast time to communicate their values to their audience. However, the significance of watching television channels as the service encounter of public service broadcasting was complicated over this period by the BBC's other strategic response to the changes in the media landscape, which was (like Channel 4) to expand its channels and services.

The BBC's brand expansions

As the BBC faced cuts to its licence fee income in the mid-late 1980s, the corporation's annual reports identified the need to generate increased revenue from its commercial arm, BBC Enterprises, in order to offset its financial shortfalls elsewhere.[14] As Michael Checkland (Director General of the BBC, 1987–92) stated of BBC Enterprises in the BBC's Annual Report and Accounts for 1990–91:

> Already the world's biggest programme seller (16,000 hours of TV programmes sold, not including America), the BBC continues to seek ways of supplementing the licence fee – through a range of products and services linked to our role as a public service broadcaster.
>
> (BBC 1991: 6)

In the late-1980s the BBC's primary commercial activities revolved around four areas: programme sales, co-productions, consumer products and broadcasting services. For example, in 1990–91 the BBC entered into 118 co-production deals, mainly with US cable and PSB partners, sold programmes to the USA through its distribution company Lionheart Television, had a slate of magazines and other consumer products based on core programming content, such as children's programme *Fireman Sam* (BBC, 1986–2007) and genres like wildlife and cookery shows, and was exploring a venture with Whitbread to develop interactive pub games (see BBC 1991: 74–76). The BBC had also begun exploiting new technologies to extend its channels overseas, including direct relays of BBC One and BBC Two to Europe and to the US cable channel A&E via satellite and cable (BBC 1988: 2). By the early 1990s the BBC was developing a joint venture with Thames Television to launch a commercially funded cable and satellite channel, which was to result in the UKTV-branded slate of channels that were developed over the decade (see Chapter 3). As Tracey argues of the BBC in the late-1980s:

> Co-production, co-financing, implicit and explicit sponsorship, new services, foreign sales, the whole lexicon of commerce invaded the Corporation. ... what was clear was that commerce as an idea of how to fund the BBC had by the late 1980s become a legitimate and increasingly important part of its financial strategy.
>
> (1998: 115)

After the 1994 White Paper on the future of the BBC encouraged the corporation to further develop its commercial activities, particularly international television services (Tracey 1998: 119), BBC Enterprises was restructured as BBC Worldwide Ltd and commercial expansion became a more overt strategy:

> As well as selling BBC programmes around the world and licensing merchandise associated with programme brands, BBC Worldwide has recently been developing a strategy to create more long-term value from licence payers' assets by creating channels, in the UK and overseas, to showcase BBC programmes.
>
> (BBC 1998: 30)

On 19 March 1998 the BBC signed a US$0.5 billion deal with Discovery to develop global channel brands that exploited the BBC's archive and programme-making expertise. The deal led to the launch of BBC America on 30 March 1998, a US subscription network owned by BBC Worldwide, but marketed and distributed by Discovery (the venture also led to the launch of the channels, Animal Planet and People and Arts, in a number of international territories). As with E4, BBC America was a brand extension that exploited the associations of the BBC in the USA with quality programming. The BBC also exploited the emergence of the internet to develop commercial services, such as the launch of beeb@thebbc, a commercial web service developed with ICL (owned by Japanese conglomerate Fujitsu), with three main sites exploiting key BBC content: *Top Gear*, *The Score* (sports) and the listings magazine *Radio Times* (BBC 1997: 50). Therefore, there were two interrelated aspects of the BBC's commercial expansion from the late-1980s: the development of new channel brands that built on the BBC's reputation and programme archive; and the exploitation of BBC content as brands that could be extended into new ventures and onto new platforms. In fact, by 1998 the BBC was increasingly selling its programming in 'branded blocks', such as 'Animal Zone' (natural history programmes) and 'Britcom' (BBC comedy), as well as exploiting key programme brands across multiple media, such as *Top of the Pops* (BBC, 1964–2006) and *Top Gear* (BBC 1999: 31).

However, the BBC's brand expansions in this era were not solely commercial. As discussed in Chapter 3, the BBC also developed a slate of BBC-branded digital channels, such as BBC News 24, BBC Three and CBBC. While the BBC's commercial expansions were intended to increase revenue for the corporation, these non-commercial expansions were part of a 10-year plan to spend 9 per cent of the total licence fee income on developing digital public service broadcasting (BBC 1997: 12) and included the development of BBC Online (launched on 15 December 1997) and interactive television (see Bennett 2008b). The BBC's activities in all three areas (digital television channels, online websites and services, and interactive television) can be understood as enhancing the BBC's core public service values. For example, the BBC claimed that BBC Three (launched in February 2003) was part of an attempt to reverse the long-term fall in consumption of BBC services by under-35s, while the BBC Asian Network (a British Asian digital radio station launched on 28 October 2002) and 1Extra (a black music digital radio station launched on 16 August 2002) aimed to address ethnic minority audiences (see BBC 2003: 10). While it could be argued that this was simply promotional rhetoric on the part of the BBC (particularly in relation to BBC Three) in order to persuade the government to endorse services that were in direct competition with commercial rivals, at the same time the BBC did have specific performance objectives set in 2000–01 to reach underserved young and minority ethnic audiences (see BBC 2002: 13–14). Furthermore, when the BBC was given the consent to offer online services in 1998 it was on the basis that it fulfil a core set of objectives, which included providing a home and acting as a trusted guide for licence payers on the web and strengthening the accountability of the BBC to, and its relationships with, licence payers (see BBC 2003: 59). This interactivity has ranged from enabling listeners to email questions to the Radio 4 news programme *Today* (BBC, 1957–), to inviting parents to share their questions and advice about parenting on message boards, to supporting online public consultations about the BBC.

While the corporate structure of the BBC differentiates its commercial and non-commercial businesses, much as Channel 4 differentiated its core public service channel from its other commercial businesses, in practice the relationship between these different services is fluid and nebulous. The BBC claimed that its aim in developing new non-commercial channels and services was to extend its presence across all platforms in an increasingly multimedia landscape, in order 'to become the UK's number one digital destination' (BBC 2002: 15). Meanwhile, although the expansion of the BBC's commercial services was justified as necessary in order to provide funds to supplement its public service programming, it also functioned to enhance the BBC's reputation as a global corporate brand. Mirroring Iosifidis' argument that the development of the BBC as a powerful global brand has significant value for the UK economy nationally and globally, the BBC's Annual Report and Accounts for 1994–95 stated of its commercial activity, 'All of this builds on our presence as a distinctive, high quality, British broadcaster on the international scene, bringing credit to Britain and raising its global profile' (BBC 1995: 61).

In an increasingly global media landscape, raising the BBC's global profile contributes to the corporation's aim to become the UK's 'number one digital destination' (BBC 2002: 15). In view of this, therefore, while the BBC's co-development of commercial UK cable, satellite and digital channels was branded as UKTV, its development of commercial services and channels overseas, such as BBC America and BBC Entertainment make use of the BBC brand name, with its global associations with trust and quality as a key selling point.[15] This also points to the way in which brand extensions can be determined by the particular market within which they are launched. Within the UK market, the BBC brand name is strongly associated with non-advertiser-funded channels. As a consequence, there is value within this market in not using the BBC brand name in advertiser-funded channel brand extensions like the UKTV channels, as this might dilute the public service values associated with the BBC. However, there is particular value in the BBC brand name overseas, justifying its use in the BBC's international channel brand extensions. Furthermore, by positioning itself on the global stage as a key British brand with significant value to Britain as a nation, the BBC is able to justify its continued existence in both cultural and economic terms.

However, if the development of a global reputation as 'one of the most trusted brands on the planet' (BBC 2000: 2) contributes to the BBC's place and status in the UK, as media consumption becomes increasingly globalized, it also confuses the distinction between the BBC's commercial and non-commercial services. The BBC has attempted to use branding to clarify the identity of its different services. For example, in 2001 the corporation rebranded its internet and interactive services as BBCi, including redesigning its web pages to give them a consistent look. The strategy increased traffic to the BBC website by 70 per cent (ibid.) and, today, the BBC's web pages share a central design and functionality that allows for specific specialization, whether for certain channels or genres (see Chapter 6). In addition, all the BBC's channel and service idents use the BBC's corporate block logo. While this creates a consistent look and feel for all the BBC's UK content, on the global platform of the web this becomes more confused. For example, while the BBC America site does not carry the distinctive black bar across the top that unites all the BBC's UK public service websites, its design borrows from that used for BBC One and it uses the BBC's corporate logo. Meanwhile, the BBC supports both a bbc.co.uk site for *Top Gear* (<http://www.bbc.co.uk/topgear>), which retains the consistent look and feel of all UK BBC online sites, and a commercial *Top Gear* site (<http://www.topgear.com>), where the BBC brand is present, yet more minimal. In the case of both the commercial *Top Gear* site and the BBC America site, advertising is present, undermining a key feature of the BBC in the UK as a public service broadcaster financed by the licence fee.[16]

Michael Tracey is particularly critical of the Conservative government's attempts in the 1990s to turn the BBC into a globally oriented multimedia corporation, arguing that this increased commercialization offered revenue possibilities to the UK, but was fatal to the public service character of the organization:

> Whether the BBC is seriously able to compete globally with the likes of Rupert Murdoch of News Corporation and John Malone of TCI is debatable. That it would be able to do so and retain a public service remit is ludicrous.
>
> (Tracey 1998: 119)

Ironically, the same commercial ambitions have also been criticized for their potential threat to a free and fair market in broadcasting. For example, Cave, Collins and Crowther (2004: 251), citing Chris Hunt of Digital Classics, argue that the BBC has both 'the market power and the will' to crowd out commercial competitors. Here, the BBC's commercial activities are seen to have two negative impacts. The BBC's development of commercial channels (they give the example of UK History, one of the UKTV channels since rebranded as Yesterday, see Chapter 3) can put smaller commercial channels operating in similar areas, such as Digital Classics, out of business. They argue that this has an impact on public service broadcasting by undermining plurality, using the example of the channels UK History, Digital Classics and The History Channel, which 'can plausibly be considered to offer programming no less public service in character than the BBC's' (Cave *et al.* 2004: 251). These same commercial activities by the BBC are also seen as likely to impinge upon commercial suppliers and hence be anti-competitive. Key to both arguments is an anxiety that the BBC has considerable power in its position as a free-to-air, licence-funded public service broadcaster, and that this power gives it an unfair advantage in the commercial market.

The BBC has always operated within a broader commercial media landscape (see Johnson 2009) and since the 1980s has been operating within a commercial broadcasting landscape. It is impossible for the BBC not to engage in some form of commercial activity, and this has always been the case. The expansion of the BBC's commercial activities since the 1980s was in direct response to demands from the government for the corporation to become more efficient and to supplement its licence fee income. Deakin and Pratten argue that the changes in broadcasting that emerged over the 1990s stemmed in part from the Treasury's desire to get more income from the regulation of broadcasting, claiming that the Treasury demanded reduced costs and increased efficiency from the BBC 'as a quid pro quo for the renewal of the BBC's Charter in 2001' (1999: 342).

Furthermore, the arguments put forward by Cave *et al.* also fail to take significant account of what might be meant by public service broadcasting. Their assumption that The History Channel, UK History and Digital Classics all offer a similar kind of public service programming fails to define exactly what public service broadcasting means. One can only presume that history in itself makes these channels' output public service, yet any viewer of UK History and The History Channel can attest to the variety, range and difference in quality in the kinds of history presented in each channel.[17] Furthermore, such an argument assumes that public service broadcasting can be defined as a set of programming, rather than as a service or ethos (one, for example, that may be embodied in the idea of the mixed programme schedule).[18]

Although Cave *et al.* argue that, if the BBC behaves anti-competitively, then diversity and pluralism are likely to be compromised, they fail to address what kind of diversity and pluralism is at stake here. While it may be that a free market might increase the diversity of programme supply, the shift to specific niche audiences in the case of the USA suggests that the market cannot necessarily be relied upon to offer a range of output addressed to the full diversity of British society. Thus, in these arguments there is insufficient exploration of public service broadcasting itself as a concept or discussion of what one might be prepared to risk or sacrifice in order to maintain the benefits of public service broadcasting. While Cave *et al.* (2004: 268) argue that many of the competition problems of the BBC stem from the desire to 'leverage dominance from one market to another', they fail to examine both the potential benefits of this leverage (for example, in helping to develop public service provision as a central part of new digital media) or the fact that such leverage is also a common aspect of most contemporary media development and is clearly evident in the activities of the large commercial global media conglomerates that are the BBC's main competitors (such as The History Channel, which is jointly owned by A&E Networks (AETN International) and BSkyB).

These arguments demonstrate the contradictions facing contemporary public service broadcasters and regulators since the 1980s. The BBC now has to operate and compete within a highly commercialized industry characterized by large media conglomerates and within a regulatory environment where there is little appetite to increase its funding and where commitment to public service broadcasting as a fundamental ethos in broadcasting has been undermined. As a broadcaster synonymous with public service broadcasting, the BBC has had to find a way to respond to external pressures from the changes to the media landscape and from government at the same time as defending public service broadcasting itself. If the core components of contemporary definitions of public service broadcasting are citizenship, universality and quality (Born and Prosser 2001: 670–71), then the BBC has needed to be able to find a place for itself where it could fulfil these criteria. It needed sufficient funds to continue to produce programming of significantly high quality. It needed a presence on the new media platforms that were threatening the centrality of television in order to assert its continued universality as a broadcaster and fulfil its role of supporting citizenship, which was increasingly enacted online. The BBC therefore had to find ways of supplementing the licence fee and of occupying a central place on the emerging new media platforms if it was to survive as a public service broadcaster.

Yet, at the same time, the expansion into commercial services by both the BBC and Channel 4 does complicate each corporation's identity and role as a public service broadcaster. Both the BBC and Channel 4 have had to expand their channels and services in order to increase revenue and in order to remain relevant and connected to their viewers. Such expansion has public service value as well as commercial value, in being used to support citizenship, extending universality of provision onto new media platforms and generating funds for programme production in order to enable continued quality of provision. For example, Graham Murdock (2004) argues that the BBC's online initiatives extend information and knowledge rights, deliberative rights and rights of participation by providing additional information and links to sources and message boards for debate on key topics, such as genetically modified crops. Yet, this expansion of channels and services vastly increases the sites where one might encounter these public service broadcasters. If the service encounter is the primary means by which people experience public services, then the BBC and Channel 4 now have a large number and range of service encounters through which the public will form opinions about them. On the one hand, this is necessary in order to generate the attention required in the digital 'attention economy'. On the other hand, it makes it much harder for each corporation to manage the service encounter. This is particularly the case on the internet where, as we have seen, a range of different identities for each corporation (and for their key programme brands) can exist at the same time.

Clearly, branding is one way in which the BBC and Channel 4 can attempt to manage the expansion of their service encounters. Both corporations have developed clear visual identities for their different channels and services that have been extended onto new media platforms (see Chapter 5). At the time of writing, Arqiva is beta-testing a new online television venture called SeeSaw, which will provide a single online portal through which viewers can access a selection of programmes from the BBC, Channel 4 and Channel 5 (as well as other content).[19] This is a commercial venture with each programme beginning with adverts that cannot be skipped (unless you pay for the content) and a SeeSaw ident. However, unlike the similar US venture Hulu (see Chapter 2), where the brand identities of the participating networks, such as NBC and ABC, are largely absent, in SeeSaw the corporate brand identities of each participant broadcaster are ever-present. The front page of the site (accessed 4 February 2011) includes channel idents for each participant that can be clicked on to see their most popular offerings. When you do so, the background changes to include the visual branding of the broadcaster that you have selected. Furthermore, the images of programme content contain a small corporate logo indicating which broadcaster it belongs to.

I want to suggest that the greater emphasis on corporate branding on SeeSaw compared to Hulu stems from the public service nature of these corporations, even though this is a commercial venture. For the networks participating in Hulu, the success of the venture primarily rests on the commercial profits that it generates. The networks can therefore decide whether it is of greater commercial benefit to include their corporate idents, or (as they have done) to create a new branded identity for the service. By contrast, although SeeSaw is a commercial venture intended to generate profits, by branding the content on Seesaw, the BBC, Channel 4 and Channel 5 ensure that the experience of viewing this material contributes as much to the service encounter of each broadcaster as the viewing of their content on their terrestrial channels. Simon Danker (BBC Worldwide's director of content partnerships) justified the corporation's involvement with SeeSaw in the following terms:

> As a nation we're becoming increasingly familiar with watching full-length content online. We're pleased to give UK viewers the chance to watch some of their favourite BBC shows whenever and wherever they want.
>
> (cited in Shepherd 2009)

Clearly, here, extending the availability of BBC content onto a wide range of platforms is seen to contribute favourably to the BBC's corporate brand identity and to enhance the corporation's aim of becoming the UK's 'number one digital destination' as much as it offers a means of generating revenue.

Conclusions

In the introduction to this chapter I asked whether branding could be seen to undermine or contribute to public service broadcasting. Over this chapter I have demonstrated that this question actually misunderstands the nature and role of branding and simplifies the current state of public service broadcasting in the UK. This chapter has demonstrated that branding has been used by the BBC and Channel 4 as a strategy in response to changes in the broadcasting landscape, rather than as an instigator of those changes. So, while branding and marketing decisions may have increasingly dominated programme production, this is because public service broadcasters have been forced to adopt market-oriented practices as a consequence of government policy. Furthermore, while branding can be used to address the viewer as a consumer, rather than a citizen, within this context of marketization, this is not a necessary consequence of the adoption of branding. Indeed, I have demonstrated the need to separate out an understanding of marketing from marketization and demonstrated that marketing and branding can be used to help public service broadcasters explain and communicate their public service values to the public and to government. Indeed, as public service broadcasting has come under threat, this has become increasingly important.

In examining the range of branding strategies used by the BBC and Channel 4 I have demonstrated that branding does not reduce public service values to banal taglines, as this misunderstands the function and role of branding. Rather, branding has been used to attempt to negotiate the increasingly complex digital media environment. Thus, branding could be understood (as Petros Iosifidis suggests) as a necessary strategy in an increasingly commercial environment. Yet, to understand the significance of this we need to unpack the use of branding in more detail. Key here has been the creation and communication of corporate brand identities, along with the branding of the specific services and channels within them. As we saw with the USA, this has the dual function of grouping together and separating different segments of one corporation. However, in the UK there is far greater emphasis on extending the corporate brand across all aspects of a corporation's operations. Hence, the BBC brand is used in both commercial and licence-funded channels by the BBC, and the Channel 4 brand is extended into a range of services and channels that are not bound by Channel 4's public service remit. What this suggests is that the traditional boundaries of public service broadcasting no longer hold. If, once, we could define public service broadcasting as those aspects of a broadcaster's activities that were bound by a public service remit by government, today this definition has crumbled, because all aspects of each corporation's activities contribute to its reputation and hence to its identity and values as a public service broadcaster. Indeed, as I have argued elsewhere (Johnson 2009), this was always the case – it is just that, in the increasingly marketized digital era, this becomes more acute. This is particularly so on the internet, where such a wide range of different businesses and activities from each broadcaster, targeted to both national and international audiences, sit side by side. Within this context, branding becomes one way in which to manage the wide range of different service encounters that are now available, ensuring in the 'attention economy' that the value of the attention of the viewer to the corporation is not lost.

Notes

1 The Peacock Committee held its meeting on 29 May 1985 and met 20 times over the subsequent year, with the final meeting taking place on 29 May 1986.

2 There were different editions of the programme for the national regions.

3 Briefly, there was a shift in broadcasting regulation from the mid-1980s onwards away from regulating to protect public service provision towards regulating to protect competition. At the same time, the principle that broadcasters that are competing for audiences should not compete for revenue was eroded, and the audience for broadcasting was increasingly conceptualized as a consumer, rather than a citizen. See Chapter 3 for a more detailed discussion of these changes.

4 Chapter 1 argued that the shift to niche demographics in US television also favoured youth and upmarket audiences over other social groups.

5 The cover contained stills from the tapping campaign of the following stars: comedian Sandi Toksvig (*The Talking Show*, *The Big One*), youth presenters Terry Christian and Katie Puckrick (*The Word*), comedian Clive Anderson (*Clive Anderson Talks Back*), sitcom actors Victoria Wicks and David Swift (*Drop the Dead Donkey*), comedian Jack Dee (*The Jack Dee Show*), sitcom actors Norman Beaton and Carmen Monroe (*Desmonds*), journalist Mary Goldring (*The Goldring Audit*), soap actor Paul Usher (*Brookside*), presenter Richard Whitely (*Countdown*), presenter Chris Evans (*The Big Breakfast*) and reporter/news anchor Jon Snow (*Channel 4 News*).

6 Over the 1990s, as Paul Rixon (2003: 55) points out, the ITC moved to force Channel 4 to show more domestic programmes and be less reliant on US imports.

7 Sky Television has copied this strategy in launching on 1 February 2011 its new channel, Sky Atlantic, which is billed as 'the home of HBO's world class television' (see <http://tv.sky.com/skyatlantic>, accessed 4 February 2011).

8 The measure of share by commercial impacts removes the non-advertising-carrying BBC channels, allowing one to identity the share of the terrestrial commercial channels, compared to their commercial non-terrestrial competitors. In the early 1990s, Channel 4 and ITV1 had a combined share of over 95 per cent of commercial impacts in the UK (Channel 5 was not introduced until 1997).

9 Of the other three, two were owned by BSkyB.

10 Chapter 5 will examine the idea of an emerging 'attention economy' in more detail.

11 The rebranding of BBC Two in 1991 is discussed in more detail in Chapter 5.

12 As we saw at the opening of this chapter, this was not the first time that the BBC had attempted to communicate its public service values on air. The differences between the 1986 'What have the BBC ever given us?' promo and the 1997 'Perfect Day' promo will be discussed in the final chapter.

13 While Born is right to argue that with this came the danger of a perceived artificiality, again this stems not from branding itself, but from how it was utilized. However, it is ironic that, at the moment when the BBC was directing increasing funds to communicating its public service brand to viewers, it was, according to Born (2004), undermining the centrality of public service values amongst its employees.

14 BBC Enterprises was set up as a division of the BBC in 1960, was incorporated in 1979 and changed its name to BBC Worldwide Ltd on 1 January 1995.

15 The BBC launched its satellite channel BBC TV Europe in 1987, relaying programmes from BBC One. The channel formed the platform from which the advertiser-funded subscription channel World Service Television was established in 1991, offering a mix of news and entertainment, and extending into Asia and the Middle East 18 months later. The channel was relaunched as BBC World in 1995 and introduced to Europe alongside the entertainment channel BBC Prime (later renamed BBC Entertainment) (Reynolds 1996: 8–9).

16 This is further complicated by the deal that the BBC made with YouTube in March 2007 to establish BBC and BBC Worldwide channels. Here, BBC Worldwide channels, which carry advertising, sit alongside (and are hard to distinguish from) non-advertiser-funded BBC channels.

17 I do not mean to imply here that UK History offers programming of greater public service value than The History Channel, but that, in order for such an argument to be made, a definition of public service broadcasting needs to be developed against which each channel may be assessed.

18 See Born and Prosser (2001) for discussion of contemporary definitions of public service broadcasting.

19 Arqiva was formed from the transmissions units of the BBC and ITV, which developed over the past 30 years into significant businesses in the areas of broadcast transmission, communications infrastructure and networked solutions for digital media. See Arqiva (2010) for a fuller history.

Part III

THE TEXTS AND INTERTEXTS OF BRANDING

5

OF IDENTS AND INTERSTITIALS

Channel branding

> We did a really interesting piece of research two or three years ago with viewers where we took a fictional programme name and said this programme is on these five channels. What was absolutely fascinating was the type of programme that people expected it to be when it was placed underneath that channel. So you could have exactly the same programme title but if it was on ITV2 you would expect it to be something, if it was on Bravo you would expect it to be something else. And that is fundamentally branding, that is all about the power of the brand and what you expect from it.
>
> (Charlie Mawer, Executive Creative Director, Red Bee Media, interview with the author, 21 May 2010)

The principal focus in this book so far has been on exploring the reasons *why* the US and UK television industries adopted branding over the 1980s and 1990s. In this final section I want to focus more explicitly on *how* branding is used by these industries. Thus far, I have argued (borrowing from Arvidsson 2006) that brands can be understood as frames of action that attempt to manage the communication and activity around branded products and services. In doing so, branding intertwines the use value and symbolic value of products and services into a branded identity that is communicated through elements of design, from packaging and product design, to promotion and advertising. In television, product design might be thought of as equating to all elements of the television programme text – its narrative, plotting, style, *mise-en-scène*, performers, music, title sequences and so on. Yet, as Television Studies has reminded us, television programmes are not experienced in a vacuum, but are 'packaged' in various ways. In the broadcast era, television programmes were experienced within the flow of broadcasting (see Williams 1975), leading to the general axiom that people 'watch television not programmes'. Therefore, we could think of the 'packaging' of television programmes as being the flow of broadcasting: how programmes were ordered in the schedules and the design of the idents, trailers, adverts and other texts between and within them. The ordering and design of broadcast flow contributed not only to the meanings of individual programmes, but also to the meanings of television in general, as both Raymond Williams and Paddy Scannell (1996) have demonstrated.

In his theorization of flow Williams (1975) argued that television does not exist as discrete programmes, but rather as a continuous flow of segments. As such, for Williams, broadcasting introduced a fundamentally different experience to the discrete event of reading a book or watching a play, in which different forms of communication (plays, news, music, trailers, adverts) are unified into a singular experience. Importantly, Williams argued that the flow of television is continuous and that the texts between programmes, such as adverts and trailers, should not be understood as interruptions to the programmes, but as part of a planned flow that makes up the experience of watching broadcast television. Scannell also argues that the broadcast programme and the schedule within which it is broadcast are inseparable, and that to understand the meanings and values of broadcast television we need to attend to the overall experience of broadcasting. In order to make the experience of broadcasting intelligible to viewers, broadcasters have learnt to align their behaviour to the places and times of viewing (1996: 9). Reflecting this, Scannell argues that broadcasting displays a 'communicative ethos' that is attentive to (and changes with) setting, place and time (both of day and over years, such as the increasing informality of address in television) (1996: 19–20).

However, despite both Williams's and Scannell's attention to the flow of broadcasting, there is relatively little analysis in either book of the role of the interstitials (the bits between the programmes) in constructing the meanings of broadcast television in general or of the individual programmes that make up its flow. Scannell focuses in particular on 'talk' as being at the heart of the communicative ethos of broadcasting, perhaps because he is equally concerned with radio as with television; but what of elements of visual and aural design, both within programmes and around them? Although there has been some excellent work on television idents and channel branding (see for example Grainge 2009 and 2010, Green 2007, Light 2004, and Selznick 2009), there is relatively little attention paid to the daily use of promotions and idents within the flow of broadcast television. We therefore have little understanding of how the kinds of texts found in between the programmes contribute to the meanings of the flow of broadcasting. Such work becomes even more pressing if one considers the impact of the changes that have taken place since Williams and Scannell were writing.

Recent television scholarship has drawn attention to the role of the ancillary texts around television, from games, toys and magazines, to trailers, posters and other forms of promotion (what Gray (2010) refers to as 'paratexts') that contribute to the meanings associated with individual programmes. Such work reminds us that, while people might 'watch television not programmes', the experience of watching television flows beyond the moment of initial broadcast. And, of course, over the past 30 years new technologies have added a further level of complication to understandings of the nature of television as a medium. The remote control, and later the DVR, increased the viewer's control over the broadcast flow so that it can now be paused or even bypassed. Programmes can be watched on VHS and DVD, with the box set contributing to the experience of bypassing broadcasting altogether (Hills 2007 and Kompare 2006). And programmes can be watched on demand and in new forms on new platforms – from mobile television, to the internet, to short-form television on YouTube (Dawson 2007). It is not just the individual programme that is affected by these changes, but also the packaging of television more broadly, now that broadcasting is not the only experience of watching television. How does the organization and design of broadcast television attempt to manage the new on-demand, everywhere possibilities of watching television in the digital era? How do the various platforms upon which television viewing now takes place package or brand the experience of watching television?

While Chapter 6 will explore the impact of the digital era on programme branding, this chapter will focus on channel branding. For one element that is relatively overlooked in Scannell's account of broadcasting is the channel – perhaps because he was writing at the end of what Ellis (2000) has termed the 'era of scarcity', when the impact of multichannel television was only just beginning to be felt. Yet, any consideration of broadcasting as a flow must account for the channel as a central organizing force. As Julie Light argues, 'Channels are integral to the way that television is structured and organized, and yet it seems that we take them almost entirely for granted, if not as viewers, then certainly as objects of study' (2004: 7). As the number of channels multiplied over the 1980s and 1990s, the need to create a clear meaning and identity for television channels increased, which (as argued in the first two parts of this book) led broadcasters to explore channel branding as a strategic response to a period of enhanced competition. Yet, at the same time, new means of viewing television (DVDs, on demand, online and so on) pull away from the channel as the organizing feature of television. In doing so, these changes also threaten to overturn our long-held assumptions about television – that we 'watch television not programmes' – that are so central to theorizations of broadcasting.[1] Such changes suggest that the programme, and not the flow of broadcasting, might be the unit of television after all.

Yet, the shift of the experience of television from the viewing of a broadcast flow to the selection of individual programmes is not complete or even inevitable. Ofcom's most recent report on public service broadcasting in the UK analysed BARB figures from 2009 to reveal that only 6 per cent of all viewing on the five terrestrial channels in the UK was time-shifted, with the figure rising to 15 per cent for individuals with a DVR (Ofcom 2010: 49).[2] At the same time, the study claimed that the average hours of total daily television viewing increased by 3 per cent between 2005 and 2009 (Ofcom 2010: 3). Although Ofcom's study does not take into account television viewing on DVD or other platforms (internet, mobile phone and so on), it does suggest that broadcasting is still the principal way in which television is viewed. This was reinforced by Ofcom's Digital Day research project, which analysed the media use of 1,138 adults over a seven-day period in April and May 2010 and found that 'scheduled TV forms 82% of all video watched' (Ofcom and Gfk 2010: 4). Nevertheless, between 2005 and 2009 the average hours of daily viewing of all public service broadcasting channels dropped by 15 per cent (Ofcom 2010: 3), and broadcasters increasingly have to deal with a media environment in which viewers *can* engage with television in multiple different ways. I want to argue that these new possibilities for viewing television are having an impact on the organization and design of broadcast television, even if broadcasting remains the principal experience of watching television.

Scannell argues that the 'relationship between broadcasters, listeners and viewers is an *unforced* relationship because it is unenforceable. Broadcasters must, before all else, always consider how they shall talk to people who have no particular reason, purpose or intention for turning on the radio or television set' (1996: 23). Over the past 30 years the 'unenforceability' of this relationship has arguably increased, with the range of options available to viewers beyond broadcasting enabling them to exert far more control and choice over what to watch, when and how. In view of this (as discussed in Chapter 4), broadcasters are having to respond to the emergence of what Michael H. Goldhaber refers to as the 'attention economy', which he claims has developed within post-industrial societies.

> It is precisely because material needs at the creature comfort level are fairly well satisfied for all those in a position to demand them that the need for attention, or what is closely related to attention, meaning or meaningfulness of life, takes on increasing importance. In other words, the energies set free by the successes of what I refer to as the money-industrial economy go more and more in the direction of obtaining attention. And that leads to growing competition for what is increasingly scarce, which is of course attention.
>
> (Goldhaber 1997)

Central here is the internet, which, for Goldhaber, offers the possibility for attention to be captured and circulated by individuals, diminishing the role of organizations in society. Yet, in many ways television (and other broadcast media) has always been concerned with obtaining attention even if, in the broadcast era, television channels did not have to work very hard to do this and (within the context of British public service broadcasting) there was even some anxiety about attempting to engage our attention all the time. After all, the models for funding commercial broadcasting have historically been based on attempting to measure and monetize viewer attention through ratings used to cost the sale of advertising space. What differs in the digital era is that audience attention for broadcasting is scarcer, as the number of sites for accessing audio-visual material has increased and individuals can more easily produce and distribute their own material and hence generate attention on a vast scale without the intervention of broadcasters. Yet, this does not mean, as Goldhaber argues, that there is no role for organizations in the attention economy. After all, if attention is scarce, then we all need ways of deciding where to pay attention and organizations can play a central role in this. Broadcasters have always attempted to capture viewer attention and enforce certain kinds of viewer behaviour. Indeed, Julie Light (2004: 112–13) argues that the traditional theorization of flow accepted by the industry was based on the idea that, at any time of day, there is an 'available audience' who have decided to watch television and for whom *what* they watch is secondary to the pleasures of television watching itself. Thus, although Scannell might be right to point out that viewers can switch off the channel if they want to, broadcasting is industrially organized on the assumption that viewers are open to manipulation by scheduling strategies precisely because they are actually unlikely to switch off. As attention has become an increasingly scarce commodity, broadcasters have adopted new strategies within the interstitials to encourage viewing and these have had a fundamental impact on the communicative ethos of broadcast television in the USA and the UK.

Furthermore (as I have argued in the previous chapters) the communicative ethos of broadcasting is constructed not just through the relationship between the broadcaster and the viewer. In the UK, the activities of the public service broadcasters are shaped in part by those who have power and authority over their very right to broadcast – the government, pressure groups, opinion makers and so on. In the USA (and to a certain extent for UK commercial broadcasters), advertisers, affiliates and shareholders are also central to the ways in which broadcasters communicate. It is perhaps a truism of commercial broadcasting in the USA that it aims to sell audiences to advertisers as well as programmes to viewers. This affects not just what programmes get made, but also how they are organized, the branding and design of each channel, even the nature of the corporate reporting of each company or corporation. Thus, the communicative ethos of broadcasting is shaped by the relationship between broadcasters, listeners/viewers *and other stakeholders*. While Scannell is correct to assert that broadcasters must consider how they talk to viewers who can simply turn off (or turn over), the precise nature of this address will be shaped by the broader context within which such broadcasting is produced. As we shall go on to see, despite significant similarities in the changes that have taken place to US and UK television, the nature of the communicative ethos in each context is strikingly different and shaped by the broader context within which each industry is situated.

Methodology

One of the reasons why there has been so little research on the interstitial breaks between (and within) programmes is the methodological difficulties of undertaking such research. While it is possible for a researcher to record contemporary examples of off-air television, undertaking historical research is far harder due to the relative lack of archival access to off-air broadcasts of television programming. In order to examine how the communicative ethos of broadcast television has changed over the last 30 years, this chapter focuses on the UK terrestrial and US national broadcasters.[3] In the UK we are fortunate that the British Film Institute's National Archive has been recording selected whole days of terrestrial television since 1988, which allowed me to examine one evening of television (approximately, from 6pm to 11pm), every five years from the end of October or start of November from 1988 to 2003, from the main terrestrial channels, BBC One, ITV1 (recorded in the Thames/London region) and Channel 4.[4] In the USA, there is no similar collection to the BFI's whole days of television. The UCLA Film and Television Archive's NAPA (News and Public Affairs) collection contains off-air recordings of news programmes made in the Los Angeles region from 1979 to 2003. This enabled me to examine off-air recordings from the same time period as the UK sample from the four major US networks, CBS, NBC, ABC and Fox. However, as these recordings were mostly only one hour of programming, which included one local and one national news programme, they offered relatively little insight into the ways in which the national networks used the transitions between programmes to communicate their channel identities.[5] Luckily the University of Texas at Austin's Instructional Media Centre (IMC) has a collection of off-air recordings of US television from 1994–97. While the IMC focused on recording selected programmes there are a few instances where it is possible to piece together one or two hours of prime-time network television for analysis.[6] This archival viewing was complemented by viewing idents, junctions and promotional media on YouTube and TVArk (<http://www.tv-ark.org.uk>), as well as analysis of an evening from each broadcaster from spring/summer 2010.[7] If analysing on-air branding is complicated by a lack of archival access, then examining how these strategies have been extended onto the web is even harder. While websites such as The Wayback Machine (<http://www.archive.org/web/web.php>) have archived webpages from 1996, it struggles to retain the layout and architecture of these sites, making it of limited use for a study of design and branding.

The difficulties of undertaking this kind of research extend beyond the accessibility of archive material. While, on the one hand, this chapter is only examining a proportion of televisual material, on the other, the amount of data generated has been daunting. The kinds of texts that one finds within the interstitials are densely edited and rapidly packed together into very short spans of time. Accounting for just this small sample of material within one chapter has involved not always being able to address some of the nuances within these texts. In addition, my analysis of the US material has been hampered by the relative inaccessibility of archived days of broadcasting, so that my claims here about US television will inevitably be drawn from a more limited range of primary sources than those about UK television. Nevertheless, from this relatively limited sample the differences between the communicative ethos of television broadcasting within each country is striking, suggesting that the national specificity of watching television remains even within today's global media landscape.

UK on-air branding: BBC One, ITV1 and Channel 4

In the 1980s, the principal role of the junctions in UK terrestrial television was to provide clarity and order to the flow of broadcasting. In 1988 there was consistency in the use of interstitial space by all three channels (see Table 5.1). Each junction contained a slide with a still image of the programme coming next in the schedules voiced by a continuity announcer, a trailer for a programme on that evening or later in the week and a channel ident over which the continuity announcer introduced the next programme. The consistent structure of the junctions regularized the experience of watching television for viewers. This was enhanced by the use of channel idents, which were short graphic sequences used to lead into every programme, accompanied by a continuity announcer explaining what was on now and next.[8] In 1988 the channel idents used by BBC One and Thames were largely unchanged from the 1960s. The Thames ident consisted of a composite skyline of London that rose from the centre of the screen to reveal the word 'Thames', which had been used since the channel started broadcasting in 1968. BBC One's ident was based on a spinning globe with the channel name underneath, which had been in use in various forms since the mid-1960s. Channel 4's ident was perhaps the most distinctive, with its computer-generated coloured blocks that flew into the screen to form the '4' logo. As

Table 5.1 Typical order of interstitials on UK terrestrial television in 1988

ITV/Thames and Channel 4	*BBC One*
Programme	Programme
Occasional slide for book/leaflet linked to programme (Channel 4)	Occasional slide for book/leaflet/video linked to programme
Slide for programme on next (sometimes with additional slide for programme on ITV/Channel 4)	Trailer
Ad break	Slide for programme on next (sometimes with additional slide for programme on BBC Two)
Trailer	
Ident and continuity announcer	Ident and continuity announcer
Programme	Programme

well as providing a consistent indication of what channel was being viewed, the idents for BBC One, Thames and Channel 4 in the 1980s also contributed to constructing an identity for each channel: Thames's place as the commercial public service broadcaster for London; BBC One's role to bring the nation together and represent British broadcasting; and Channel 4's remit to serve a wide range of different viewers (represented by the different coloured blocks) on one channel.

However, Channel 4's 1980s ident was also hailed as 'the first expression of a properly-branded television channel' (Myerson 1997: 15). It was produced in six different versions that varied the movement of the blocks (rotating, imploding, exploding and so on) and developed as part of a consistent presentation style to be used for all on-air interstitial graphics, from slides and menus, to the weather map and clock (see Lambie-Nairn 1997: 69). This helped 'to establish a unique personality for the station' (Lambie-Nairn 1997: 69) and contributed to the visual pleasure of the ident, so that it became more than just a functional visual signifier and acted as a form (albeit limited) of entertainment.[9] This was not a common feature of other channel idents at this time. For example, in 1988 the BBC One ident appeared in just one form (a spinning globe with 'BBC1' in text underneath), while BBC One used different graphics for its slides (with 'BBC1' in vertical gold text on the left hand side) and for its menu of the evening's viewing (beginning with an animated graphic of a large, metallic blue '1'). Meanwhile, its trailers did not include any BBC One logos at all. Thames began some of its trailers with an animated graphic of a blue metal box, embossed with the Thames logo, opening, but this was not used consistently or in the slides for programmes on next, which had their own graphic style. Thus, BBC One and ITV/Thames did not have a consistent graphic style for their channels in the 1980s.

The development of an entertaining ident that conveyed a unique personality for Channel 4 and that was extended across all the design elements of the junctions contributed to the construction of the channel as a brand that communicated a set of values to the viewer. However, the ident was developed separately from the channel's brand strategy, reflecting a broader tendency within the television industry in the 1980s to separate marketing from on-screen presentation (Lambie-Nairn 1997: 71). Furthermore, Charlie Mawer (Executive Creative Director, Red Bee Media) argues that there was much consistency in the 1980s between Channel 4's attitude towards idents and that of the other UK terrestrial broadcasters. Describing Lambie-Nairn's original Channel 4 idents, he argues:

> it's still a reasonably recessive piece of brand communication that is just a gloriously visual piece of logo type-work really. So I think that sort of held sway really, that it was about bringing neatness and order to what are always extraordinarily busy, diverse, bulging at the seams brands to contain. So I think Martin's [Lambie-Nairn's]

> view on branding was very much driven by that sense of bringing order to chaos and neatness and clarity all of which all four channels had in abundance. Possibly what they didn't have as much which they need to do now is to communicate what they stood for and what role they were to have in people's lives.
>
> (interview with author, 21 May 2010)

The argument that a primary function of the channel ident might be to bring clarity and order is reinforced by the musical stings used to accompany the channel idents for Channel 4 and ITV/Thames in 1988. Thames had used the same brass fanfare since the 1960s, which accompanied the movement of the ident before the continuity announcer spoke. Channel 4 also used a fanfare motif. As with Channel 4's visual ident, the musical fanfare was simple enough to enable variation, with arrangements that were orchestral, rock and reggae (Fanthome 2007: 259).[10] Mark Brownrigg and Peter Meech suggest that the fanfare, which had been the dominant aural underscoring to UK idents since the arrival of the new ITV franchises in the 1950s, 'is instantly recognisable, bears seemingly infinite repetition and creates an excited enthusiasm for what comes next' (2002: 347). The repeated short fanfares, often using brass instruments, addressed the inattentive and provided a memorable aural cue that a programme was about to start. The lack of music on BBC One's idents at this time is likely to be tied to the lack of advertising. A key role of the junctions is to manage the flow of viewer attention. Because Channel 4 and ITV carry advertising, viewers were more likely to graze or be distracted during the ad breaks, and the musical fanfares of each channel were a useful aural signal to the viewer of what channel they were on and that the programme was about to start.

Alongside the use of musical fanfares, order and clarity was also provided by continuity announcers who would speak over the ident in order to introduce the programme about to be aired. The continuity announcer is a long-standing tradition across European public service broadcasters, acting as a consistent and personal guide through the evening's viewing. Hilde Van Den Bulck (2010) argues that the continuity announcer functions as an ambassador for public service broadcasting and plays a key role in carrying the image of the channel, a role that for European public service broadcasters was tied to the construction of national identity. In 1988 the presentational style of the continuity announcers on all three channels was relatively formal, with an emphasis on providing clear information, rather than conveying the personality of the announcer.[11] This emphasis on the informational function of the interstitials was also apparent in the trailers in 1988. At this time there was a consistent style for the trailers across all three channels, with a voice-over describing the programme and when it was on, intercut with extracts and dialogue from the programme. All trailers ended with text and a voice-over giving title, day and time of broadcast.

Over the 1990s, the role of the junctions in UK terrestrial television began to change in two ways. First, there was an increasing emphasis on creating a brand identity and personality for channels over and above their programming. Again Lambie-Nairn pioneered this move with the redesign of BBC Two's idents in 1991. One key difference between Lambie-Nairn's approach to rebranding BBC Two and his development of Channel 4's ident in 1982 was its basis in audience research. This revealed that audience perceptions of BBC Two were that it was 'boring', 'heavy', 'quiet', 'middle-class', 'snobbish' and 'highbrow' (Lambie-Nairn 1997: 122). The new BBC Two idents unveiled on 16 February 1991 (alongside new idents for BBC One) attempted to construct and communicate a new identity for the channel as 'witty, innovative, surprising' (Lambie-Nairn 1997: 125). The design was based on a large sans serif 2 initially depicted in nine different scenarios (having paint thrown at it, lit up in neon, lying under a rippling silk cloth, and so on), but all sharing a cool viridian green colour palette. While such variation in the idents had been used in 1982 for Channel 4, the BBC Two rebrand constructed the 2 more overtly as a character.

> After only six months on-air, audience research showed that the BBC2 figure had become a talking point; people often identified their own favourite 'character', and the channel itself was perceived as sophisticated, witty and stylish: a complete transformation in its popular image had been achieved.
>
> (Lambie-Nairn 1997: 129)

In 1993 BBC Two launched a new set of these idents that further exploited the construction of the sans serif 2 as a character. One featured the 2 as a fluffy toy that nodded, barked (in a high-pitch tone) and flipped in the air. In another, the 2 appeared as a radio-controlled car that whizzed around the screen, while, in a third, it was wired up with charges that exploded in turn, catapulting it repeatedly into the air. These idents used conventions of entertainment to communicate a channel identity in a way that was designed to be memorable and emotionally engaging.

These idents also pioneered in their use of music, turning away from the fanfare towards musical sounds directly linked to the images, but united in their use of 'Bell-like sonorities, quasi-minimalist pulses, warm, dark-timbered synth textures, heavily "treated" sound (echoes, pitch modulations, distortions etc.) and a fluid hypnotic approach to the combination of elements' (Brownrigg and Meech 2002: 348–49). As Brownrigg and Meech go on to argue, 'the overall tone is reflective and tranquil rather than blaring and self-important. The single, monolithic utterance of many ident fanfares, including Channel 4's, has been rejected in favour of a mix of musical elements adapted and arranged to suit each different visual design, yet still recognisably of a piece' (2002: 349).[12] Over the 1990s, the continuity announcements also changed, becoming more informal and ambiguous, often relating to an aspect of the programme, rather than mentioning its title, or using popular abbreviations of long-running programme titles (such as 'Corrie' for *Coronation Street* (ITV, 1960–)). This change in tone also contributed to conveying a sense of the personality of the channel to the viewer, while also speaking to them in their own language, emphasizing the connection between viewer and channel, rather than adopting a paternalistic attitude.

These BBC Two idents pointed to a shift in the visual and aural style of idents on British television that is evident in the subsequent rebranding of all the terrestrial channels over the 1990s. First, the ident functioned as a form of entertainment in itself – a short scenario in which the channel logo played the role of a character – extending the moves that Channel 4's block logo made in this direction. Second, the ident was produced in a range of variations, enhancing its role as entertainment, while allowing adaptation to the tone of the programming being broadcast. Finally, in the aural and visual design of the idents, contemplation and serenity was emphasized over the sharp excitement and differentiation of the fanfare. By 2010 these three aspects of design (entertainment, variation and contemplation) are evident in the idents for all the UK terrestrial channels and, in particular, the emphasis on contemplation and reflection has been enhanced. For example, in Channel 4's idents the camera moves through different landscapes within which the 4 block logo is gradually and momentarily revealed, formed out of aspects of the environment, from neon signs, to pylons, to bales of hay, accompanied by fluid, hypnotic soundscapes.[13] As such, the ident communicates a more complex identity for the channel, as well as functioning as a contemplative pause between programmes, rather than as a monolithic utterance of the channel's identity. Branding is particularly useful within the public service context of the mixed programme schedule because brands function to connect together different products and services within one set of values (see Lury 2004). The channel idents developed for UK terrestrial broadcasters had to be fluid enough to unify a range of clustered content, while also providing a useful tool within the flow of broadcasting to enable shifts in tone from, for example, comedy to current affairs.

The second change in the role of the junctions over the 1990s was a shift in the scheduling strategies adopted. In the UK from the mid-1990s a new art of scheduling emerged in response to increased competition. Strategies such as stripping (placing the same genre or programme at the same time every day), zoning (placing certain kinds of content within particular days and times) and theming (creating special blocks of programming around specific themes) all aimed to make the schedule more memorable for viewers (Light 2004: 120–26). These contributed to what Ytreberg terms the 'continuity' function of junctions: 'a set of strategies for keeping viewers tuned to one or more channels through the schedule's duration' (2002: 286). However, as Light argues, these strategies also contributed to the construction of brand identities for channels beyond individual programmes: 'the growth of zoning, stripping and theming associated channels with specific types of programming' (2004: 132). Over the 1990s the principal role of the junctions in UK terrestrial television shifted from providing clarity and order to the flow of broadcasting, to constructing branded identities that conveyed a personality for the channel over and above its individual programmes.[14]

Julie Light argues that, by the early 2000s, there was consensus at the BBC that 'a brand and its values should drive consistent brand communications both on and off air' (2004: 140–41) and that channel brands were those through which the BBC believed it could derive most value. In a world where viewers had to choose from an escalating number of new channels, channel brands were seen by the BBC as valuable signposts that supported the corporation's broader goal to be a 'trusted guide' within the newly emerging digital landscape (Light 2004: 145). More generally for European public service broadcasters, Ytreberg argues that the 'allure of television branding lay in its promise to differentiate the broadcaster from its competition in appealing terms' (2002: 298). And, of course, at this time public service broadcasters across Europe were facing competition from new commercial satellite, cable and digital channels, many of which had adopted clear branded identities.[15] However, by the early 2000s the British terrestrial broadcasters had also expanded onto digital themselves, with new channels, websites and services. As argued in Chapters 3 and 4, this placed an increased emphasis on branding as a means of uniting these different services within one corporate brand, while also creating separate brand identities for them. Furthermore, it increased the need for broadcast terrestrial television to promote these new services, particularly for the BBC, which had a specific remit to encourage the up-take of digital technologies in the UK.

In the 1980s it was common for ITV and Channel 4, and BBC One and BBC Two, to cross-promote each other's programmes, and the interstitials also included slides for spin-off products (mainly books, videos and pamphlets) produced by the broadcasters to accompany their programmes, as well as trailers for the two main listings magazines, *TV Times* and *Radio Times*. However, from 1998, and particularly in the sample evenings from 2003 and 2010 analysed for this chapter, cross-promotion became a far more dominant aspect of the breaks between programmes, as the broadcasters used the terrestrial channels to promote their new digital channels and services.[16] By 2010 it had become as common for BBC One, ITV1 and Channel 4 to trail whole channels/services as to trail individual programmes. Despite anxieties that in the digital era the television channel is becoming irrelevant (see for example, Ytreberg 2002), this suggests that British terrestrial broadcasters still believe that there is as much value in creating and promoting a channel as a destination with a sense of personality and a connection with its audience, as there is in promoting one individual programme.

Table 5.2 Typical order of interstitials on UK terrestrial television in 2010

ITV1	*Channel 4*	*BBC One*
Programme with occasional in programme pointer	Programme with occasional in programme pointer	Programme with occasional in programme pointer
End credit squeeze with menu of what's on next over different ITV channels/ services or continuity announcer over credits	End credit squeeze with menu of what's on next over different Channel 4 channels/ services or continuity announcer over credits	End credit squeeze with menu of what's on next over different BBC channels/ services or announcer over credits
Ident sting	Trailer, ending with Channel 4 logo	Trailers – usually at least two for whole services as well as individual programmes, often with a digital on-screen graphic (DOG)
Ad break	Ad break	
Ident sting	Ident sting	
Trailers – usually two for whole services as well as individual programmes, all with a DOG	Trailer, ending with Channel 4 logo	
Ident and continuity announcer	Ident and continuity announcer	Ident and continuity announcer
Programme	Programme	Programme

However, cross-promotion was not just apparent in the trailers, but also in the new continuity strategies that emerged in the junctions on British terrestrial television over the 2000s, as can be seen in Table 5.2.[17] By 2010, slides were rarely used anymore in the junctions. They had been replaced by end credit squeezes (menus within the end credits of programmes), continuity announcements over the credits, and in programme pointers (pop-up banners over the last few minutes of a programme), all informing the viewer of what is coming up next across a far wider range of channels and services. There are far more trailers, with ITV1 and Channel 4 also running trailers in the ad breaks within programmes. The ident also takes a more prominent place, with ITV1 and Channel 4 using brief ident stings (silent versions of the ident of 1–3 seconds duration) around the ad breaks. It has become common for trailers to include a DOG (digital on-screen graphic, sometimes referred to as a BUG) of the channel logo in the corner of the screen, and trailers are frequently for whole channels or services.[18]

Continuity announcements over credits began around 1993 as the terrestrial broadcasters were preparing for increased competition from satellite and cable channels.[19] In my sample, by 1998 BBC One was employing end-credit squeezes containing short trailers for the premiere of its new Sunday night drama, *Vanity Fair* (BBC, 1998). By 2003, all three channels were using end credit squeezes, which were now more likely to contain menus with information about the evening's schedule, or what was on now and next on the different channels owned by that broadcaster. While some producers attempted to prevent end credit squeezes by including programme content in the credits (such as sketches in the credits for *The Fast Show* (BBC, 1994–2000)), in June 2007 the BBC introduced production guidelines to accompany its new end credit strategy (Bryant 2009). It is now common for end titles to be produced to accommodate the end credit squeeze, with the credits for soap operas *Emmerdale* (ITV, 1989–)[20] and *Coronation Street* running along the bottom of the screen to allow space for the ITV menus above, and the credits for *Hollyoaks* (Channel 4, 1995–) and *Big Brother* (Channel 4, 2000–) running up the left of the screen to allow for Channel 4's menus on the right.

In many ways end credit squeezes have simply replaced the slides used within the interstitial breaks in the 1980s in order to manage the increasing number of channels and services owned by each broadcaster and the anxiety about audience churn in an age of choice about what and when to watch. However, while in the 1980s the emphasis was on clearly indicating to the viewer what was on now and next, today the possible choices available to the viewer are vastly increased and the construction of the end credit squeezes reflects this. Rather than simply informing the viewer of what is on next on the channel and its related channels, there is a much stronger sense of targeting what is promoted to the perceived viewer. For example, the menu over the end credits of *EastEnders* (BBC, 1985–) on BBC One at 7.30pm on 15 June 2010 listed what was on next on BBC One (the soap opera *Holby City* (BBC, 1999 –)) and BBC Three (the film *Win a Date with Tad Hamilton!* (2004)), promoting content within a similar genre (soap opera) or targeted demographically (*EastEnders* gives BBC One some of its youngest demographics and is also repeated on BBC Three). Over on ITV1 on 14 June 2010, the end credits for a double bill of *Coronation Street* (with an episode of *Countryside* (ITV, 2009–) hammocked in between) were squeezed for a menu promoting the on-demand ITVPlayer as a service where viewers can catch up with episodes of *Coronation Street* that they have missed.[21]

The pressure to promote a far wider range of channels and services has also led to an increased need for clear logos and graphic signifiers for each channel and service. In addition to channel logos that accompany all menus and most trailers (often as DOGs in the corner or along the bottom of the screen), all three broadcasters have adopted different colours to accompany the trailers and menus for their channels. For example, the BBC uses red for BBC One, viridian green for BBC Two, pink for BBC Three, and black for BBC Four. Channel 4 uses light blue for Channel 4, purple for E4, red for FilmFour, and dark green for More4. Trailers for programmes to be transmitted on these digital channels make use of their specific channel graphics, idents, soundscapes and often continuity announcers, clearly tying the programme to the identity of the channel. At the same time, however, trailers for programmes often include information about other services provided by the broadcaster, such as on-demand and mobile services and URLs for websites, so that individual programmes are frequently promoted as transmedia texts linked to a wide range of channels and services.

The graphic design and logos for each channel are also carried over onto new media platforms, although with varying degrees of emphasis. The web pages for ITV's channels make use of the colour palettes designed for each channel ident, but emphasis is also placed on creating a clean white style that is consistent across the ITV site overall, while the pages for ITV's online on-demand service, the ITVPlayer, makes use of its own distinctive black graphic style, which is also used for on-air trailers for the service. Channel 4's individual channel web pages also use the design elements from each channel. However, this is most apparent for E4 and 4Music, those channels that are most overtly targeted at an audience likely to engage with television online. Overall, on both ITV's and Channel 4's websites there is less graphic consistency (in terms of both layout and the use of colour and type) than on the BBC. In 2008 the BBC embarked on a project called 'Global Visual Language 2.0' that aimed to unify the visual and interactional design of its internet and mobile websites, including its on-demand service, the iPlayer. Central to the project was creating a more consistent visual and navigational system for each web page that gave the BBC a distinctive cross-platform identity, simplified the journeys that viewers took across the BBC's platforms, and yet was flexible enough to accommodate the visual identities of the BBC's existing brands. As Bronwyn van der Mervwe claims, 'We wanted to create something that is flexible enough to allow all our brands their full expression whilst uniting them into a coherent user experience' (2010). All BBC web pages, including the iPlayer, now share the same navigational bar across the top, which helps the viewer to travel between the different sections of the BBC's website, from channel and programme pages, to the iPlayer and news. Yet, each of the BBC's channel websites is framed by the graphic design used on its on-air idents. For example, BBC One uses a red circular graphic in all of its on-air idents and menus, which also forms the background of its webpage and creates a consistent identity that travels from the broadcast to the online experience of engaging with the channel. Thus, it is on the BBC that the emphasis on communicating distinctive branded personalities and constructing clear journeys for its viewers through its different platforms has been extended most directly from broadcast to online (and onto its mobile services).

However, the terrestrial broadcasters have not just extended their channel brand identities onto their own websites, but also onto the new sites for accessing media content, such as YouTube. There are YouTube channels for Channel 4, 4oD, E4, ITV1 and ITV2, which all use design elements from each broadcast channel or service. For example, ITV1's YouTube channel features the ITV1 logo and is framed by the black and gold version of its ident used on air. By contrast, the BBC doesn't replicate its broadcast channels on YouTube, but rather extends its corporate identities and programme brands with BBC channels and BBC Worldwide channels. The extension of channel brand identities online extends from the design of the online interfaces to the actual content available for streaming and/or downloading. Each programme on the BBC iPlayer begins with an ident for the channel on which it was originally broadcast. However, as with its YouTube channels, the BBC does not include idents at the beginning of the clips that it makes available through YouTube. On the ITVPlayer, the service ident for the ITVPlayer fades into a channel ident before the adverts and then the programme are screened, and on ITV's YouTube channels each clip begins with the relevant channel ident. When Channel 4's content is viewed online (on YouTube or on 4oD on Channel 4's website), adverts are followed by an ident for 4oD that borrows from the style of the Channel 4 idents described above.[22] This suggests that there is some variation in the ways in which the terrestrial broadcasters are extending their identities online and the extent to which channels are valued as a way of framing the experience of watching their content online.[23]

Where once the communicative ethos of the on-air junctions on British broadcast terrestrial television was based on ordering, and informing the viewer about, the flow of programming, in the digital era the junctions have now taken on a new role: managing viewer behaviour by constructing channels with clear brand personalities that are communicated to viewers in ways that entertain them and arrest their attention, and developing design elements (logo, colour, typography, layout) that encourage certain journeys across the different platforms owned by the broadcaster. While the extent to which this has been translated onto new media platforms, such as the internet and mobile phone, varies between the UK terrestrial broadcasters, the construction of a consistent and distinctive look, feel and sound for each channel has now become a fundamental aspect of the communicative ethos of British broadcasting. Yet, this shift was not inevitable. As we shall go on to see, very similar industrial shifts within the USA over the 1990s (see Chapters 1 and 2) have not led to the same changes to the communicative ethos of network television.

US on-air branding: NBC, ABC, CBS and Fox

If the communicative ethos of the UK terrestrial channels' junctions in the 1980s was based on clarity and order, in the USA the emphasis tended towards persuasion. Although the US network junctions contained many of the same texts as the UK (idents/logos, trailers, continuity announcers and advertisements), the most common text was the programme trailer. As in the UK, these tended to focus on informing the viewer; what Eastman refers to as the 'what' (description of the programme), 'who' (the main stars) and 'when' (the transmission time and day) of programme trailers (2006: 134).[24] The use of channel idents of 10–30 seconds leading into each programme is not a regular feature of the communicative ethos of US network television as it is in the UK. Rather, channel identities are mainly communicated through network logos (referred to as station IDs) and network promos. The US networks all have long-standing and strong brand logos. CBS adopted its 'eye' logo in 1951, NBC developed is 'peacock' logo in 1956 to accompany its introduction of colour television, and ABC used its stylized circle logo for the first time in 1962.[25] As in the UK, these logos do serve to provide clarity to the interstitials. They are used on programme trailers and at the end of in-house productions to reiterate the channel being viewed. Since the 1990s these logos have also appeared as DOGs in the corner of the screen throughout network programming, and hence function to clearly communicate to the viewer what network they are watching.[26] The integration of local station and network logos (see Chapter 1) was part of an attempt to increase the consistency of this across the whole of a channel's broadcasting, rather than having local programming refer to 'channel 2', while networked programming referred to 'CBS', as was common in the 1980s.

However, these logos by themselves do little to convey the identity of each network. This has historically been the role of network promos, 2–3 minute-long films that aired in the junctions, particularly at the start of each season. These promos were based around specially devised slogans, such as ABC's 'Still the one' in 1977 and 1979, NBC's 'Proud as a peacock' in 1979, and CBS's 'We're looking good' in 1979.[27] For example, ABC's 1983 promo centred on an African-American man being left to babysit his young grand-daughter. After making the largest sandwich that they could, they sat down to watch *Happy Days* (ABC, 1974–84) on ABC. The scene is edited to a ballad that proclaims 'that special feeling for you and me, that special feeling on ABC', ending with a new animated version of the ABC circle logo. The promo is designed to associate ABC and the experience of watching the channel with happy domestic life and what Selznick (2010) calls the 'wholesome family'. By contrast, NBC's 1982 promo combined rapidly edited extracts from the network's fall season line-up and its logo to a catchy pop song that extolled the quality and range of the network's programming, repeatedly exclaiming 'we're NBC, just watch us now!' Here, the emphasis is on conveying to the viewer the excitement and fun that could be theirs if they just watched NBC 'now!' Barbara Selznick (2010) argues that these network promotional films can be best understood as 'positioning'. Positioning refers to the relationship of a product to its market competitors. A frequent element of these campaigns is to position each network in the minds of the audience as 'still the one', 'looking good' or 'the place to be' (from NBC in 1990). In this sense, both of these films do convey an identity for each channel. Yet, the principal aim here (and one that is particularly explicit in the NBC example) is to persuade viewers to watch the network.

Furthermore, these campaigns were often updated annually, so that, although the US networks had highly distinctive and recognizable channel logos, the network's identity and positioning was being frequently revised.

As in the UK, over the 1990s the US networks did turn to channel branding in response to the rise of new channels and increased deregulation (see Chapters 1 and 2). The turn towards branding aimed to construct and communicate a more explicit identity for each network, which is exemplified by ABC's 'yellow' campaign, discussed briefly in Chapter 1. The campaign launched in 1997 and made extensive use of the colour yellow in on- and off-air marketing, accompanied by ironic slogans about television viewing, such as 'Before TV, two world wars. After TV, zero' and 'If it's so bad for you, why is there one in every living room.' For the 1998–99 season the slogans became warmer and less ironic and the campaign was extended throughout the design of the interstitials on the broadcast channel (Alan Cohen, ABC Executive VP/Marketing cited in Sharkey 1998). The campaign, created by Chiat\Day, was based on audience research that suggested 'that Americans found the networks to be identity-less, and that the usual image promos – goony phrases, big logos, stars and clips of shows and laugh tracks – made them time out' (Lippert 1997: 20, 82). As with the adoption of channel branding on UK terrestrial television, the ABC yellow campaign attempted to construct an identity for the channel that imbued all its activities. The emphasis was on creating a personality for the channel that was cheeky, fun and spoke directly to the viewer in their own language. In addition, the campaign aimed to make the interstitials entertaining. As Alan Cohen, ABC Executive VP/Marketing explained, it was 'a whole new way to use our promotional time to entertain people so they're less likely to reach for the remote' (cited in Elliott 1998).

However, as discussed in Chapter 1, the ABC yellow campaign was controversial when it launched (see for example, Anon. 1998 and Huff 1998). The trade press argued that channel branding was only valuable for highly targeted and differentiated niche cable channels and that viewers watch television programmes not television channels. Or, as Lewis Grossberger claimed in *Media Week*:

> People don't watch networks! People watch programs! NBC gets high ratings because it has *Seinfeld* and *ER*, not because people think NBC is cool.
>
> (1997)

This scepticism within the trade press about the value of branding for the major networks is reflected in the samples of US network television viewed for this chapter from the 1990s and 2000s, where there was little evidence of the coordinated on-air branding campaigns that were emerging at the same time in the UK. Although ABC and NBC included specially shot idents in the 1990s, the graphic style of these was not used consistently throughout the interstitials. Indeed, across all channels it was far more common for network programme promotions to make use of the title graphics of the individual programme, with the network logo simply added over the final frame. Thus, promoting a brand identity for the programme appeared to be more important than promoting a consistent channel brand identity. On US network television the communicative ethos would appear to privilege the programme over the channel.

As in the UK, the 1990s also saw changes to the scheduling practices of US network television. Donald M. Davis and James R. Walker (1990) noted that, in the late 1980s, the networks were already adopting strategies designed to discourage viewers from switching channels between programmes, following a decline in network audience share. These included running fewer promos between programmes and postponing the title sequence in favour of opening the programme with a teaser or other short scene.[28] Susan Tyler Eastman, Jeffrey Neal-Lunsford and Karen Riggs (1995) analysed these strategies further by undertaking quantitative analysis of the transitions between programmes on the four networks in the 1992–93 and 1993–94 seasons. They argue that, from 1992, the networks began systematically altering the structure of the ends and starts of programmes and experimenting with the transitions between programmes. Eastman *et al.* (1995) noted strategies such as 'hot switching' (where one programme leads immediately into the next without any break), 'cold starts' (when a programme begins with a scene and postpones its title sequences), the elimination or squeezing of programme credits, continuity over the credits and the introduction of post-credit scenes. While in the UK over the early 1990s the amount of time given to promotions and idents in prime-time terrestrial television increased, in the USA the trade press began to report a decline in non-programme time on network television (Eastman *et al.* 1995), and an analysis of four weeks of network transitions in 1994 and 1995 suggested that the mean length of the break between programmes had declined from 90 seconds to 70 seconds (Eastman *et al.* 1997). This does not mean that the networks stopped promoting programmes during this time. Rather, programme promotions moved from the transitions between programmes into the ad breaks within programmes. Although these strategies were introduced sporadically over the 1990s and involved renegotiating contracts with programme producers and affiliates, each of them was in evidence in my samples from the 1990s and by 2010 they had become even more common on the networks.[29]

The adoption of these strategies across all four networks over the 1990s suggests that, for the US networks, a key function of the interstitials was to manage viewer flow and that the need to use the interstitials to retain the audience from one programme to the next became even more important with the rise of increased competition for viewer attention. Branding strategies for segments of the schedules, such as NBC's Thursday night 'Must See TV' campaign, support this function of the interstitials by encouraging viewers to tune in for an evening of coordinated and linked programming. By contrast, idents and other forms of channel branding potentially run counter to share maintenance. While the networks were experimenting with strategies designed to reduce the perception of breaks between programme ends and starts, idents potentially act as intervals in the flow of programming.

Writing in 1975, Raymond Williams saw the BBC's spinning globe ident as an example of a declining technique of placing intervals between discrete programme units in order to distinguish them (1975: 89–90). Williams described true intervals as, 'usually marked by some conventional sound or picture to show that the general service was still active. There was the sound of bells or the sight of waves breaking, and these marked the intervals between discrete programme units' (ibid.). He argued that, with the arrival of commercial television in the UK in 1955, the concept of the interval became inadequate to describe the complex flow of adverts and trailers that now appeared between programmes. Although the increasing range of texts within the interstitials since the 1990s has arguably further undermined the idea of the interval in broadcast television, it has not disappeared completely. Indeed, as we saw above, the trend in British broadcasting over the last two decades has been towards producing more contemplative idents that function in part as a pause and change of tone in the flow between programmes and between promotional texts and programmes. Although these idents are not true intervals as Williams describes them, they do slow down the movement of the flow, hence functioning as a shift in tempo and mood akin to the intervals of early British broadcasting. Charlie Mawer argued that on UK television, idents can:

> help those uncomfortable gear changes between programmes and between individual trailers, to give moments for you to catch your breath from the past programme or build up anticipation for the next one or simply to go from a hard hitting factual programme at 8 o'clock to a light comedy at 9. It's kind of like a sip of water between courses, really.
>
> (interview with the author, 21 May 2010)

The description of idents providing a 'sip of water between courses' is likely to be quite alien to anyone familiar with US broadcast network television, where the pace of the interstitials is far more rapid than on UK television.[30] With the emphasis in US network television firmly placed on managing share maintenance, there is little space for the kinds of contemplative idents found on UK terrestrial television.

The role of channel branding and idents on network television is further problematized by the economics of US broadcast television. For the US networks, all non-programme time is potentially revenue-generating, advertising sales time. Therefore, although the networks don't have to pay directly to use their own airtime for promotions and idents, any time used by the network or its affiliates between or within programmes is a potential loss in advertising revenue.[31] As a consequence, media planning in the USA is particularly concerned with the bottom line and with ensuring that the non-advertising texts within the interstitials are generating revenue.[32] Eastman, Ferguson and Klein argue that, since the 1990s, the networks have cut back on their self-promotion, largely because of increased pressure within the new media conglomerates to focus on the bottom line:

> Owners [of networks] now see promotion as an expense that must result in direct, not indirect, benefits on the profit side of the ledger. In consequence, the industry has moved away from promotion as a domestic branding tool to emphasize short-term profits.
>
> (2006: 17)

They argue that the emphasis on branding in the 1990s has been largely replaced by a shift towards cross-promotion in which the large media conglomerates now use their different holdings to cross-promote their range of programmes and services (2006: 16). As in the UK, cross-promotion became an increasing feature of the interstitials on US network television from the late 1990s, including the promotion of brand extensions, such as the cable channel MSNBC News, a joint venture between NBC and Microsoft, and other channels owned by the parent company, such as ABC's promotion of programmes on Lifetime, a cable channel owned by Disney. The 2000s also saw an increase in the cross-promotion of non-television services, including local station websites, Facebook sites and multiplatform news services (such as a trailer for a Fox Chicago News iPhone app), and by 2010 all four networks regularly included URLs for their websites in their network logos, in programme pointers (IPPs) and programme promotions. As in the UK, there is also variation in the ways in which the US networks have extended their channels online. All four networks have websites, with NBC, CBS and Fox also extending their channels onto YouTube, and NBC, CBS and ABC offering channel sites on Facebook. Although these sites utilize design elements from their station IDs, on the whole this is limited to background colour (black for ABC, white for Fox) and the use of the network logo, rather than a distinctive visual design that is carried over from broadcast to online.[33]

Although Joshua Green argues that ABC's 'Start Here' rebranding campaign re-imagined 'the television network itself as a multiplatform object' (2007), this was far more limited than the use of the junctions by the UK broadcasters to construct journeys for its viewers across a range of platforms. Green describes the campaign, which launched in 2007, as follows:

> 'Start Here' presents ABC as the launching point for engaging with their content regardless of platform. Built around a graphics package featuring revolving icons representing a TV, computer, iPod, and cell phone, it features a prominent 'play button' on the flip-side of the ABC medallion and a reminder to viewers the network is the official source for accessing content. Expressly offering viewers the promise of content available 'anytime, anywhere,' the campaign attempts to establish the significance of the network in an era of textual and viewer mobility.
>
> (2007)

One promo from 2007 contained clips from the network's fall season line-up (such as *Ugly Betty*, *Desperate Housewives*, and *Lost* (2004–10)) displayed on revolving circular icons with images of an iPod, computer, television and cell phone intercut with captions proclaiming 'your favourite shows', 'wherever', 'whenever'. These icons finally merged into a small play button that spun around to reveal the ABC logo as the words 'start here' wiped out to the right. In my sample from 2010, the ABC logo with 'start here' was included after every programme trailer. Although some of these trailers included ABC's URL, they did not utilize the multiplatform element of the 'start here' campaign. However, this did emerge in the use of IPPs within the programmes themselves. Hence, during the drama series *Flash Forward* (2009–10), the ABC DOG was replaced by a small computer icon next to a banner stating 'Ask Flash Forward. Answers at ABC.com.' Other IPPs promoting television programmes on the network later that day or week similarly used the television icon from the campaign. Across the evening's viewing, therefore, an identity was constructed for ABC as the starting point for accessing content across a range of platforms. However, the journeys offered here were relatively limited compared to those offered within the UK junctions in 2010 and the focus was on promoting specific programmes, while channel branding was relegated to the ends of trailers and small DOGs and IPPs.

On the US networks, therefore, the changes wrought by digital have also altered the communicative ethos of broadcast television, but here the main impact has been to heighten the emphasis placed on persuasion by continuing to prioritize programme promotion and adopting new scheduling strategies designed to enhance share maintenance. Yet, ironically, while the promotion of programme viewing is so central to US television, the strategies adopted to promote programmes increasingly undermine the actual experience of watching television. This is particularly apparent in the use of in programme pointers, which have been adopted by all the networks after each advert break to promote forthcoming programmes. These often utilize intrusive sounds and graphics. For example, as one of the *Big Brother* (CBS, 2000–) contestants emotionally came out as gay during the first few minutes of *Big Brother* on CBS on 11 July 2010, an in programme pointer promoting the new Autumn series of *Hawaii Five-0* (CBS, 2010–) appeared. This intrusive IPP consisted of a graphic of a wave washing over the bottom of the screen and turning into a sea-coloured banner that rippled like water accompanied by the sounds of flowing water and the title graphic for the programme, with the day of broadcast and channel logo. A later in programme pointer during *The Mentalist* (CBS, 2008–) on the same channel promoting the new Autumn series *The Defenders* (CBS, 2010–) included images of the two central characters against a cityscape that intruded over the bottom third of the screen. While the US networks have not adopted on-air channel branding as extensively as the UK terrestrial channels, the experience of watching television remains a key means through which a broadcaster communicates its identity and values to the viewer. In their emphasis on keeping viewers watching and on programme promotion, the US networks create a viewing experience that is far from the 'special feeling' once promoted by ABC, but rather functions to undermine the key value of any television network – which is the experience of watching television.[34]

One reason for this may be the place of the programme within the economy of America's media conglomerates. Kunz (2009: 644) demonstrated that, over the four seasons from 2004–5 to 2007–8, the six major media conglomerates in the USA (National Amusements, NBC Universal, News Corp., Sony, Time Warner and Walt Disney Co.) 'had a financial interest in between 94.7% and 89.4% of programmes with attributed ownership, not counting movies, live sporting events, and encore presentations' in the debut prime-time schedules of the six mainstream networks (NBC, CBS, ABC, Fox, UPN/WB or CW).[35] As we shall explore in more depth in Chapter 6, these programmes function as potential sites of revenue for these media conglomerates well beyond the advertising sales of their initial broadcast. The television network is, then, just one site and one business through which revenue might be generated, while the programme can potentially generate revenue across a wide range of different sites and businesses. Within this economic model, not only is there particular value in promoting the programme over the network, but arguably there is also value in offering differentiated experiences of watching the programme. While the initial broadcast contains adverts, IPPs and other promotional texts that might disrupt the viewing experience, the network can promote the value of buying the DVD without adverts, or the on-demand version (such as on Hulu), where you can chose when to view the ads. As such, the network television broadcast is positioned as the site for a 'first-look' at programming that can then be experienced across a range of different revenue-generating platforms.

Conclusions

The reasons for the differences in the use of interstitial space on the UK terrestrial channels and the US networks are complex. It is perhaps surprising that, in the UK context, channel branding is seen as particularly useful for uniting the range of programming provided in the public service broadcaster's mixed programme schedule, whereas in the USA the far less pronounced variety of programming found on the networks is seen as undermining the usefulness of channel branding. One reason for this is the different place that the programme holds within the US and UK television industries. The UK terrestrial broadcasters base their schedules on the production of a wide range of different kinds of programmes. By contrast, the norm in the USA is for the networks to commission a relatively limited (in comparison with UK terrestrial television) slate of serialized programmes that forms the basis of its schedules for each year. Even though the 1990s saw an increase in serialization and the development of new strategies such as zoning and theming, there is far less seriality and far more variety on UK terrestrial television than on the US networks. As such, the programme plays a far more central role in US television, and network identities are far more dependent on the particular set of series being offered each season. Furthermore, the US networks generate revenue from the sale of advertising space within specific programmes and from the repurposing of programming itself, both of which place an emphasis on the programme over the channel as the central unit of broadcasting.

In the USA, the increasing emphasis placed by the large media conglomerates that own the networks on the bottom line has tended to lead to strategies whose effects can be measured.[36] The continued prioritization of programme promotion and the tendency to see channel branding in opposition to good programming also suggests that normative judgements have played a significant role in the strategies adopted by US broadcasters.[37] In the UK, the identities of the public service channels are intricately tied to the identities of each broadcaster and hence play a significant role in contributing to their broader public and corporate identities. For the public service broadcasters, therefore, their television channels are the embodiment of their public service values. With the emphasis that branding places on constructing and communicating values to the public and to key decision makers, it is perhaps unsurprising that Britain's public service broadcasters should brand their channels. Over and above this, however, all the UK's public service broadcasters have developed a slate of new channels and services that placed increased pressure on the need to have distinctive yet unified channel identities that could be cross-promoted to viewers.

However, we are in a period of transition, where the impact of digital on television viewing is still unknown, as the variation in strategies for extending UK channel brands onto new media platforms suggests. Indeed, in 2009 NBC adopted a channel branding strategy that is strikingly similar to the channel brand identities created by the UK terrestrial broadcasters. NBC's 'More colorful' rebrand was created by Capacity in 2009 as an explicit attempt to construct a consistent visual design for the network based on vertical bars of colour drawn from the network's famous 'peacock' logo. The most striking aspect of this rebrand is the way in which it is extended across all aspects of its junctions, as well as being used in off-air promotion and online services. For example, Capacity created 'colourbursts', vibrant flashes of the coloured bars and the NBC peacock logo, that open every promo, are built into the endtags and are used online to create 'an almost subconscious notification to the viewer that an NBC promo is starting or that important information is coming up' (Capacity 2010). When NBC launched this new strategy it was struggling in the ratings with a series of unsuccessful programmes that *Hollywood Reporter* claimed were creating a reputation for 'lousy programming' (Hibberd 2008) that was affecting its ability to attract talent to the network. As such, NBC's adoption of a more extensive rebranding campaign could be seen as an explicit strategy to rebuild the image of the network in the eyes of both viewers and the industry more broadly. Unfortunately, programming strategies adopted at the same time (such as moving its popular talk show *Jay Leno* to 10pm, a slot usually reserved for more costly scripted drama) were criticized as a blatant attempt to save money and undermined the network's attempt to revive its brand reputation, reinforcing the argument that any branding campaign has to correspond to the actual product produced (see for example, Hibberd 2008). It is notable that the ABC yellow rebrand and the NBC 'more colorful' rebrand were both introduced by networks struggling in the ratings, suggesting that such branding campaigns are not seen as standard industrial practice in the USA, but are adopted at times of crisis. I would therefore hesitate to see NBC's 'more colorful' campaign as an indication of a shift in attitudes towards channel branding in the USA.

Despite these differences, however, in both the USA and the UK, the place of the television channel has shifted, becoming just one platform of many through which television programmes can be viewed. With this shift, the communicative ethos of broadcasting has also changed, positioning the television channel as a multiplatform object that can steer the viewer in a larger journey of engaging with television content. Yet, as television programmes are increasingly extended across multiple media platforms, it becomes harder for the television channel to frame all the possible encounters with television programming. While this has led to a range of different strategies for the development and extension of channel brands (as we have seen), it also shifts the position of the programme within the television industry. As a consequence, programme branding has emerged as another means of managing the new, extended experiences of engaging with television. How branding is applied to the television programme itself, will be the subject of the next chapter.

Notes

1 It could be argued that the recent discourses around quality television could be tied to the diminishing centrality of broadcasting, in that an environment of distinction can now be created around television, where programmes can be easily plucked out of the flow as

'special' and repackaged in aesthetically pleasing box sets for re-viewing, thus escaping the seemingly endless ephemerality of broadcasting to attain an aura of quality (see Hills 2007).

2 BARB defines time-shifted viewing as the 'viewing of programmes recorded and subsequently played back within seven days, as well as viewing after pausing or rewinding live TV' (Ofcom 2010: 50). As viewing outside the seven-day window is not accounted for, the proportion of time-shifted viewing could be higher in reality.

3 This methodological decision allows for an analysis of the ways in which channels that emerged largely in the broadcast era have had to adapt to the new demands of the digital era. However, there is certainly a need for more research into the strategies used by new digital channels in each context. In particular, it would be valuable to assess the extent to which the communicative ethos of global channels (such as the Discovery channels or MTV) varies according to the localized context of reception.

4 This time of year was selected as the period when the broadcasters had established their autumn season of programmes and where there were no significant public holidays or festivals. The days selected were Tuesday 1 November 1988, Monday 1 November 1993, Sunday 1 November 1998, Tuesday 14 October 2003. In addition, I examined the launch night for Channel 4 on Tuesday 2 November 1982. The precise dates were determined by the availability of material in the archive, which means that it did include one Sunday (1 November 1998), which has a slightly different scheduling pattern to a weekday and which also coincided with the launch of Channel 4's new digital channel, FilmFour, which was broadcast on Channel 4 from 7pm, thus limiting the usefulness of this particular evening.

5 The evenings selected were 31 October 1982, 1 November 1988, 1 November 1993, 31 October 1998, 14 October 2003 for NBC and CBS; 1 November 1982, 1 November 1988, 2 November 1993, 3 November 1998, 14 October 2003 for ABC; and 1 November 1988, 1 November 1993, 1 November 1998, 14 October 2003 for Fox. Priority was given to evenings where the archive had recorded more than one programme onto a single tape.

6 The evenings analysed were ABC on 18 October 1996 (9–10pm); NBC on 3 December 1994 (8.30–10pm) and 22 May 1997 (8–9pm); CBS on 13 February 1995 (8.30–9.30pm); and Fox on 10 October 1996 (8.30–9.30pm).

7 While YouTube contains a large number of junctions and idents, I have not relied on these as a primary source, as it can be hard to verify the provenance of the clips. TVArk is a more reliable source for UK idents, but only includes a few examples of the idents being used within the interstitials. In order to gather contemporary off-air recordings from the USA I had to rely on the goodwill of friends and family, and would like to thank Madeleine Noland, Max Dawson, Avi Santo and Jonathan Gray.

8 The continuity announcer would occasionally mention what was on the sister channel. In the 1980s BBC One and BBC Two, and Channel 4 and ITV would cross-promote each other's programmes.

9 The entertainment possibilities of the Channel 4 ident were memorably exploited in a television advert for Hamlet cigars in the mid-1980s. Hamlet had been running a campaign in which a series of mishaps were represented, culminating in the protagonist taking solace in smoking a Hamlet cigar. In the Channel 4 Hamlet ad, the coloured blocks of the Channel 4 ident flew into the screen but formed a '5'. After trying for a second time and once again failing to form the iconic '4' logo, the blocks formed into a face as a cigar flew in for it to smoke and the Hamlet music faded up.

10 There are earlier examples of this from Thames, such as a version of the Thames fanfare that was recorded by the orchestra used for *Des O'Connor Tonight* (BBC, 1977–82, Thames, 1983–2002) to allow the ident to link seamlessly into the programme's opening credits.

11 Channel 4 did innovate in using a wider range of regional accents in its continuity announcements, but they remained largely formal in tone and style in the 1980s.

12 Examples of these idents can be found at TVArk's website, <http://www.tv-ark.org.uk> (accessed 23 December 2010).

13 Over the 1990s there was considerable experimentation with the style and tone of idents, with all three channels trying out using stars and/or ordinary people in their idents, as well as with different graphic devices. It is beyond the scope of this chapter to explore this in detail, but Christine Fanthome's (2007) outline of the development of the Channel 4 ident gives some indication of the different kinds of strategies adopted.

14 See Chapters 3 and 4 for a detailed discussion of why public service broadcasters turned to channel branding over the 1990s.

15 Light claims that, in her interviews with BBC personnel over the late 1990s, MTV was held up as the example of effective channel branding in television (2004: 144).

16 In 2005 Ofcom published two reports about the promotional activities across 14 UK television channels (terrestrial and digital) (Communications Research Group 2005) and viewers' attitudes towards promotion (The Knowledge Agency Ltd. 2005). The report into promotional activities claimed that 5 per cent of promotions on ITV were cross-promotion, rising to 11 per cent for Channel 4, 30 per cent for BBC One and 39 per cent for BBC Two. The greater percentage of cross-promotions on the BBC's terrestrial channels can be accounted for by the higher number of services (radio, television and new media) that the BBC has to promote (Communications Research Group 2005: 13).

17 There is far more variation in the order and use of these different strategies by all three channels in 2010 than in the 1980s, as well as in the use of menus at different moments indicating what is on now and next.

18 The terminology used here comes from an interview by the author with Charlie Mawer, Executive Creative Director, Red Bee Media. DOGs tend not to be used on BBC One, ITV1 and Channel 4 apart from in trailers, but are a common feature throughout all the programming on digital television in the UK.

19 In his analysis of the changes to the credits on British television, Steve Bryant (2009) identified examples from as early as 1991 on Channel 4 of continuity announcements emerging over the end credits of programmes. However, such strategies became more commonly used across all terrestrial channels from 1993.

20 *Emmerdale* changed its name from *Emmerdale Farm* in 1989. *Emmerdale Farm* had been broadcast since 1972.

21 This ties in with the rise of media planning, which Julie Light argues emerged in the BBC in the late 1990s and in which 'BBC channel junctions were planned according to marketing principles' (2004: 153).

22 Each 4oD ident is accompanied by a continuity announcer who tells you that you are watching 4oD through a particular service, such as 'on YouTube' or 'on Virgin Media'.

23 The UK terrestrial broadcasters also offer mobile services. Again, the centrality of the channel here varies, with the BBC offering mobile versions of its website, including its channel pages, and ITV and Channel 4 offering specific mobile sites that are largely based on programme-specific or themed content. Meanwhile, the use of Facebook and Twitter by the UK terrestrial broadcasters tends to be based around specific programmes and will be discussed in more detail in Chapter 6.

24 It is worth noting that network television junctions also include very short (5–10 second) trailers for that evening's local news programmes that often just consist of a newscaster outlining one or two headlines, sometimes intercut with images from each story. It is rare for these to explicitly mention channel name or number, with the programme title only appearing in on-screen graphics and logos. This points to the consistency of the scheduling on US network television, where it can be assumed that audiences know when the local news programme will be broadcast.

25 In each case the networks had initially experimented with different logos (and NBC continued to experiment until the late 1970s) before settling on the ones that are still in use today.

26 In 1993 ABC was the first network to display its logo as a DOG for the first five seconds after the commercial break in its entertainment shows, and in all promos, network newscasts and news programmes (Eastman *et al.* 1995).

27 The networks also produced shorter versions of these promotional films using the same music and taglines, combined with an animated network logo.

28 Surprisingly Davis and Walker's quantitative analysis of share maintenance (the maintenance of audience share from one broadcast programme to another) suggested that, while share maintenance decreased between 1983 and 1985, this trend reversed between 1986 and 1988. This suggests that the increase in competition from cable channels and the growing adoption of VCR and remote control technology did not completely disrupt traditional viewing habits.

29 In my sample from 2010, NBC and ABC used hot switching and NBC, ABC and CBS used cold starts and continuity announcements over end credits.

30 In addition to the strategies adopted since the late 1980s to accelerate the flow, it is also more common for US network television to run trailers of five or ten seconds' length, and these trailers also tend to be more rapidly edited.

31 The ABC yellow campaign included a short on-air promo that actually drew attention to this fact, including a spot that exclaimed, 'This spot is costing us money, but if money were all we were interested in, we wouldn't be in the entertainment business, now, would we?' (cited in Lippert 1997: 20).

32 Although ITV and Channel 4 are funded by advertising, the amount of advertising that they can carry is regulated by Ofcom and so there are not the same kinds of financial pressures on the use of the interstitials for promotion and branding as in the UK (see Grant *et al.* 2010).

33 Of course such cross-promotion occurs not just in advertising, but also within the content of programmes, newspaper and magazine articles, radio shows and so on. As we shall see in the next chapter, conglomerates are increasingly seeking to extend the value of their media properties, blurring the line between promotion and text.

34 In both the USA and the UK, the use of in programme pointers, end credit squeezes and DOGs are the subject of complaints by viewers. See for example the complaints about IPPs (referred to as 'violators') on <http://www.televisionwithoutpity.com> by US viewers (such as ScribblerGuy 2009 and jw7579 2009), and the letters of complaint in the *Radio Times* in the UK about end credit squeezes in the 18 September and 2 October 2010 editions.

35 In 2006 WB and UPN merged into a new network, The CW.

36 As Julie Light (2004) points out, however, there are some problems with the ways in which the networks measure the success of their share maintenance strategies, as it is impossible to know whether it was this factor that led to a programme's success or failure.

37 In her study of the scheduling changes adopted by Nordic broadcasters over the 1990s Espen Ytreberg points to the central role that normatively based judgements played in the decision-making processes (2002: 295).

6

LONGEVITY, TRANSFERABILITY AND MULTIPLICITY

Programme brands

> [T]he potential for any particular content package to be leveraged across multiple media platforms has ceased to be merely a desirable product asset. Rather, it has emerged as the indispensable characteristic of blockbuster media content.
>
> (Murray 2005: 416)

> [M]uch of the logic of the media industries is oriented to the search for (or invention of) content brands like *The Spice Girls* or *Britney Spears* that can easily be extended across different media platforms and used for product tie-ins and cross-promotions. The purpose of such strategies is to create a network of intertextual links that suggests a coherent modality of use or enjoyment for the product.
>
> (Arvidsson 2006: 77)

The extension of content across the widest range of platforms and products has become an increasingly important part of the contemporary US and UK television industries. New media platforms, such as the internet and mobile devices, have provided new opportunities for exploiting television programming. These media offer the possibility of increasing revenue through economies of scope by 'exploiting the same content or intellectual property across more than one form of output' (Doyle 2002: 63). As broadcasters in the USA and UK have seen their revenues dwindle (whether in the decline in audience share and profits from advertising or cuts in the licence fee), creating additional revenue from programme content has become a central part of the economics of television production. As Derek Kompare argues, 'Rather than only function as draws for advertisers, television programs are now seen as multi-faceted properties that can spark several complimentary revenue streams' (2005: 213).

However, the extension of programmes not only amplifies the revenue streams for television content, it also offers the possibility of creating new relationships with viewers in an attempt to capture and retain splintering audiences. Sharon Marie Ross refers to this as an attempt by broadcasters to generate 'tele-participation': 'By the late 1990s, networks – both broadcast and cable – sought to retain viewers by creating a more intense relationship between the audience and a show, increasingly through multiplatforming that gave television programs life in the world of film, print, the Internet, etc' (2008: 5). The attempt to generate new relationships with viewers through the extension of programme content is also apparent in the context of public service broadcasting in the UK. For example, the BBC has placed more emphasis on extending the 'long tail' of its content beyond the initial transmission slot (for example, by creating a webpage for every programme broadcast on the BBC website, <http://www.bbc.co.uk>) and allowing increased audience interaction with programming through enabling content on the iPlayer to be shared and embedded by viewers. It is within this context that the television programme itself has become a focus for industry branding strategies. Yet, what do we mean by programme branding and what are the consequences of developing television programmes as brands?

What is at stake in programme branding?

In her analysis of the development of marketing over the second half of the 1970s and the 1980s, Celia Lury notes the shift from branding stand-alone products to branding product ranges, so that 'the brand emerges as *the organisation of a set of relations between products or services*' (Lury 2004: 26, italics in original). Branding began to be increasingly used as a medium for new product development, with Lury giving the examples of the extension of the Mars chocolate bar brand into ice cream and the Persil detergent brand into washing-up liquid (2004: 27). The nature of the television programme as an object makes the role of programme branding slightly different. In standard economic accounts of broadcasting the primary output of television is regarded as the *programme service*, which has the attributes of a 'public-good' in that:

> the way it is consumed by an individual viewer does not reduce its supply for everyone else. The essential quality from which the consumer value of a television broadcast derives is not physical. Instead, it is in the meanings or messages conveyed. These are immaterial and do not get used up in the act of consumption.
>
> (Doyle 2002: 61).[1]

This understanding of the economics of television does not tell the whole story. After all, since the early days of television, the programmes that made up a television service often existed in a physical form (on film, videotape, or in digital storage). With the development of video recording (especially home video in the late 1970s and 1980s) and in particular the emergence of DVDs in the 1990s, the television programme as a material object became increasingly important to the television industry, and archives of programming became more valuable. Furthermore, the contemporary practice of extending television programmes across multiple media means that the television service is no longer the primary output of television. Indeed, with conglomeration the television programme can function as just one aspect of a broader product range designed to increase profits across a number of differentiated media companies. Therefore, within the television industry, as within the consumer products industries cited by Lury, branding emerges as a way of organizing the relationship between the different products or texts that now make up a 'television programme'.

However, the extension of television programmes onto other media is not that new. Johnson (2009) and Santo (2010) have demonstrated that, as early as the 1940s and 1950s, radio and television programmes in the UK and USA were being extended onto a range of different products, from toys and games, to cartoon strips and novels. So, what is so different about the extension of television programmes in the digital era? One feature of the contemporary media industry's extension of programming onto other media that has been singled out as a new development is the emergence of transmedia storytelling. Initially developed by Henry Jenkins in relation to *The Matrix* (1999, 2003) franchise, transmedia storytelling is the production of a story 'across multiple media platforms, with each new text making a distinctive and valuable contribution to the whole' (2006: 95–96). For Jenkins, what differentiates transmedia storytelling from earlier forms of merchandising and licensing is that there is an attempt to create a larger, single and coherently organized fiction that is delivered across multiple platforms. Jenkins argues that, while 'the current licensing system typically generates works that are redundant' (2006: 105) in that they fail to offer character or plot development, transmedia storytelling fulfils a desire in audiences for extended storyworlds in which all of the component texts 'offer new insights and new experiences' (ibid.).[2]

Elizabeth Evans (2011) has developed Jenkins's model by arguing that transmedia storytelling can be distinguished from other kinds of programme extensions in three ways: narrative, authorship and temporality. For Evans, therefore, transmedia texts are characterized by a narrative universe that is shared across different media platforms in a temporally coherent manner and identified with a single author (whether a broadcaster, production company, or individual). She gives the example of *Dr Who* to clarify the difference between transmedia storytelling and earlier forms of licensing and merchandising. While the original *Dr Who* (BBC, 1963–89) series generated a range of spin-off texts, such as films, novelizations and toys, these were produced under licence. There were often contradictions in the narrative universe of the television episodes and the spin-off texts, such as the first *Dr Who* spin-off film, *Dr Who and the Daleks* (1965), depicting the Doctor as a human inventor, rather than an alien. By contrast, the new *Dr Who* (BBC, 2005–) series was produced by the BBC as a number of transmedia texts, including short prequels (Tardisodes) that could be viewed online or on a portable media device, a website that included behind-the-scenes footage, extra information and opportunities to participate, and an online game. These different texts expanded the same coherent narrative universe, were presented as being authored by the BBC and were temporally coherent, with viewers encouraged to download the Tardisodes, then watch the episode, and then access the website and play the games before the next instalment. Furthermore, Evans argues that transmedia storytelling is not the only new development in the extension of television programmes. She also points to the emergence of 'transmedia distribution': the distribution of the same text (for example a television programme) onto a range of different media platforms (broadcast television, the internet, mobile television) by both viewers and users.

However, while these studies usefully delineate the new practices opened up in the digital era, these have not supplanted earlier models for extending television (and film) onto other media. The new *Dr Who* series has been licensed to produce trading card games (*Battles in Time*), comics for the US market (through a partnership between BBC Worldwide and IDW Publishing) and a wide range of merchandise (from T-shirts and pyjamas, to action figures, games and lunch boxes). All these different extensions of the *Dr Who* programme sit alongside the various texts which would fit within the parameters of transmedia storytelling and distribution. Indeed Jonathan Gray argues that Television Studies needs to attend not just to the new transmedia texts of television, but to all of the 'paratexts' that 'establish frames and filters through which we look at, listen to, and interpret' (2010: 3) television programmes. As well as licensed merchandise, Gray would include here the wide range of promotional texts that surround programmes, from billboards and trailers, to more complex marketing campaigns that use Facebook or alternative reality gaming. As Gray argues, these paratexts 'are not simply add-ons, spinoffs, and also-rans: they create texts, they manage them, and they fill them with many of the meanings that we associate with them' (2010: 6). If we think about the television programme as part of a network of paratexts, then we can better account for the ways in which the meanings associated with and around those programmes are generated.

While television programmes have always been paratextual, the digital era has made television's paratextuality more visible. This, combined with the industry's increased dependence on the extension of television programmes to generate revenue and engage audiences, is what has led to the shift towards developing programmes as brands. Adam Arvidsson argues that branding is 'essentially about putting public communication to work in ways that either *add to* or *reproduce* the particular qualities that the brand embodies' (2006: 67). He goes on to argue that 'The easiest way to do this is to quite simply appropriate the *common* that people spontaneously produce in their use of branded consumer goods' (2006: 68). Central to Arvidsson's argument here is that, at some level, all human communication is mediatized, making use of (at the very least) language, gestures and so on that shape the meanings that are communicated. Arvidsson goes on to argue that media culture connects 'diverse communication processes to each other and thus making them unfold within a common ambience' (2006: 37). Brand management attempts to harness this 'common' by:

> proposing branded goods as tools, or building blocks whereby consumers can create their own meanings. What people pay for, the idea goes, is not so much the brand itself as what they can produce with it: what they can *become* with it. ... Customers are thus expected to add more or less personal dimensions to the brand, to accommodate it in their life-world, to produce something – a feeling, a personal relation, an experience – with it.
>
> (Arvidsson 2006: 68)

The value of television for its viewers has always been the experiences and feelings created through the act of watching. Developing television programmes as brands is concerned with extending and multiplying these experiences.

John Thornton Caldwell describes how in the USA, from pre-production right through to distribution and exhibition, programmes are developed as 'diversified entertainment properties' (2008: 232–33) with scripts analysed for their opportunities for exploitation across multiple markets. However, such programme extensions are not simply determined by market logic. Take *Britain From Above* (BBC, 2008), a BBC documentary produced by Lion Television and developed explicitly as a transmedia programme. The series used global positioning satellite tracking and ground-breaking computer imaging to provide audio-visual representations of various migrations across Britain, from the GPS (global positioning system) traces of air traffic, to the shipping paths through the straights of Dover, and the talk that travels through the national telephone exchange. The different stories of *Britain From Above* were packaged into 60-minute and 30-minute documentaries shown over three weeks from 10 August 2008 on BBC One, BBC Two and BBC Four that were also available for one week after transmission on the BBC iPlayer and released on DVD in September 2008. However, they were also unbundled into five-minute stories made available through a BBC website, <http://www.bbc.co.uk/britainfromabove> (accessed 23 December 2010), alongside additional short films not included in the televised documentaries. The website offered multiple routes into the content, allowing viewers to select stories by theme (such as technology or space), or by location, using an interactive map. Not only did the website allow viewers to select those stories most personal to them, they could also embed these short films into their own websites or blogs, 'to accommodate it in their life-world' (Arvidsson 2006: 68). The website also provided behind-the-scenes footage, articles about those involved in the production, facts and figures related to the stories and slideshows highlighting the work of Jason Hawkes, the aerial photographer for the series. These all provided different ways of extending engagement with the series, offering viewers a wider range of different kinds of experiences related to the programme brand, which were complimented by a book accompanying the series, published by Pavilion, with a foreword by the presenter of the series, Andrew Marr. The book explicitly positions itself as offering new pleasures:

> The book has some distinct advantages over the series – readers have the leisure to pore over images in detail, to play spot-the-difference with the 'then and now' images in the *Rewinds* chapter, and to marvel at the array of fascinating statistics unearthed by *Britain From Above*.
>
> (Harrison 2008: 13)

These different elements of *Britain From Above* accord with Jenkins's and Evans's models of transmedia storytelling, with each element of the programme functioning to offer new experiences that contributed to the overall aim of offering new perspectives on Britain through spectacular images produced by cutting-edge technology.

However, the transmedia expansion of the series does not stop here. The production company that produced the series has a page dedicated to the programme, which largely reinforces the BBC's rhetoric about the series as a landmark piece of cross-platform commissioning, but positions it alongside other Lion Television productions (Lion Television 2010). The corporate websites for both Cityscape (2010), the company responsible for some of the aerial shots in the series, and 422 South (2009), the company that produced the CGI sequences, carry extracts and behind-the-scenes footage from the programme courtesy of the BBC in order to showcase their work. While these sites emphasize the innovative technology that went into the production of the series, the Bring IT On (2010) website, which promotes careers in IT for 14–19-year-olds, uses the series to emphasize the impact that technology has on our everyday lives. By contrast, when the series was transmitted on the UKTV digital channel Blighty, the programme was framed within the channel's broader brand identity as the home of all things British. While the BBC's website describes the series as an 'epic journey revealing the secrets, patterns and hidden rhythms of our lives from a striking new perspective' (BBC 2010), Blighty's website promoted the show with an image of Andrew Marr doing a tandem skydive with a caption that firmly situated the series as entertainment:

> Is it a bird? Is it a plane? Erm, no it's neither. It's Blighty from a birdseye view, and there's not a man with pants over his tights flying through the sky in sight … Ahem, actually there is … Anyway, what we're trying to say is enjoy a spectacular view of Britain like you've never seen it before. Tally ho, chocks away!
>
> (Blighty 2010)

Furthermore, while the initial transmedia extensions of *Britain From Above* were temporally coherent, with the programme and the website launched together to offer an extended range of experiences for the viewer, the non-broadcast content has a long tail, remaining accessible two years after the initial broadcast.

While these different sites reframe *Britain From Above*, potentially shaping the meanings associated with the series, they do not undermine or contradict the overall aim of the programme brand to use cutting-edge technology to offer new perspectives on Britain as a nation. Furthermore, they could be said to contribute to the BBC's broader public service remit. As James Bennett argues of the BBC in the digital era:

> its position as a portal should be used not just to direct user/viewser-flows to its own proprietary content or that of content affiliates, but be more open than this – lending its trusted brand to connect users to independent and other media in a way that will help structure the choices made by 'DIY citizens' beyond fulfilling mere consumerism: to interface the nation with one another.
>
> (2008a: 290)

It is important, here, to avoid falling into simplistic dualisms that might position the commercial exploitations of programme brands as inherently consumerist. After all, although the sale of *Britain From Above* by the BBC to Blighty was part of a financial exchange to generate revenue for the BBC, Blighty's framing of the series within rhetoric of entertainment may have drawn viewers to the series who were put off by the more serious tone of the BBC's own promotion. The BBC also provided a playlist of short stories from the series on YouTube as part of a larger deal that allows the BBC to share in the advertising revenue generated by traffic to its programmes on the site. While, again, these are part of a commercial deal, YouTube offers the additional feature of enabling viewers to comment on and discuss the films. While this generated some complaints about errors in the commentary, other comments praised the innovation of the series and offered support for the BBC and the licence fee.[3]

However, the difficulty of sustaining the open position proposed by Bennett is that it creates the possibility that the programme and/or corporate brand might be damaged through the viewer's productive engagement with it. As Arvidsson argues:

> an important task for brand management is to ensure that the ongoing production of a common social world on the part of consumers proceeds in ways that reproduce a distinctive *brand image*, and that strengthens the *brand equity* – the productive potential that the brand has in the minds of consumers – which is understood as the most important factor behind brand value.
>
> (2006: 74)

This task is made more pressing in the digital era because the internet makes the common social world produced by consumers around media brands far more visible. Hence, the comments on YouTube make visible debates about the value of BBC programmes that would previously have been largely conducted in private.[4] While *Britain From Above* provides an example in which the extensions of the series worked to reinforce the central values of the programme and the corporate brand, this is not always the case.

Sharon Marie Ross (2008: 94) gives the example of an unsuccessful programme brand extension offered by sponsors of *American Idol 2* (Fox, 2003–4), citing research undertaken by Initiative into the show's fans (Koerner 2005). This research revealed that the most engaging attributes of the show for fans were not the ability to vote, but rather the core personalities on the show – the judges and contestants.[5] AT&T's sponsor spot focused on the voting elements of the series, depicting a ditzy blonde girl harassing the participants in the show while appealing to viewers to vote using AT&T's SMS text-messaging service. Koerner (2005: 12) claims that the campaign actually undermined the value of the AT&T brand by insulting fans who read the spots as an affront to their fandom. While, in this example, it was largely the sponsor's brand image that was damaged, Caldwell (2008: 62) provides an example of a programme brand extension that damaged the brand identity of the series itself: NBC's production of a fake fan blog-site to promote buzz in advance of the premiere of its new quality drama series *Studio 60 on the Sunset Strip* (2006–7). The Defaker.com site purported to be reporting gossip from the show's fictional universe, but the poor quality of the blogs, which paraphrased press releases and tried to pass off production stills as surveillance photos, was quickly identified as false. The Gawker website, which provides gossip from within the media industries in the USA, reproduced an exchange from Defaker.com that illustrates the ways in which the site undermined the expectations of the fans:

> I know Albie and Tripp were huge deals at Studio 60 back before they went big-time Hollywood movie mogul, but that's ancient history. Can they still bring the funny? And will Harriet still be on her A-game now that her ex is her boss? I'll be tuning in Friday nights to find out.
> Posted by: Swann | September 20, 2006 03:14 AM
>
> This is lame, you can't even get stills from the set? You had to use screengrabs? Get it right guys and put some effort into your viral-marketing bull.
> Posted by: oliver | September 20, 2006 04:42 AM
>
> (cited in Mark 2006)

This exchange demonstrates the ways in which extensions can undermine the value of a programme brand not just by contradicting or undermining the integrity of the storyworld (as in the example of the *Dr Who* film above), but also by undermining the broader values associated with the brand: in this case, the expectation that the same level of care and attention would have gone into the production of the promotional blog as into the production of the series itself.

These examples reveal a further characteristic of the contemporary television industry, which is that production and distribution have become far more dynamic and open-ended. Victoria Jaye (BBC Head of Fiction and Entertainment Multiplatform Commissioning) argues that the benefit of multiplatform for the BBC is in offering new ways for audiences to access, discover, consume and engage with broadcast content (interview with author, 1 June 2010). As we saw with the example of *Britain From Above*, multiplatform allows the broadcaster to place its content where the viewer is in order to extend points of access. Similar strategies have been adopted by the US networks. For example, for the 2005–6 season of *Lost*, the programme could be viewed as broadcast on ABC or on ABC-HD, time-shifted through a PVR, downloaded from iTunes for US$1.99 per episode the day after first transmission, or watched for free with embedded ads on ABC's website. Meanwhile, earlier seasons could be bought on DVD for the cost of around US$2 per episode and *Lost* recap episodes were broadcast to bring new viewers up to speed. You could also view free video promos for the series on ABC's website, watch streamed clips and mobisodes on your mobile phone, download *Lost* podcasts where the producers and cast discussed the series and read text recaps of the series online (Slocum 2006: 30). Within this new mode of production, as Marshall argues, 'Instead of an end product, there is a serial form of production where each product in the series is linked through a network of cross-promotion' (2002: 70). Rather than a single product, therefore, there is a network of on-going production.

A good example of this is *E20* (BBC, 2010–), a multiplatform spin-off from the BBC's long-running soap opera *EastEnders*. The series was conceived by the programme's executive producer Diederick Santer as a way of nurturing new talent on- and off-screen (Rushton 2009). *E20* introduced new young characters into the storyworld of *EastEnders*, but developed storylines for them that were largely separate, with only small amounts of cross-over between each series.[6] *E20* allowed the producers of *EastEnders* to explore the narrative world of the series from the perspective of young outsiders and aimed in part to appeal specifically to the younger demographic that watched *EastEnders* (broadcast four times a week on BBC One) but little else on the BBC's terrestrial channels. The production began with a competition for young Londoners to take part in a summer school to write the series. It was followed with a second competition, launched on Radio 1 on 13 November 2009, for remixes of the *EastEnders* theme tune to be used as the *E20* theme tune. On 23 December 2009 the BBC set up a Facebook site for *E20*, posting links to photos of the new cast. Before the first episode aired online on the BBC's *E20* website on 8 January 2010, the BBC posted trailers about the series on Facebook and encouraged discussion and debate about the characters by, for example, asking viewers to vote for their favourite.[7] This interaction continued over the first season, with the BBC posting information about new additions to the website (such as behind-the-scenes footage, previews, extra scenes and new episodes) as well as interacting with the fans posting on the site. This included responding to complaints about the length of episodes, thanking those who praised the show and posing questions designed to stimulate the kinds of discussion already taking place on the site, such as asking which character is the sexiest or which characters should get together. On 8 April 2010 the BBC posted to the Facebook site that a second season had been commissioned and over the next few months regularly posted updates and links to trailers and behind-the-scenes footage for the new season. This included (from 28 July 2010) links to new Twitter sites for characters from both seasons of the show. These tweets were in character, allowing the viewers to get to know the new characters for season 2 before the first episode aired. The production of *E20*, therefore, extended beyond the commissioning, writing, filming and editing of a drama series. The production process not only included a far wider range of texts, but it also spilt out from the creation of the drama itself to include character tweets, extra scenes, behind-the-scenes footage and online interaction. And this interaction was not confined to the period when the show initially aired. By making the episodes of *E20* permanently available online, and by extending the experience of the programme beyond the watching of the episodes, *E20* perfectly illustrates a non-linear and open-ended form of production.

Celia Lury argues that brands provide 'a means by which products enter into a processual relationship both with individuals and with entities, activities or fields that exceed the individual, providing the basis for a sustained, ongoing relationship between "production" and "consumption"' (2004: 46–47). As a programme brand, *E20* framed a set of complex and open relationships between viewers and a wide range of different kinds of texts, providing a mechanism or framework that presented the programme's episodes as an open-ended site for both production and consumption. While fan scholars have demonstrated that these kinds of relationships between texts and audiences have a long history, *E20* provides just one example of the ways in which they are being integrated into the production and distribution practices of the television industry. Through its use of Facebook and Twitter, the BBC situated *E20* as 'very much a part of that world which the young generation occupies' (Victoria Jaye, interview with the author, 1 June 2010), placing the programme brand into a site that forms part of the everyday social interactions of the individuals who follow the series online.[8]

Increasingly, producers and executives are using the visibility of viewers' engagement with television programmes online to generate audience feedback that can be used to shape the development of the programme brand. As Ross argues in relation to *American Idol*:

> by providing viewers with the opportunity to discuss how and why they tele-participate through online forums, producers have their own opportunity to monitor those discussions. As well (and as their website specifies), producers can use elements of those discussions for promotional purposes. At a more thematic level, by emphasizing the active participation of the viewer ('*You* vote, *you* decide ... *You* discuss'), the show positions itself and its network as 'benevolent' (for lack of a better term) – graciously inviting the viewer to be producerly.
>
> (2008: 89)

However, just as certain brand extensions can undermine the value of the programme brand, the opportunities for interaction between producer and viewer also have the potential to undermine the brand. For example, Sharon Ross describes how the Fox network used summaries of the message boards for *The O.C.* (Fox, 2003–7) during the teen drama's second series to inform changes to the style and content of the show, without taking into account the complex dynamics of these online communities, which are often far from representative of the programme's overall audience (2008: 147–48). Indeed, a panel of television scriptwriters at the Society for Cinema and Media Studies conference at Los Angeles in 2010 claimed that, while they read message boards, they did not let the negative comments influence their creative work and even claimed that fan criticism was positive in that it indicated that the viewer was emotionally engaged with the show.[9] Yet, Ross's audience research indicated that one of the key pleasures for fans in participating online was 'the opportunity to be heard by individuals and groups within the television industry' (2008: 74). Indeed, if branding depends on harnessing the 'common' that viewers produce in their engagement with television programmes, then the online discussions that take place around programmes contribute to the programme's brand values. At the same time, changing a show in response to online discussions could actually undermine the core attributes of that programme brand.

A good illustration of this dynamic comes from the BBC's magazine show *Top Gear*, proclaimed by BBC Worldwide as their first 'Global Brand' (Bonner 2010: 33). *Top Gear* is an example of what Brett Mills (2010) has recently termed 'invisible television', long-running and high-rating television programmes that are overlooked within Television Studies. The series began on the BBC in 1978 as a half-hour magazine show of three to four individual films with an emphasis on information about new car launches and car safety (Bonner 2010 and Wood 2005). After a ratings slump in the early 2000s the programme was reformatted by Andy Wilman who brought back popular presenter (and friend) Jeremy Clarkson and transformed the programme into what Wood describes as a 'testosterone-fuelled rollercoaster entertainment show loaded with interviews, stunts and characters' (2005: 20). Clarkson was subsequently joined by James May and Richard Hammond. Bonner (2010) argues that this gave the show different registers of masculinity and enhanced its comic potential by allowing May and Hammond to off-set and ridicule Clarkson's more aggressively dominant personality. The programme also settled into a narrative structure that combined car-related news with stunts and regular features, such as the Stig (an unnamed racing driver who tests the latest high-end cars), Star in a Reasonably Priced Car (where celebrities get the opportunity to race a car around a track) and the Cool Wall (where Clarkson and Hammond debate the coolness of new car releases).

In 2005 *Top Gear* won an Emmy for best non-scripted entertainment show at the international awards in New York (Matthews 2005: 3). According to the BBC, in the UK 40 per cent of the audience for the series is female (Wilde 2009: 23). When broadcast on the BBC in the UK, *Top Gear* regularly gets audiences of 5–6 million and a 20 per cent share of the viewing population and in 2008–9 it was BBC Worldwide's top-selling programme (Anon. 2010). The series has been sold to over 100 countries (Rushton 2008: 3), tops the iTunes chart in every territory in which it has been released (including Germany, France, the USA and Canada) and local versions have been produced in Australia, Russia and the USA (Anon. 2010).[10] The series has been extensively extended onto other media, including a YouTube site, three BBC Worldwide sites (one for the UK, one for the USA and one for Australia), as well as a bbc.co.uk programme site, a live show and an extensive range of merchandise. In addition, the series has a strong fan following, including two very active fan sites with message boards: FinalGear.com (which also includes the other UK terrestrial motoring show, *Fifth Gear*) and TopGearShow.com.

On 20 December 2009, the Executive Producer for the series, Andy Wilman, posted one of his regular blogs on the BBC Worldwide UK *Top Gear* site (<http://www.topgear.com>) responding to criticisms on fan forums that the series had lost its direction. In particular, Wilman was responding to a long post on the Final Gear website from Monk, who felt that the show had lost sight of its core audience, writing:

> The true purpose of *Top Gear* isn't to make a programme that will appeal to viewers of competitive Sunday-night programmes; it is to make a programme designed to appeal to a certain demographic of the populace that loves cars. *Top Gear* is crippled by the fact that it masquerades as a car programme but tries to appeal to an audience of people who do not care about cars.
>
> (Monk, citied in Wilman 2009)

Wilman's response was not to accede to these complaints, but to use them as a springboard to justify why the programme has the format it has and where he felt it had been strong and weak in the past:

> although we understand the complaints, it doesn't necessarily mean we're going to do anything about them. Believe me that's not arrogance on our part, but the fact is we're not wedding DJs taking requests, and for good reason, because no good telly in the history of man was ever created that way. … However when we do agree with where the viewers are coming from, then we could be in business. Personally, for example, I do believe we've now got the presenters playing to their TV cartoon characters a bit too much – Jezza the walking nuclear bomb, Richard the daft Norman Wisdom, and James the bumbling professor. I like those characters, but I too would like to see more of them as they were in Bonneville, or in Botswana or in the US Special.
>
> (Wilman 2009)

Wilman's blog reinforces the core aspects of the programme's brand, while simultaneously demonstrating to the online fans that he is listening to and engaging with their opinions. It thus functions as one facet of brand management, engaging with and encouraging participation from the fans, while simultaneously strengthening the core values of the programme brand.

This example further demonstrates that, once we start to think about programmes as brands, then the broadcast programme itself becomes decentred as the primary site through which the meanings of the programme are conveyed and located. Rather, there is a conflation between the programme and its paratexts. Max Dawson argues that the US network's production of short-form content for the web and mobile phone has produced a form of 'promotainment' that blurs the boundaries between entertainment and promotion:

> Are the *Family Guy* clips Fox posts on Hulu short-form content, or a kind of branded entertainment? Are the *Lost* recaps on ABC.com there to refresh regular viewers' memories between seasons, or as free samples meant to entice new viewers? Are the Susan Boyle YouTube clips a grass-roots viral sensation, or promos meant to prime the American audience for *America's Got Talent*?
>
> (Dawson 2009)

While (as we saw in Chapter 5) the programme trailers broadcast on the US networks are explicitly positioned as advertisements, Dawson argues that this kind of short-form content found on the web frequently attempts to obscure its promotional function, whether in the form of the viral marketing discussed above around *Studio 60* or in the webisodes produced for *Dr Who* that appear as short-form prequels to the episodes themselves.

Turning to the writer's strike in 2007–8, Dawson demonstrates how the policing of the boundaries between what is a programme and what is promotion has significant impact for labour relations in the US media industries. When NBC produced a short-form web spin-off of *The Office* in 2006 (*The Accountants*), they positioned the series for the public as original online content, while internally categorizing it as promotion, so that its writers were ineligible for compensation or residuals. The strike resulted in the Writers Guild of America (WGA) and the Alliance of Motion Picture and Televison Producers (AMPTP) establishing a new agreement to cover writing for new media (see Dawson 2009). Dawson warns that recent academic work on transmedia television is in danger of a similar slippage between content and promotion that identifies 'every paratext, no matter what its provenance or function, as transmedia content. … One danger is that we lose sight of the specificity of the promotional text, and equally troubling, of the specificity of the conditions under which promos are produced' (ibid.). The writer's strike provides an example of the ways in which the terminology used to describe certain media texts can have powerful resonances within the politics of the production cultures within which they are produced.

Yet, at the same time, I want to argue that to simply position some forms of content as promotional and some forms of content as not promotional is equally to ignore the contexts within which the extended texts of television are now produced and consumed. Rather than attempting to police the boundaries between what counts as promotion and what counts as the 'primary text' or 'content', we should be considering the different and multiple functions that media texts are now invited to play. 'Promotional' should not be used as a category to pigeon-hole a particular text, but rather should be understood as one of the many functions that a media text can play. This is because, it seems to me, the answer to Dawson's questions above about *Family Guy* clips, *Lost* recaps and Susan Boyle clips is that all of these different texts perform both of the functions that he ascribes to them. For example, the *Lost* recaps play an important narrative function for both regular and new viewers in summarizing what has gone before and highlighting key themes and characters that will be important over the seasons to come. Yet, this narrative function also (and at the same time) has a promotional function, enticing new and regular viewers and creating anticipation and awareness of the new season of the series. In branding terms, all these different examples of short-form content can be seen as texts that condense and promote the core values of the programme brand for viewers. Thinking about promotion as a function of all texts is particularly important, because there remains a tendency within academic studies to view promotional texts dismissively as marketing that lacks the authorial integrity and creativity of the primary texts of the film or television programme. Such an argument in some ways replicates the fight between the WGA and the US networks about the labour involved in the production of web content, in that promotional texts are positioned as unauthored and lacking in the creativity and originality of the primary television programmes. Examining the ways in which all texts can have both promotional and non-promotional functions can help to value the creative labour involved in the production of texts previously dismissed as 'just advertising'.

So far I have argued that the extension of programmes onto multiple media has become an increasingly important aspect of contemporary television production. Programme branding organizes the relationships between all the different products and services that now make up a television programme, from new forms of transmedia storytelling, to older forms of franchising, such as format sales, licensed merchandise and spin-off products. Brand management attempts to ensure that all these different extensions contribute to the overall image of the brand. However, brands only gain value through the uses and meanings attributed to them by the public. Therefore, programme branding is an attempt not just to organize the relationships between programme extensions, but also to manage the uses to which these products are put by the public. As our engagement with media products is made increasingly visible through the internet, this becomes more pressing. Programme brands organize the public's engagement with branded products through extending and multiplying the experiences surrounding television programmes. In doing so, the production and distribution of branded products becomes more open-ended. Rather than a single product that is produced and then distributed, the relationship between production and distribution becomes more dynamic, enabling and utilizing the input of viewers along the way. Yet, at the same time, this complicates previously held distinctions between content and promotion, forcing us to explore the ways in which all texts might take on multiple functions depending on how they are positioned by producers and used by viewers.

What emerges from this account of programme branding is that the programme brand is not a static, singular object. Rather, the brand is an intangible object that exists in material form (as a set of branded media artefacts, for example), but gains meaning through the exchange between producers and consumers. Yet, this relationship is not necessarily open and equal. As Jenkins argues, producers are increasingly inviting participation from viewers, while at the same time attempting to control or circumscribe the nature of this participation. For example, in the late 1990s and early 2000s Fox threatened a number of websites such as <http://www.vidiot.com> that enabled fans to download video and audio clips from popular television shows, including a number of Fox programmes. Fox claimed that these fan sites violated the copyright and trade mark rights that the corporation had in these programmes. In a similar vein, Jenkins (2006) describes how Warner Bros wrote to a number of *Harry Potter* sites after it purchased the film rights to the book series in 2001, threatening to close sites that infringed its copyright and trade mark rights, even though many of these sites were run by teenage fans. Here, these companies were attempting to use trade mark and copyright law to control what viewers did with their programme brands. The reasons for these attempts to control the use of programme brands relate to the ways in which brands are protected in law.

The primary forms of legal protection for programme brands are copyright and trade mark law. Copyright law protects the programme itself and its scripts, but it generally does not cover other aspects of a programme brand, such as titles, logos or character names, which a corporation may want to licence for use on other products.[11] These more intangible aspects of a programme brand are covered by trade mark law. Trade mark law protects the distinctive graphic signs, such as logos, type-faces, colours and designs, used to distinguish branded goods and services (see Lury 2004: 99–100). As all brands are signified in part by graphic logos, trade mark law is the primary means through which brands are legally constituted and protected. While the channel brands discussed in the last chapter would be signified by logos and idents, programme brands tend to be signified by title names and graphics, such as the distinctive *Top Gear* title design or the *Buffy the Vampire Slayer* (WB, 1997–2001, UPN, 2001–3) logo produced in its own typeface.

The origins of trade mark law lie in protecting consumers from copycat products appropriating the distinctiveness of a successful brand. However, as Celia Lury argues, 'trade mark law does more than protect the mark owner from unfair forms of competition. It makes it possible for mark owners to exploit new forms of production and exchange' (2004: 123) such as the licensing of a programme name to appear on another company's products. At the same time, the producer has to establish 'the reputation, distinctiveness and originality' of the trade mark in order to have it registered (Robertson and Nicol 2002: 336). Furthermore, as the protection offered by trade mark law is potentially indefinite (unlike copyright law), the producer needs to prevent the dilution of its trade marks in order to ensure that the trade mark retains the distinctiveness necessary to be protected by law (see Coombe 1998). Steve Jones argues that trade mark law, in allowing the owner to protect the uses of his/her property, combines the notion of ownership with the notion of propriety or correct behaviour. He argues that intellectual property intertwines the two etymological roots of the word 'property': 'derived from the Latin proprius, meaning "one's own", the word property was a doublet for propriety in More's Utopia' (Jones, cited in Coombe and Herman 2001: 923). The implication is that the improper use of a sign or property might damage the property and its owner. Thus, corporations like Fox and Warner Bros police the uses of their programme brands for two reasons. First, to financially protect their investment in order to justify the fees that they charge other companies for licensing such activity. Second, to ensure consistent meanings associated with the programme and to prevent any dilution of the value and distinctiveness of their marks. Yet, the paradox is that such activities lead to widespread criticism of and negative publicity for such media conglomerates for constraining the creative activities of the very viewers and consumers that contribute to the franchises' success and who are operating, not for profit, but for pleasure. Furthermore, as Coombe and Herman (2001) argue, the internet actually facilitates and makes visible such critical discourse. The attempt to protect the distinctiveness of these media brands by constraining fan engagement with them potentially undermines the very 'common' through which brands gain their value.

What makes a programme a 'programme brand'?

If branding is becoming a more important aspect of television production, what impact might this have on programme production? Are there certain kinds of television programmes that are more suited to branding than others? As we have seen, programme branding emerges as a strategy to manage the extended texts of the television programme and the more complex and open-ended relationships between production, distribution and consumption. While not all contemporary television programmes are developed as brands, I want to argue that those that are have three central characteristics: longevity; transferability; and multiplicity. As we have seen, the television industry is increasingly seeking to increase the long tail of its programmes by extending them onto multiple media, selling them as formats for overseas production and distributing them across a range of platforms, often in multiple forms. As Ian Grutchfield (Brand Manager, *Dr Who*, BBC Cymru Wales) argues, 'The programme needs to be big enough to justify the approach. … I have said to producers, don't bother looking for lots of spin-offs or indeed lots of commercial returns for something that isn't planned to run and run' (interview with the author, 8 November 2010). On the whole, then, branding favours serialized productions and, certainly, the key programme brands in the UK and the USA over the past few years, such as reality television shows like *The Apprentice* (NBC, 2004 –, BBC, 2005 –) and *American Idol*, or dramas such as *Dr Who* and *Lost*, have been long-running series.

While most US television production is serialized, the UK's public service broadcasters have both a tradition and a remit for producing single programmes. Yet, as we saw in Chapter 5, one strategy adopted by the UK's public service broadcasters in response to the increased competition and audience fragmentation of the digital era was to developed strands and zones within the schedules to make one-off programmes easier to find. These zones have also been developed as brands. For example, in 1998 Channel 4 created T4, a zone in its daytime weekend schedules specifically targeted at a youth audience. Originally created to form a brand around the omnibus of teen soap opera *Hollyoaks*, T4 also shows US and UK reality programmes, dramas and entertainment, introduced by presenters and distinguished with its own logo, idents and visual style. T4 has since been extended online, with its own website, Twitter updates, Facebook pages and clips on YouTube, as well as a live show, *T4's Stars of 2010* at Earls Court in London on 21 November 2010. Meanwhile, BBC Worldwide cites BBC Earth as one of its Global Brands. BBC Earth is an umbrella brand under which the BBC exploits its range of natural history content across DVDs, books and other products, including a branded block on US cable channel BBC America.

In addition to having a long tail, programme brands need to provide opportunities for extension: what Ian Grutchfield (Brand Manager, *Dr Who*, BBC Cymru Wales) refers to as having 'transferrable characteristics' (interview with the author, 8 November 2010). Such transferability could relate to format sales, unbundling and providing opportunities for product placement and cross-promotion as in much reality television such as *The Apprentice*, or it might lie in the possibilities for transmedia extensions and merchandise as in much drama such as *Dr Who*. Simone Murray argues that the commodification of television programmes undermines their complexity (2005: 416–17). While it is tempting to presuppose that programme brands must be relatively simplistic constructs that can be reduced to a single idea, tagline or logo, I want to argue that, actually, branding encourages the production of programmes with what Sharon Ross calls an 'aesthetics of multiplicity' (2008: 20–26). As argued above, in extending its content onto multiple media the television industry aims not only to increase its revenues, but also to create new and more engaged relationships with viewers. Sharon Ross argues that:

> Shows that have marked tele-participation feature narratives with multiple points of view, typically through the use of ensemble casts, and often, but not always, through complex narrative structures. These programs also often focus on incomplete stories, typically relying on seriality and interruption.
>
> (2008: 255–56)

In placing increased emphasis on the on-going and open-ended relationships between viewers and programmes, programme branding favours those texts that are most likely to offer multiple points of engagement for viewers.

These three characteristics of programme brands seem to particularly describe two forms of programming that have emerged as central to the contemporary US and UK television industries: serialized drama and reality television. However, programme branding is not restricted to these two forms of television. Indeed, one of the most successful global programme brands is the motoring show *Top Gear*, discussed briefly above. I want to go on to demonstrate that *Top Gear* perfectly exemplifies the characteristics of programme branding outlined above and that examining the programme as a brand can help to draw out the meanings of the series. Although *Top Gear* is ostensibly a motoring show, the redesign of the programme in the early 2000s placed a strong emphasis on entertainment. The combination of motoring knowledge and the pleasures of cars and driving is apparent in both of the key elements of the programme brand: the presenters and the structure of the series.

Francis Bonner argues that *Top Gear* is 'presenter-*dominated*' (2010: 33, italics in the original), with the three male presenters (Jeremy Clarkson, Richard Hammond and James May) functioning as a comic trio. Yet, at the same time, each presenter has extensive motoring knowledge that is drawn on throughout the series. The combination of comedy and motoring know-how is equally apparent in the fourth regular character in the series: the Stig. Dressed in a racing suit and full-face crash helmet that obscures his identity, the Stig is an iconic unnamed racing driver who tests the high-end cars featured on the show and takes part in many of the stunts. Over the years, the identity of the Stig has become a key aspect of the entertainment of the show, with Clarkson introducing him each week with increasingly absurd facts: 'some say that he is Mac compatible and that he once punched a horse to the floor. All we know is, he's called the Stig.' At the same time, he is positioned as a talented and experienced driver who teaches the celebrities on the show to drive at speed and tests the latest high-end cars.[12] While the whole tone of the series combines the fun and hedonism of cars and driving with regular motoring news and information, the structure allows different elements to be emphasized. Regular features such as the Cool Wall and road tests provide a space to examine the performance and style of new high-end cars, while the weekly inclusion of stunts, such as creating a space shuttle out of a Reliant Robin, emphasize sheer boyish fun.

Although *Top Gear* had already been running since 1978 (although not continuously), these elements of the rebrand of the series contribute to its continued longevity, offering a format that provides consistent pleasures that can be updated each season, with new stunts and new car releases. With any long-running series the programme needs to remain fresh. In addition to responding to viewer comments, the series does this through its brand extensions. For example, the Cool Wall iPhone app allows viewers to construct their own Cool Wall from over 350 cars. The app provides information about each car, with quotes from *Top Gear*, and allows you to measure your own ratings against the programme's presenters. While the Cool Wall app allows viewers to engage in the world of the series and hence extend its pleasures beyond the moment of broadcast (what I have elsewhere called an example of diegetic merchandising, Johnson 2007), other extensions, such as the online car reviews and news enable the programme brand to remain constantly up to date. For example, TopGear.com has a news section that provides motoring news and clips, such as photos of Sebastian Vettel's 2010 Formula One season to celebrate him becoming the youngest F1 champion in history in November 2010, and footage of a modified Lamborghini Gallardo crashing at over 100 mph in Texas in October 2010. These brand extensions help to keep the *Top Gear* experience fresh and relevant for viewers.

These brand extensions also demonstrate some of the transferable characteristics of *Top Gear*. Central here are the three presenters, each with his own persona that is extended through a range of books and DVDs. Not all these are branded as *Top Gear* merchandise, but they all contribute to the construction of the personas that are so central to the series. For example, Clarkson is positioned as arrogant, confident and most likely to spout the anti-environmental and reactionary politics that are sometimes associated with the series (see Bonner 2010), a persona that is extended in his four-volume book series (*How Hard Can it Be?: The World According to Clarkson*). Meanwhile, Richard Hammond's softer and more metrosexual persona (which is emphasized in his presentation of children's programme, *Blast Lab*) is apparent in his book, *As You Do*, which combines his account of taking part in *Top Gear* stunts with amusing anecdotes about his family life. Meanwhile, the Stig, as an iconic character that can be easily licensed, forms the basis of most of the toys and games for the series. These are largely aimed at men and boys, ranging from a Stig lunch bag, soap on a rope and bendy toy, to mugs, a memory stick and mouse mats.

However, the transferability of the series also emerges in its format. Each episode is made up of a series of regular elements that can be unbundled into short online content. There are road tests of new cars, usually combining a five-minute filmed segment of one of the presenters driving the car and commenting on its features with a timed drive of the car by the Stig around the *Top Gear* track ranked against the other cars tested. 'Star in a Reasonably Priced Car' is a ten-minute segment in which a celebrity is interviewed by Clarkson and then races a car around the *Top Gear* track with their time ranked against other celebrities. The news segment sees Clarkson, May and Hammond gathered in the studio to discuss the latest motoring news, again for around 5–10 minutes. There are also filmed stunts, such as playing football with the new Toyota Aygo or trying to destroy a Toyota Hilux, and longer challenges, usually broadcast in two parts, in which the presenters are given motoring-related challenges, such as designing their own motor homes or racing from Switzerland to Blackpool on one tank of fuel. In addition to the usual episode format there are 'special' episodes, such as the polar special in which the team attempted to race to the North Pole or the Vietnam special, where they attempted to travel the length of the country by motorbike. The segmentation of the regular episodes allows them to be easily unbundled. The BBC Worldwide *Top Gear* website, the bbc.co.uk *Top Gear* webpage and the *Top Gear* site on YouTube all carry clips from the show categorized by segment (news, challenges, celebrities, tests etc.). Indeed, in 2008 *Top Gear* was given its own dedicated BBC Worldwide YouTube site in recognition of its popularity online. Links to clips are also placed on the *Top Gear* Facebook site which has over 5.5 million fans.[13]

The openness of the series to unbundling has also assisted its sale overseas. In 2007 BBC Worldwide sold 39 hours of *Top Gear* footage to Korean broadcaster TU Media's satellite digital multimedia broadcasting (S-DMB) service which allows viewers to watch segments from the programme on mobile phones, laptops and digital cameras (Rogers 2007: 12). *Top Gear* is thus an example of the unbundled text that Dawson argues is 'exemplary of an emergent mobile television aesthetic that exploits the segmental quality of the television text to reconfigure integral media commodities into flexible forms expressly constructed so as to flow freely between screens' (2007: 239). Furthermore, *Top Gear*'s transferability extends beyond the unbundling of the episodes onto new media platforms. The development of a series of regular transferable elements has also facilitated the sale of the series as a format that can be adapted for other media. In addition to the development of local versions of the series in the USA, Australia and Russia, a *Top Gear* magazine competes successfully in the UK as a men's lifestyle magazine against titles such as *FHM* and *Men's Health* (Anon. 2007: 2) and has been published in 22 countries. And in 2008 the BBC launched an internationally touring *Top Gear* live event, tied into motoring shows with stunts, films and appearances from the presenters.

Top Gear's transferability is hinged upon an aesthetic of multiplicity. The three different presenters offer multiple points of access to the show, whether through the bullish and iconoclastic Clarkson, the metrosexual Hammond or the bumbling masculinity of May, while the Stig has particular appeal to children, all of which helps to extend the appeal of the show beyond the presumed middle-aged male audience for motoring programmes. The DVD releases emphasize the entertainment aspect of the show, selecting the challenges and stunts that are most overtly narrative driven and open to repeat viewing with a wide appeal. These were the sections that in Bonner's small-scale audience research about the series had the greatest appeal to female viewers, who tended to watch the show with their male partners and children (2010: 37). Meanwhile, the road tests and news segments, which are more topical and more specifically targeted at those interested in motoring, are grouped together online, where you can read *Top Gear* car reviews, view related *Top Gear* road tests and stunts and search for new or used models for sale in your local area (<http://www.topgear.com/uk/car-reviews>). Indeed, the most popular video categories on TopGear.com are the road tests and the Stig (any videos featuring the Stig as a character).

Yet, the multiplicity of the series extends beyond just the characters and the structure to the tone and address found across the programme brand. Bonner notes that, within the episodes of the programme itself, the world created is a socially conservative and politically reactionary one. Cars are often derided as being 'gay' or for women and the show's revelling in fast, powerful cars positions it as anti-environmentalist. Yet, at the same time, as Bonner argues, these positions are constantly situated within a comic register:

> Read 'straight', it endorses a conservative male viewer feeling beleaguered in a changing world. Concentrating on the moment of disavowal enables a more progressive viewer to register that it is a self-mocking production, not to be taken seriously.
>
> (2010: 43)

Yet, while I would argue that Bonner is right that the series offers these different reading positions, I would also suggest that they are not seen as mutually exclusive. Rather, I would argue that what is at work within *Top Gear* is a constant negotiation of the brand's aesthetic of multiplicity. At one level, it is important that each element of *Top Gear*'s extensions fits within the core characteristics of the programme brand. Yet, at the same time, the multiplicity of the series particularly facilitates the extension of the programme onto multiple media and to divergent audiences. The segmentation of the broadcast show is particularly useful here, in that it allows specific elements to be exploited in ways that seem relatively incongruous. The Stig is a good example, in that this character has been turned into a range of non-motoring related merchandise and even a book, *Where's the Stig?*, based on the *Where's Wally?* series, in which readers have to locate the Stig within detailed crowd pictures. Yet, while these extensions would seem to pull against the pleasures of the broadcast programme, there is something in the tone of address that remains the same. Across the entire *Top Gear* programme brand there is a tone of irreverence and fun. The editor of TopGear.com argues that there was a deliberate attempt to replicate the tone as well as the content of the programme when designing the website: 'We've adopted something of the irreverent attitude of Jeremy Clarkson and his fellow presenters … . We've made it more of an alternative motoring site with an emphasis on lifestyle and entertainment' (Paul Regan, cited in Anon. 2006a: 2). While this is heightened or lessened depending on the specific text (being least overt in the car reviews), it remains consistent across the wide range of texts that make up the programme brand and can be understood as a paratext that frames engagement with all aspects of the show. Furthermore, the irreverent comedy of the series is a central point of discussion and pleasure in the forums on both FinalGear.com and TopGearShow.com.

This irreverent comic register is central to the aesthetic of multiplicity of the series. The reactionary politics spouted by Clarkson (for example) are positioned within a comic register, whether through the banter between the three presenters, the ironic and self-mocking text framing Clarkson's contributions on TopGear.com, or in his exaggerated performed persona. As such, the series does endorse a conservative discourse of beleaguered masculinity, while *at the same time* mocking that very position. In presenting these multiple perspectives the series allows viewers to occupy both positions simultaneously and to shift between positions as they engage with the different texts associated with the *Top Gear* brand. In doing so, it opens that conservative or reactionary position up for exploration from a range of perspectives, allowing it expression, while simultaneously holding it up for critique. Far from undermining its complexity, the *Top Gear* brand is constructed through an aesthetics of multiplicity that enables discourses of masculinity and conservative politics to be worked through by a wide range of different viewers from a variety of perspectives.

Conclusions

In the contemporary television landscape, where the set in the living room is being repositioned as just one site through which viewers engage with television content, it is likely that programme brands with longevity, transferability and multiplicity that facilitate extensions across multiple texts and platforms will become more common. While the adoption of programme branding is certainly fuelled in the USA and the UK by the desire to increase the revenue produced from one commission, over this chapter I have attempted to demonstrate that examining programmes as brands can reveal a lot more than simply the economic conditions within which they were produced. Branding is not simply a means of financially exploiting programmes. Rather, it can be understood as a response to the new conditions emerging with the television industry in which the broadcast text is just one aspect of a more dynamic and open-ended context of production and consumption for programme brands that have a much longer life across a far wider range of texts. These programme brands invite multiplicity, not just in their formal construction (for example being made up of multiple segments that can be unbundled and/or transferred onto other products), but also in their address to viewers. By attempting to create programme brands that harness the common social experiences engaged in by viewers, programme branding favours texts that offer multiple points of access and multiple points of engagement. Increasingly, to understand these new texts of television, we need to explore the complex and sometimes contradictory experiences that they offer to viewers and the ways in which these are managed by the programme brand.

Notes

1 As discussed in Chapter 1, the second product in traditional accounts of the economics of broadcast television is the audience and, in commercial advertiser-funded models of broadcasting, access to the audience is sold to advertisers (Doyle 2002: 60). Part I complicated this understanding of the economics of television by arguing that the channel emerges in the cable era as a product that can be sold to cable operators.

2 Jenkins does not provide any evidence to back up the assertion that audiences want all the components of a transmedia text to offer new insights and experiences. Indeed, later in the

same chapter he acknowledges the deeper meanings and experiences that licensed merchandise (such as toys and games) can provide for viewers through play (2006: 146).

3 See, for example, the comments by caffeine and BobTheMunificent on 'Looking Down – Britain From Above – BBC', YouTube. Online. Available HTTP: <http://www.youtube.com/watch?v=cVkhc3J7zNk&p=F5D324185EE73FEC> (accessed 5 November 2010).

4 The difficulty for the BBC as a public service broadcaster is that it needs to negotiate a position in which it is seen to open up its content, while also needing to ensure that the activities that viewers engage with around its content do not undermine its broader corporate values (see Johnson 2009).

5 This accords with Evans's (2011) research, which suggests that the characters are central to audience engagement with transmedia drama.

6 Characters from season 1 of *E20* subsequently joined the regular *EastEnders* cast.

7 The first season of *E20* initially aired online in 12 twice-weekly short episodes. The BBC also made omnibuses of season 1 available on three consecutive Sundays in January through their 'Red Button' interactive service and on the iPlayer. The episodes were also posted on the BBC YouTube site and made available via BBC Mobile. Episodes from season 2 were also broadcast on BBC Three.

8 As of 6 November 2010, the *E20* Facebook site had 36,278 friends.

9 The panel was titled 'The More Things Change … : Writing for Television in the 21st Century' and consisted of Kevin Murphy, Noreen Halpern, Mark Brown, Neal Baer and Lisa Seidman.

10 The first season of the local version of *Top Gear* in Australia was the second most-watched show on SBS in 2008–9, beaten only by the UK version of the series (Anon. 2010).

11 In simple terms, copyright law protects works of art and so, in order for a name, title or character to be protected through copyright, it would have to be designed with 'such distinctive lettering that the design of the name is itself an artistic work' (Flint *et al.* 2006: 549–50).

12 Historically there has been considerable speculation about the identity of the Stig. The BBC's contract with the drivers who portray the Stig includes a confidentiality clause in order to maintain the anonymity so central to the character's persona. In 2003 Perry McCarthy was dropped as the Stig after his identity was revealed. In August 2010 the BBC entered into a legal battle after McCarthy's replacement (later revealed to be Ben Collins) announced his intention to publish his autobiography.

13 The BBC also has a Stig Facebook site and a *Top Gear* Twitter site.

WHAT'S AT STAKE IN TELEVISION BRANDING?

In the final chapter of this book I want to draw together some of the more theoretical arguments developed over the previous chapters to ask: what are we actually referring to when we talk about television branding? What are television brands? What do they do and what do they tell us about television? Central to the theorization of branding developed over this book is the argument that brands are far more than just logos, designs or taglines added to products and services in order to market them to consumers. To be sure, branding does use packaging, promotion, design and logos to communicate an identity and set of values related to the product/service to the consumer. And, historically, branding was developed to distinguish products from the competition and to encourage consumer loyalty by acting as a guarantee of quality and appealing to values shared by the consumer. However, in constructing a set of values around a product designed to create consumer loyalty, brands are effectively attempting to shape what people do with and say about a branded product. Brands are thus frames of action (Arvidsson 2006) that manage the relationships around branded products and services. Brands frame our engagement with a product or service, from shaping our expectations, to constructing the terms with which we might talk about a service or use a product. The interface of the brand (Lury 2004) shapes not just the consumer's engagement with the product, but all aspects of the production and socio-cultural circulation of products and services. Therefore, brands now increasingly frame production, the way in which employees talk about their work, the terms of press criticism and policy discourses, as well as the relationship between the consumer and the branded product/service itself. As a frame or interface, the brand cannot be pinpointed as a singular object or thing. While brands do have material manifestations (as packaged goods, logos and so on), ultimately the brand is an intangible cultural form that gains value through its socio-cultural uses.

Branding as an industrial strategy, therefore, attempts to attach financial value to our engagement with branded products and services, and brand management is concerned with attempting to control and circumscribe the activities around brands. This is done in part through product design, packaging and promotion, but also through other activities that respond to the more open and dynamic mode of contemporary production, such as developing brand extensions or responding directly to the activities of the consumer. Such brand management is encouraged by the legal production of the brand: trade mark law. Trade marks can only be legally protected if they are distinctive. Therefore, brand owners police the uses of brands in order to protect the distinctiveness of their trade marks. However, while branding can attempt to determine the use and symbolic value attached to a product or service, ultimately it can only suggest how they should be used or understood. Brands only gain meaning and value through what people do with and say about them. Therefore, while the activities of brand managers can harness the positive values, attributes and uses of branded products and services, attempts to police the activities around brands too closely can potentially undermine the very means through which brands gain value: through the activities of consumers.

Traditional brand theory, developed in relation to the consumer industries, differentiates between product and service brands. Berry argues that, 'In packaged goods, the product is the primary brand. However, with services, the company is the primary brand' (Berry 2000: 128). The main reason for this different location of the brand is that services are intangible and so cannot be packaged and displayed in quite the same way as packaged goods. While, with both service and product brands, it is primarily the experience of the service or product itself through which the brand gains value, crucially Berry argues that 'with services, the company as a whole is usually viewed as the provider of the experience' (2000: 130). As a consequence, while product brands are located around a particular packaged good or product range (such as Nike trainers), service brands tend to be associated with the company that provides the service (such as British Airways or Federal Express). Berry includes CNN and Disney as examples of service brands, and in many ways television is a service, with the television industry providing the service of television viewing to its audience. However, while most services involve a face-to-face encounter, the service encounter of television is mediated by the technology of television itself.[1]

Historically, the service encounter for the television industry has been the television channel. This complicates the relationship between the company and the service, with the service being associated with both the corporation that provides the service (the BBC) and the channel through which the service is delivered (BBC One, BBC Two). The channel has, therefore, been central to the corporate brand identities of broadcasters, as well as shaping viewers' experiences of watching television programmes. However, because the service being provided by television is the experience of watching television programmes, the identities of channels (and the meanings and values attributed to them) are determined to a significant extent by the programmes themselves, framed by interstitial texts between and within the flow of programmes, such as channel idents, station IDs, trailers and so on. One consequence of the nature of television as a service, therefore, is that there is a complex interrelationship between the broadcaster, the television channel and the television programme, with the channel historically acting as the central site through which television was encountered. It is, therefore, unsurprising that the channel has been a focus of branding in the US and the UK television industries.

In the broadcast era, when a small number of broadcasters dominated the television industries in the USA and UK, there was far less need for channels to construct and communicate clear brand identities, although all the channels in the UK and USA did have logos that distinguished them from their competitors. The US and UK television industries turned towards branding as a more central strategy in part because the nature of the television channel changed. In both countries the cable/satellite era ushered in a vast increase in the number of channels, creating more competition for audiences and a greater need to construct and communicate a clear channel identity with which the viewer could identify in order to attempt to create viewer loyalty. Traditional economic theory argues that television is a dual-product market: selling programmes to audiences through a television service and selling audiences to advertisers through the sale of airtime (Doyle 2002). The satellite/cable era introduced a third product into television, the television channel itself, as advertiser-funded cable and satellite channels, such as MTV and the UKTV channels, needed to be carried by cable/satellite operators in order to reach significant audiences. Branding functioned to manage the relationship between the television channel and these three different constituencies. Branding campaigns were developed based on market research in order to construct and communicate an identity and personality for the television channel to audiences over and above the programmes broadcast, through promos, trailers and the creation of interstitial material such as idents and station IDs. These branding campaigns also attempted to communicate the values of the channel to advertisers and/or cable/satellite operators. For example, MTV and Fox additionally produced material that explained the commercial value of their target audience (see Chapter 1) and ITV attempted to construct a brand identity that united its regional franchises in order to emphasize to advertisers its ability to reach mass audiences (see Chapter 3).

The construction of the channel as a brand also facilitated the development of channel brand extensions, and the example of MTV usefully illustrates the issues at stake in understanding television channel branding. From 1987 MTV began to expand its brand into new markets. Having initially planned to feed the US MTV channel to Europe via satellite, MTV altered its strategy and instead launched a new channel targeted specifically at Europe: MTV Europe (Powell 1987: 26). Initially, MTV Europe was marred by inconsistencies in cable penetration and the problems of programming across the different countries, languages and music tastes of Europe. However, MTV's solid brand name and its track record in attracting young audiences significantly facilitated its success.[2] Indeed Josephson claims of MTV Europe three years after its launch that 'the brand awareness of MTV has increased to the point that advertisers are coming to the network to develop special campaigns for the channel's youthful demographic' (1990: 20). MTV's broad strategy in launching MTV Europe, of adapting its brand to the demands of the local audience, has been adopted by the network as it has expanded into other new markets. For example, Alex Okosi, Vice President of MTV Africa claims of the channel 'we are not expanding internationally as a big company moving in and pushing American content, our platform is to provide a place for young African Artists to shine' (cited in Mandell 2005: 45). This strategy of 'glocalization' involves using local staff as well as adapting to local programming preferences and social differences. For example, Bill Roedy describes the plans for MTV Arabia (a joint venture between Viacom and Arab Media Group, the largest media group in the United Arab Emirates) as an adaptation of MTV's youthful, irreverent brand to the cultural sensitivities of the Middle East:

> MTV being what it is, there will be some edginess to it, but it has to be respectful of local culture. That is why we are having a call to prayer every Friday on the channel and why there will be an interpretation of Ramadan in a youthful-generation way. Hip hop happens to be very big in the region so we'll do that, too.
>
> (cited in Bulkley 2007: 27)

Bulkley claims that 25 per cent of the content for MTV Arabia will be locally produced and all of the VJs (video jockeys) will be Arabs (ibid).[3]

This would seem to suggest that, while the brand is functioning as a frame for the programming, promotion and production of MTV, this is a two-way relationship in which the brand also adapts to the needs of local actors. Hence, the MTV brand acts as an interface between MTV and the local environment within which its programming is produced and consumed. This would support recent studies on the globalization of television broadcasting, which characterize globalization as 'a two-way process involving "push" and "pull" or "exchanges" of power between global and local actors' (Chang 2003: 2). In her study of attempts by global broadcasters to enter the Asian market over the past two decades, Yu-li Chang argues that 'Rather than regarding globalization as a process that uniformly subverts local imperatives, it is a process of "glocalization" in which the local exercises influences in constituting the global' (2003: 28).

However, Balaji's research on MTV Desi suggests that the interface of the brand is not as open as Chang argues. MTV Desi was a channel launched in 2005 targeted at second-generation South Asian Americans. Balaji argues that, while it is 'nearly impossible to define a common South Asian

American culture', there is a prevalence of consistent images associated with Indians and Indianness (such as bindis, yoga, bhangra and Bollywood) that have 'led to a media-created notion of identity' for this diverse group of peoples (2008: 25). She argues that MTV's launch of MTV Desi came at a time when advertisers were becoming aware of the value of this community as 'the richest demographic by income in the United States' (Balaji 2008: 27), but that this inevitably led to a focus on a specific group of rich and upwardly mobile 'Desis'. Indeed, Balaji argues that the use of the term Desi was strategic, in that it simplified this diverse community into a singular identity while simultaneously using a term with which many South Asian Americans would feel comfortable. However, while Balaji sees MTV Desi as part of MTV's broader strategy of glocalization, she also uses it as an example of the failure of this strategy 'because of the network's attempts to homogenize a diverse diasporic population' (2008: 33). In February 2007 MTV closed MTV World, which included MTV Desi, MTV Chi (for Chinese-Americans) and MTV K (for Korean Americans), and it would appear that this attempt at glocalization was a failure.

Yet Balaji's conclusions do not do justice to the richness of analysis in her account of MTV Desi's rise and fall. Significantly, although Balaji cites MTV Desi as an example of glocalization, the programmes that she describes from the channel are not ones produced specifically by and for a South Asian American audience, but rather programmes imported from other MTV networks (such as *Baap of Bakra* imported from MTV India) that were often adapted from US MTV programming in the first place (*Baap of Bakra* is a version of *Punk'd*). Balaji is right to assert that these programmes failed to reflect the diversity and complexity of the South Asian American audience. Her attribution of this failure to MTV's use of branding is more problematic. Balaji argues that, in launching MTV Desi, 'MTV reconstructed the term [Desi] into a brand' (2008: 29). In doing so, MTV co-opted a term whose meaning varied across the South Asian American audience. Drawing on Eileen Meehan (2005), she argues that MTV Desi lacked originality and creativity because it was the only channel within its particular market and because its need to retain brand associations with MTV restricted its ability to be truly innovative (Balaji 2008: 32). Yet, such an argument is based on the assumption that brands are top-down cultural constructs, rather than interfaces or frames, and Balaji's account of the failure of MTV Desi points to the need for brands to function as effective frames for their audiences' actions if they are to be successful.

Over and above this, Balaji argues that, in turning Desi into a brand, MTV attempted to commodify South Asian American identity. As networks and advertisers have increasingly attempted to target their products more directly, identity has become a marketable commodity and branding, in being a key tool in niche marketing, has become a central part of this process of commodification. However, to argue that the US television industry attempts to commodify identity and difference is not to argue that identity now only exists as a commodity. Audience studies have taught us that the relationship between media and identity is highly complex. This does not mean that we should not be concerned about the increasing commercialization of the US television industry and its impact on society and culture, as political economists such as McChesney (2008) argue. In fact, in both the USA and the UK there has been a shift towards focusing programming strategies onto upscale audiences with disposable income in an attempt to generate revenue in an increasingly crowded market. It is therefore not surprising that MTV Desi should be particularly targeting upscale South Asian Americans, and it is questionable whether an unregulated commercial system can ever fully address the needs of audiences with limited financial means. Neither does it mean that large global conglomerates such as MTV are not attempting to control the meanings and uses of its audiences' engagement with its products and services and that by doing so they might construct certain meanings and uses as economic commodities with commercial value. However, as Balaji's example of MTV Desi indicates, if audiences do not engage with a brand, if the meanings and uses attached to that brand and valued by the corporation are not adopted by the audience, then that brand is likely to fail. While it has been beyond the scope of this book (which takes the industry's use of branding as its focus) to examine in detail how people make use of brands, key to an understanding of television branding is a recognition of branding as two-way process, albeit one in which the divisions of power are not equal.[4]

While, as the example of MTV demonstrates, branding has emerged as a key industrial strategy for the US cable television industry over the past 30 years, its adoption by US network television has been more problematic. Although the networks turned to branding over the 1990s after they had seen a significant fall in their ratings, they were still primarily mass broadcasters whose value to advertisers lay in their reach. One of the consequences of this was that, while the national networks adopted branding campaigns, these were often far less focused than those adopted by cable companies. As Selznick (2010) argues, these rebrands were often about reasserting existing values of Americaness, togetherness and national unity, rather than the construction of an identity that is targeted at a specific audience and channel, as with MTV. Part of the issue here is also that the networks tend to broadcast a wider range of programming than niche cable channels such as MTV, and their brand identities need to encompass this range in order to accurately reflect the service offered. One consequence of this is the strategy of branding segments of the schedules – such as NBC's branding of Thursday nights as 'Must See TV' in the mid-1990s – which have been more warmly received within the industry than attempts to create a brand identity for a whole network, such as ABC's 'yellow' campaign in 1997 (see Chapters 1 and 5).

However, it is not simply the wider range of programming offered by network television that has militated against the adoption of channel branding. In the UK, where the terrestrial public service channels offer a far wider range of programming than the US networks, the construction of a consistent and distinctive brand identity for each channel has become a central aspect of the communicative ethos of British broadcasting. Rather, the adoption of branding within each country reveals fundamental differences in the nature of each industry. In the broadcast era, the US networks and the UK public service terrestrial channels dominated the delivery of television programming through a small number of channels. However, the service provided by each was distinctly different. US network television has historically been structured in seasons, beginning each autumn with a slate of new and returning series of around 26 episodes, mixed in with news, mini-series, films, sports and television movies. These seasons ran until the spring, with the summer consisting largely of repeats and reruns. By contrast, UK public service broadcasting was founded upon the principle of the mixed programme schedule, with a wide range of genres and programme forms shown throughout the year and certain forms of programming (such as news, children's and religious programmes) being mandated through regulation.[5] In addition, although the UK included channels funded by the licence fee (BBC One and BBC Two) and channels funded by advertising (the ITV regional franchises), these were regulated by a similar public service remit, with additional limits for ITV on the amount of advertising that could be broadcast. Both ITV and the BBC had to demonstrate to the regulators that they were fulfilling their public service remit in terms of the quantities of certain types of programmes broadcast and in terms of the qualities of the programmes broadcast. These differing histories continue to shape the communicative ethos of UK terrestrial and US network television today.

In the UK the television service provided through the channel was the central means through which regulators assessed the public service provided by the terrestrial broadcasters. As a consequence, the channel has an important function within UK public service broadcasting as a central site through which public service provision is evaluated by both viewers and regulators. The communicative ethos of the terrestrial channels, therefore, has to conform to the values of public service broadcasting, which extends beyond individual programmes to encompass a broader broadcasting ethos. When the BBC and Channel 4 adopted channel branding in the 1990s they had to balance the creation of channel identities that would be attractive to audiences with their public service remits. For Channel 4, this involved developing a brand identity that appealed to the commercially valuable youth and upmarket audiences, while asserting that this was in accordance with its public service remit to be different from other television channels (see Chapter 4).

If Channel 4's branding strategies attempted to balance commercial and public service pressures, the BBC's adoption of branding emerged more directly in response to threats to public service broadcasting over the 1980s. And, while Channel 4 initially focused on channel branding, the BBC (as a corporation with television and radio channels) also developed corporate branding strategies. Although branding, with its associations with marketing for commercial gain, might seem inappropriate for a publicly funded corporation such as the BBC, the BBC used its corporate branding campaigns to communicate the value of the BBC, the licence fee and public service broadcasting. That these campaigns were aimed as much at government and opinion formers as the general public is evident from the shifts in rhetoric apparent in the BBC's high-profile corporate branding promos in the 1980s and 1990s.[6] As discussed in Chapter 4, in 1986 the BBC produced a film based on the Monty Python sketch 'What have the Romans ever given us?', which ended with the tagline 'The BBC. Is 16p a day really too much to ask?' Here, the value of public service broadcasting is clearly positioned in economic terms at a moment in history when a hostile Conservative government was considering removing the licence fee and replacing it with advertising. By 1997, when the BBC produced its 'Perfect Day' promo, in which a wide range of different artists performed the famous Lou Reed song, the tagline read: 'Whatever your musical taste it is catered for by the BBC. This is only possible because of the unique way the BBC is paid for by you. BBC. You make it what it is.' There is a clear shift in tone here from emphasizing the value of the BBC in economic terms in a period of rapid privatization and marketization, to creating an identity for the BBC that incorporates its audience at a time when there was a political shift towards evaluating public services through the attitudes and opinions of the public.

While the UK terrestrial broadcasters' adoption of branding over the 1980s and 1990s was shaped in part by the need to communicate their public service values to audiences and to other stakeholders, such as the regulator and government, this was far less the case for the US networks that were relatively unregulated. However, the US networks did need to persuade viewers to watch their programmes, advertisers to buy airtime within those programmes and local stations to affiliate with the network. One consequence of this is the different place of the programme within US network television. Historically the promotion of identities for the US networks has been primarily based on the programming mix offered each season, with a heavy concentration of promotional activity in advance of the new autumn season each year. Furthermore, the US networks generate revenue from the sale of advertising within specific programmes, placing an emphasis on promoting programmes (both to advertisers and audiences) and maintaining audience share through scheduling strategies designed to deter audiences from switching channels. The communicative ethos of US network television is far more overtly based on persuasion than that of the UK terrestrial channels, with the programme forming the basis of this promotional activity.

The emphasis on the programme was heightened as the US networks entered the cable/satellite and, particularly, the digital eras. The rise in the number of channels over the 1980s and 1990s increased the need for content, while changes in regulation allowed the networks to retain financial interests in the programmes that they broadcast. At the same time, the rise of large media conglomerates with businesses across a range of media industries meant that syndication buyers and sellers were often now part of the same company. In addition, the digital era ushered in new platforms for the distribution of television programmes, such as the internet and portable media devices, decentring the television channel as the site through which television viewing took place. As a consequence, the programme became an increasingly valuable commodity within the US television industry and the repurposing of programming became a central source of income for media conglomerates. It is within this context that the programme itself has emerged as a brand disaggregated from the television channel. However, the development of programme branding functions not just to increase the revenues that can be generated from programming by distributing and extending the programme across multiple media, but also to exploit the possibilities offered by new media technologies to create and monetize the relationships between programmes and viewers. As television audiences have splintered, new media technologies such as the mobile phone and internet offer new possibilities for engaging with television content, as well as making visible many of the activities associated with television viewing, such as gossip, discussion and play. The US media conglomerates have attempted to exploit this potential through the creation of programme brands that extend engagement with the television programme, through unbundling, the creation of web/mobile content and forums, and the licensing of ancillary merchandise. Such strategies aim to attract viewers by placing programme content on the sites that viewers frequent (such as social networking sites), to retain viewers by encouraging more intense relationships with programming and to monetize the activities associated with television viewing by providing advertisers with new ways of engaging with their target audience.

Programme brands point to the decentring of the television channel as the principal site of access for television viewing. In the USA, television channels are just one part of the large media conglomerates that emerged in the 1990s, while television programmes can generate revenue across a range of different businesses. Thus, the US networks have become just one site for the distribution of programming, offering a 'first view' of content that is often also made available online and (subsequently) repurposed on DVD and other channels. The development of programme brands can undermine the brand identities of channels, where that identity is determined to a significant extent by its programming mix. As we saw in Chapter 1, while HBO has become increasingly dependent on revenue from the repurposing of its content, this potentially undermines its channel brand identity as the exclusive home of quality programming.

Furthermore, the emergence of digital technologies has shifted television from being a push medium (where content is delivered to viewers in a linear form on broadcast channels) to also being a pull medium (where viewers can select the content that they wish to watch on a range of platforms). Within the digital era, then, the database emerges as a means of organizing content for viewing, placing emphasis on the means through which viewers find and select programmes to view. The success of programming therefore increasingly depends on the ways in which it is distributed and promoted. In the emerging 'attention economy' (Goldhaber 1997) the US television industry is still negotiating how best to position itself. While the programme brand has emerged as a valuable commodity that can be exploited across a wide range of media, television channels still remain an important site through which programming is viewed and have been extended onto the web and repositioned as portals for engaging with television content in a range of ways. At the same time, the development of new service brands such as Hulu incorporate a number of different activities associated with television viewing within one site. Unlike the television channels in the USA, Hulu has developed a brand identity that emphasizes the *experience* of watching television over any particular content provided. However, even in the case of Hulu, the relationship between programming and service brand identities is complex, with users on Hulu's discussion forums often comparing Hulu with its main rival, Netflix, in terms of the specific programmes (as well as the platforms, costs and modes of delivery) offered by each service.

Although the UK terrestrial broadcasters have developed more coherent channel brand identities than the US networks, the branding of programmes has also emerged as a key strategy over the cable/satellite and digital eras. While, as in the USA, this has placed a strain on the relationship between channels and the programmes that they air, it has also problematized the relationship between the public service channels and the corporations that own them. All the UK public service broadcasters have developed new channels and services for digital television, the internet and portable media devices. However, not all these services are regulated by a public service remit with, for example, the BBC developing commercial channels overseas, such as BBC America. Branding has emerged as one way of managing the relationship between these different services. For example, within the UK market the BBC has not used its corporate name to brand the commercial 'UKTV' channels that it developed with Flextech (UKTV is now a joint venture between BBC Worldwide and Virgin Media). However, the BBC has used the associations that its name carries with quality programming in developing commercial brands in overseas markets, whether in programme brands, such as BBC Earth, or channel brands, such as BBC World and BBC America.

While the global media landscape offers opportunities for the BBC to exploit its corporate brand overseas, at the same time the boundaries between different national markets has become blurred. This is particularly the case online where the different channel and service brands owned by the UK's public service broadcasters can sit alongside each other, undermining the separation of public service and commercial brands. One of the BBC's key programme brands, *Top Gear*, provides a useful illustration of this. In terms of broadcast television, *Top Gear* is a key programme brand for BBC Two, for Dave (part of UKTV) and for BBC America, as well as being one of BBC Worldwide's key content brands. A Google search for *Top Gear* on 5 June 2010 resulted in a number of different sites, the first of which was the BBC Worldwide *Top Gear* site which exists in three versions, for the UK, the USA and Australia, all of which carry advertising. The UK site carries the BBC corporate logo, while the US site is branded as a BBC America site. Meanwhile, the Australian site is hosted by ninemsn (a joint venture between PBL Media and Microsoft) as well as carrying the BBC corporate logo. The Google search also provided a link to the bbc.co.uk *Top Gear* site, which does not carry advertising and is clearly branded with the BBC Two logo and designed to fit into the generic design of the BBC's UK website (see Chapter 5). However, there is also a Dave website for *Top Gear*, which does not include the BBC logo, and a BBC Worldwide *Top Gear* channel on YouTube, while the programme is also available on the BBC on-demand service, the iPlayer.

The fact that all these sites (except the Dave site) carry the BBC logo suggests an attempt to use corporate branding to integrate these different service encounters with a key BBC programme brand. Yet, at the same time, the service encounters also carry quite different values – carrying ads or not, offering interaction or not – and are also framed by other brands (such as YouTube, ninemsn, Dave) that have their own values, which may or may not marry with the BBC's corporate brand values. In the digital era, as the example of *Top Gear* demonstrates, the relationships between corporate brands (the BBC) and programme brands (*Top Gear*) and the various channel and service brands that provide the service encounter for that corporation have become increasingly complex. Where once the BBC's public service television and radio channels provided the central site through which their public service provision was evaluated, in the digital era these service encounters have vastly increased and now include services that are and are not bound by a public service remit. As the service encounter for the BBC is extended across a wider and wider range of products and services, branding attempts to construct and manage the relations *between* these different products and services in order to control what we think about the individual products and services, as well as the BBC more broadly as a corporate brand.

The UK public service broadcasters' expansion into commercial businesses was encouraged by government broadcasting policy over the 1980s and 1990s, particularly as a means of subsidizing the BBC's licence fee income. Furthermore, as in the USA, the expansion into new channels (such as the BBC's digital channels) and services (such as websites, Facebook pages and YouTube channels) helps to drive viewers to content within the attention economy. At the same time, however, the extension of public service corporate brands (such as the BBC and Channel 4) challenges the traditional boundaries of public service broadcasting. Where once public service broadcasting could be defined as those aspects of a broadcaster's activities that were covered by a public service remit, in the digital era this definition becomes problematic, as all aspects of a corporation's activities potentially contribute to its corporate brand and, therefore, to its identity and values as a public service broadcaster.

The development of programme brands also poses potential threats to public service broadcasting. Chapter 6 demonstrated that programme brands tend to be characterized by longevity, transferability and multiplicity. These characteristics facilitate the extension of the programme onto multiple platforms. Programmes need to be long running enough to create an extended relationship with viewers over time; to have characteristics (such as characters or narrative forms) that can be transferred onto different media, whether through being unbundled into short clips, adapted as a game or book, or licensed onto consumer goods; and to offer multiple forms of engagement for a range of viewers. As both US and UK broadcasters turn towards programme branding as a central mode of revenue generation, it is likely that programmes with these characteristics will be increasingly valued. Indeed, it is unsurprising that these characteristics are often found in two forms of programming that have proved successful in the digital era: reality television and quality drama series. While these characteristics in themselves are not inherently anathema to the values of public service broadcasting, the prevalence of certain types of programming would run counter to the mixed provision of a wide range of different forms of programme characteristic of UK public service television. Having said that, as argued above, within the UK, programme branding functions alongside channel/service and corporate branding. As a result, broader public service values should prevent the demands of programme branding from undermining the mixed programme schedule, as long as those public service values are recognized and valued by the public, government and regulators.

In the digital era, broadcasters have to contend with a far more complex television landscape than in the broadcast era, in which the very nature of television as a medium has changed. This book has charted some of the ways in which the television industries in the USA and UK have attempted to use branding to manage the changes that have taken place over the cable/satellite and digital eras. While most branding theory distinguishes between product, service and corporate branding, it is possible to differentiate three kinds of television brands: corporate, channel/service and programme. Importantly, these three brands are not separate entities. Rather, because of the nature of television as a service, these different brands are intricately interconnected. One value of studying television branding, therefore, is that it demands a more holistic analysis of television as a cultural form. First, branding functions as an interface between the producer, corporation, programme, service or channel being branded and the audience for that brand. As such, analysis of the cultural operation of a brand invites examination of its industrial production, textual form and socio-cultural context of reception. Second, because the corporate, channel/service and programme brands in television are complexly interrelated, the study of any one particular brand has to account for these broader constituencies, such as examining how a programme brand has been extended across a range of different services and channels or contributes to the brand equity of multiple corporations. Third, charting the complex interrelationships between corporate, channel and programme brands allows an insight into the broader shifts that have taken place within the US and UK television industries and helps to highlight key differences between the USA's commercial market and the UK's more public service-oriented system. An examination of the uses of branding can help us to understand how television (as an industry, technology, textual form and socio-cultural object) has changed since the broadcast era and to account for the more complex nature of television as an object of study in the digital era.

Notes

1 The mediatization of the service encounter is becoming an increasingly common aspect of contemporary service brands, as more companies conduct their business online, so that the service encounter shifts from being face-to-face to being conducted through an electronic interface.

2 See Hujic (1999) for an analysis of MTV Europe's attempt to develop a programming strategy for a pan-European youth audience.

3 MTV Arabia is part of a broader strategy on the part of Viacom (which owns MTV) that also includes launching an Arabian version of Nickelodeon, themed hotels, theme park segments, consumer products and films (Bulkley 2007).

4 There is certainly the need for more work that examines the social and cultural engagement with media brands and is informed by recent developments in audience research.

5 This is not to argue that the seasons are irrelevant for UK television. New series are often launched in September/October and January, with the summer months also more likely to contain repeats or less high-profile programming. Furthermore, since the 1990s the US television industry has experimented with running half-seasons of 13 episodes and launching series mid-season or over the summer. However, in the USA the networks' identities remain significantly defined by the slate of high-profile original television series of 13 or 26 episodes that they broadcast each year. By contrast, in the UK series more typically run for 6–13 episodes and there is a far wider range of programming broadcast throughout the year.

6 The BBC had promoted itself to key stakeholders in the past with films such as *The Voice of Britain* (produced by the GPO Film Unit in 1935) and *This is the BBC* (1959). There is therefore a history of corporate branding at the BBC that remains relatively under-researched. However, its promotional films of the 1980s and 1990s were situated overtly as part of a larger corporate rebranding strategy that also included the branding of its television and radio channels, as well as core departments, such as sports.

BIBLIOGRAPHY

422 South (2009) *Britain From Above*, 1 January 2009. Online. Available HTTP: <http://www.422.com/gallery/article/114/1> (accessed 2 November 2010).

Anon. (2010) 'International Programme Sales', *Broadcast*, 29 January 2010. Online. Available: <http://www.broadcastnow.co.uk/news/international/international-programme-sales/5010219.article> (accessed 23 December 2010).

——(2009) 'Gossip Girl and Ellen DeGeneres Head for YouTube', *Brand Republic*, 20 August 2009. Online. Available: <http://www.brandrepublic.com/news/928215/Gossip-Girl-Ellen-DeGeneres-head-YouTube/?DCMP=ILC-SEARCH> (accessed 22 December 2010).

——(2008) 'Dave', *Campaign (UK)*, 12 December 2008.

——(2007) 'Top Gear is Star Magazine Performer', *Ariel*, 20 February 2007: 2.

——(2006a) 'TopGear.com the Consumer Choice', *Ariel*, 10 October 2006: 2.

——(2006b) 'A Dose of Reality: Special Report', *Adweek*, 10 April 2006. Online. Available: <http://www.adweek.com/aw/esearch/article_display.jsp?vnu_content_id=1002314333> (accessed 22 December 2010).

——(2001) 'Enhanced Service for the UKTV Channels', *Televisual*, November 2001: 9.

——(2000) 'UKDrama Set to Benefit from Sky and UKTV Tie-up', *Media Week*, 14 April 2000: 6.

——(1998) 'Nets "Yellow" With Envy', *Advertising Age*, 9 November 1998.

——(1997a) 'Channel 5 Special: Modern Mainstream TV', *Broadcast Special Supplement*, 28 March 1997: 1–20.

——(1997b) 'Fox on the Run', *The Hollywood Reporter Special Issue Fox 10th Anniversary*, 13 May 1997: S1–S12.

——(1995) 'True Fans', *Economist*, 337(7944), 9 December 1995.

——(1990) 'How BSB was KOed', *Economist*, 11 October 1990, 317(7680): 79.

——(1987) 'Fox Broadcasting Co.: The Birth of a Network?', *Broadcasting*, 6 April 1987: 88–90.

Arqiva (2010) 'Heritage', Arqiva website. Online. Available: <http://www.arqiva.com/corporate/heritage/> (accessed 23 December 2010).

Arvidsson, A. (2006) *Brands: Meaning and Value in Media Culture*, London: Routledge.

Attenborough, R. (1991) 'Chairman's Statement', *Report and Accounts 1991*, Channel 4 Television Corporation.

Balaji, M. (2008) 'Bollyville, U.S.A.: The Commodification of the Other and MTV's Construction of the "Ideal Type" Desi', *Democratic Communiqué*, 22(1): 23–40.

Banet-Weiser, S., Chris, C. and Freitas, A. (2007) *Cable Visions: Television Beyond Broadcasting*, New York and London: New York University Press.

Barker, P. (1995) 'Brand Recognition', *Cable and Satellite Europe*, February 1995: 24–28.

Bashford, S. (2005) 'Making More of C4', *Broadcast*, 29 September 2005: 23.

BBC (2010) *Britain From Above* webpage. Online. Available: <http://www.bbc.co.uk/britainfromabove/about/index.shtml> (accessed 2 November 2010).

——(2006) *Royal Charter for the Continuance of the British Broadcasting Corporation*, BBC, October 2006.

——(2005) *Annual Report and Accounts 2004–05*, BBC.

——(2004) *Annual Report and Accounts 2003–04*, BBC.

——(2003) *Annual Report and Accounts 2002–03*, BBC.

——(2002) *Annual Report and Accounts 2001–02*, BBC.

——(2000) *Annual Report and Accounts 1999–2000*, BBC.

——(1999) *Annual Report and Accounts 1998–99*, BBC.

——(1998) *Annual Report and Accounts 1997–98*, BBC.

——(1997) *Annual Report and Accounts 1996–97*, BBC.

——(1995) *Annual Report and Accounts 1994–95*, BBC.

——(1992) *Annual Report and Accounts 1991–92*, BBC.

——(1991) *Annual Report and Accounts 1990–91*, BBC.

——(1988) *Annual Report and Accounts 1987–88*, BBC.

BBC Worldwide (2010) 'About BBC Worldwide'. Online. Available HTTP: <http://www.bbcworldwide.com/> (accessed 18 February 2010).

Becker, A. (2007) 'ABC's Sweeney on Digital Plans', *Broadcasting and Cable*, September 24 2007: 3.

Bennett, J. (2008a) 'Interfacing the Nation: Remediating Public Service Broadcasting in the Digital Television Age', *Convergence*, 14(3): 271–88.

——(2008b) 'Your Window on the World: The Emergence of Red-button Interactive Television in the UK', *Convergence*, 14(2): 161–82.

Bentley, S. (1999) 'ITV Reinforces Network Identity', *Marketing Week*, 19 August 1999. Online. Available: <http://www.marketingweek.co.uk/home/itv-reinforces-network-identity/2014493. article> (accessed 23 December 2010).

Berger, W. (1997) 'At 25, Excellence and Big Budgets for a Late Bloomer', *New York Times*, 9 November 1997. Online. Available: <http://www.nytimes.com/1997/11/09/movies/television-at-25-excellence-and-big-budgets-for-a-late-bloomer.html> (accessed 22 December 2010).

Berry, L.L. (2000) 'Cultivating Service Brand Equity', *Journal of the Academy of Marketing Science*, 28(1): 128–37.

Billard, M. (1983) 'MTV's Super Market', *Film Comment*, 19(4), 1 July 1983: 48–51.

Blighty (2010) *Britain From Above* webpage. Online. Available: <http://uktv.co.uk/blighty/homepage/sid/7105> (accessed 2 November 2010).

Boddy, W. (2004) *New Media and Popular Imagination: Launching Radio, Television, and Digital Media in the United States*, Oxford: Oxford University Press.

Bonner, F. (2010) '*Top Gear*: Why Does the Most Popular Programme Not Deserve Scrutiny?', *Critical Studies in Television*, 5(1): 32–45.

Born, G. (2004) *Uncertain Vision: Birt, Dyke and the Reinvention of the BBC*, London: Secker and Warburg.

Born, G. and Prosser, T. (2001) 'Culture and Consumerism: Citizenship, Public Service Broadcasting and the BBC's Fair Trading Obligations', *The Modern Law Review*, 64(5): 657–87.

Bose, M. (1996) 'How the Dish Ran Away With the Ratings', *Director*, November 1996, 50(4).

Bowden, A. (2002) 'Branding Sacred Cows', *Transdiffusion*, 2010. Online. Available HTTP: <http://www.transdiffusion.org/emc/ident/contemporary/cows.php> (accessed 3 February 2010).

Bring IT On (2010) *Digital Stories: Britain From Above*. Online. Available: <http://bringitonni.info/digital-stories/britain-from-above/> (accessed 2 November 2010).

Broadcasting Act 1990, 1 November 1990. Online. Available: <http://www.legislation.gov.uk/ukpga/1990/42/contents/enacted> (accessed 23 December 2010).

Brownrigg, M. and Meech, P. (2002) 'From Fanfare to Funfair: The Changing Sound World of UK Television Idents', *Popular Music*, 21(3): 345–55.

Bryant, S. (2009) 'TV's Credit Crunch: The Slow Death of End Credits on British Television and How Some Programmes Fought It', paper presented to *The Promotional Surround: logos, promos, idents, trailers* conference, University of Nottingham, June 2009.

Bulkley, K. (2007) 'TV Prospectors Eye up Arabia', *Television*, 44(10): 26–27.

Caldwell, J.T. (2008) *Production Culture: Industrial Reflexivity and Critical Practice in Film and Television*, Durham and London: Duke University Press.

——(2004) 'Branding', in H. Newcomb (ed.), *Encyclopaedia of Television: Volume 1, A-C*, 2nd edn, New York: Fitzroy Dearborn.

——(1995) *Televisuality*, New Brunswick, New Jersey: Rutgers University Press.

Capacity (2010) 'NBC More Colorful Case Study', Capacity website. Online. Available: <http://www.capacity.tv/process/nbc-more-colorful-case-study/> (accessed 7 October 2010).

Carroll, N. (2003) *Engaging the Moving Image*, New Haven and London: Yale University Press.

Cavanagh, A. (2007) *Sociology in the Age of the Internet*, Berkshire: Open University Press.

Cave, M., Collins, R. and Crowther, P. (2004) 'Regulating the BBC', *Telecommunications Policy*, 28(3–4): 249–72.

Chang, Y. (2003) '"Glocalization" of Television: Programming Strategies of Global Television Broadcasters in Asia', *Asian Journal of Communication*, 13(1): 1–36.

Channel 4 (2001) *Report and Financial Statements 2001*, Channel 4 Television Corporation.

—— (2000) *Report and Financial Statements 2000*, Channel 4 Television Corporation.

—— (1993) *Report and Financial Statements 1993*, Channel 4 Television Corporation.

—— (1991) *Report and Accounts 1991*, Channel 4 Television Company Ltd.

Chan-Olmsted, S.M. (2001) 'Perceptions of Branding Among Television Station Managers: An Exploratory Analysis', *Journal of Broadcasting and Electronic Media*, 45(1): 75–92.

Christophers, B. (2008) 'Television's Power Relations in the Transition to Digital: The Case of the United Kingdom', *Television and New Media*, 9(3): 239–57.

Cityscape (2010) *Britain From Above*. Online. Available: <http://www.cityscapedigital.co.uk/component/content/article/59-bbc-britain-from-above> (accessed 2 November 2010).

Clemens, J. (1990) 'Watch This Space', *The Listener*, 25 January 1990: 46.

Collins, R. (2009) 'Paradigm Found: The Peacock Report and the Genesis of a New Model of UK broadcasting Policy' in T. O'Malley and J. Jones (eds), *The Peacock Committee and UK Broadcasting Policy*, London: Palgrave Macmillan.

Communications Research Group (2005) *Analysis of Current Promotional Activity on Television: A Report of the Key Findings of a Content Analysis Study*, Ofcom, 6 December 2005. Online. Available: <http://stakeholders.ofcom.org.uk/binaries/research/tv-research/promoactivity.pdf> (accessed 2 October 2010).

Considine, P. (1997) 'BBC Takes the Pay-TV Plunge', *Broadcast*, 31 October 1997: 16–17.

Coombe, R.J. and Herman, A. (2001) 'Culture Wars on the Net: Intellectual Property and Corporate Propriety in Digital Environments', *The South Atlantic Quarterly*, 100(4): 919–47.

Coombe, R. (1998) *The Cultural Life of Intellectual Properties: Authorship, Appropriation and the Law*, Durham: Duke University Press.

Crawford, A. (1997) 'Marketing Focus: Can These Men Save ITV?', *Marketing*, 30 October 1997. Online. Available: <http://www.marketingmagazine.co.uk/news/65078/MARKETING-FOCUS-men-save-ITV-ratings-falling-advertising-costs-rising-clients-demanding-change-ITV-rsquos-new-team-faces-tough-task-writes-Anne-Marie-Crawford/?DCMP=ILC-SEARCH> (accessed 23 December 2010).

Creeber, G. (2004) *Serial Television: Big Drama on the Small Screen*, BFI: London.

Davies, J. (1997a) 'Smash-mouth Broadcasting', *The Hollywood Reporter Special Issue Fox 10th Anniversary*, 347(23), 13 May 1997: S16, S36.

——(1997b) 'Guerrilla Marketing', *The Hollywood Reporter Special Issue Fox 10th Anniversary*, 347(23), 13 May 1997: S30–S32.

Davis, D.M. and Walker, J.R. (1990) 'Countering the New Media: The Resurgence in Share Maintenance in Primetime Network Television', *Journal of Broadcasting and Electronic Media*, 34(4): 487–93.

Dawson, M. (2009) 'Between Promos and Content: Renegotiating the Television Text', paper presented to *The Promotional Surround: logos, promos, idents, trailers* conference, University of Nottingham, June 2009. Online. Available: <http://www.communication.northwestern.edu/faculty/?PID=MaxDawson&type=alpha> (accessed 23 December 2010).

——(2007) 'Little Player, Big Shows: Format, Narration, and Style on Television's New Smaller Screens', *Convergence*, 13(3): 231–50.

Deakin, S. and Pratten, S. (1999) 'Reinventing the Market? Competition and Regulatory Change in Broadcasting', *Journal of Law and Society*, 26(3): 323–50.

Dignam, C. (1997) 'Why TV is Turning on the Power of Marketing', *Media Week*, 21 November 1997: 8–9.

Douglas, T. (1997) 'Terrestrials Switch on Branding Strategy to Fight Off New Rivals', *Marketing Week*, 28 March 1997. Online. Available: <http://www.marketingweek.co.uk/home/terrestrials-switch-on-branding-strategy-to-fight-off-new-rivals/2008549.article> (accessed 23 December 2010).

Doyle, G. (2002) *Understanding Media Economics*, London: Sage.

Dreyfus, H.L. (2001) *On the Internet*, London and New York: Routledge.

Eastman, S.T. (2006) 'Designing On-air, Print, and Online Promotion', in S.T. Eastman, D.A. Ferguson and R.A. Klein (eds), *Media Promotion and Marketing for Broadcasting, Cable, and the Internet*, 5th edn, Burlington, MA and Oxford: Focal Press.

Eastman, S.T., Ferguson, D.A. and Klein, R.A. (2006) 'Promoting the Media: Scope and Goals' in S.T. Eastman, D.A. Ferguson and R.A. Klein (eds), *Media Promotion and Marketing for Broadcasting, Cable, and the Internet*, 5th edn, Burlington, MA and Oxford: Focal Press.

Eastman, S.T., Neal-Lunsford, J. and Riggs, K.E. (1995) 'Coping with Grazing: Prime-time Strategies for Accelerated Program Transitions', *Journal of Broadcasting and Electronic Media*, 39(1): 91–109.

Eastman, S.T., Newton, G.D., Riggs, K.E. and Neal-Lunsford, J. (1997) 'Accelerating the Flow: A Transition Effect in Programming Theory?', *Journal of Broadcasting and Electronic Media*, 41(2): 265–84.

Ebenkamp, B. (2003) 'Marketers of the Year: Todd Cunningham, Tina Exarhos, Grian Graden and Van Toffler', *Brandweek*, 20 October 2003. Online. Available: <http://www.allbusiness.com/marketing-advertising/branding-brand-development/4680893–1.html> (accessed 22 December 2010).

Edgerley, K. (1997) 'Presentation '96 – Promotion in a Competitive Environment', *Diffusion*, Spring 1997: 51–52.

Elliott, S. (1998) 'ABC Stays With Old Yellow, But It's In An "Evolved" Form', *The New York Times*, 11 June 1998. Online. Available: <http://www.nytimes.com/1998/06/11/business/media-business-advertising-abc-stays-with-old-yellow-but-it-s-evolved-form.html> (accessed 22 December 2010).

Ellis, J. (2000) *Seeing Things: Television in the Age of Uncertainty*, London: I.B.Tauris.

Evans, E. (2011) *Transmedia Television*, Abingdon, Oxon and New York: Routledge.

Fanthome, C. (2007) 'Creating an Iconic Brand: An Account of the History, Development, Context and Significance of Channel 4's Idents', *Journal of Media Practice*, 8(3): 255–71.

——(2003) *Channel 5: The Early Years*, Luton: University of Luton Press.

Farber, S. (1987) 'Fox Chases the Ratings Rabbit', *American Film*, 12(5): 31–34.

Fiddy, D. (2001) *Missing Believed Wiped: Searching For the Lost Treasures of British Television*, London: BFI.

Finnigan, D. (2001) 'A Year of Sundays for Hollywood', *Brandweek*, 15 October 2001. Online. Available: <http://www.brandweek.com/bw/esearch/article_display.jsp?vnu_content_id=1083556> (accessed 22 December 2010).

Flint, M., Fitzpatrick, N. and Thorne, C. (2006) *A User's Guide to Copyright*. 6th edn, Haywards Heath, West Sussex: Tottel Publishing.

Fry, A. (2010) 'Earning From On-demand', *Broadcast*, 10 March 2010. Online. Available: <http://www.broadcastnow.co.uk/earning-from-on-demand/5011672.article> (accessed 23 December 2010).

Gibson, J. (1999) 'Get Your Kit On', *The Guardian*, 8 June 1999.

Goldhaber, M.H. (1997) 'The Attention Economy and the Net', *First Monday*, 2(7), 7 April 1997. Online. Available: <http://firstmonday.org/htbin/cgiwrap/bin/ojs/index.php/fm/article/viewArticle/519/440%20> (accessed 29 September 2010).

Gomery, D. (2006) 'Surviving Cable and Satellite TV: The Broadcast Networks Thrive', in D. Gomery and L. Hockley (eds), *Television Industries*, London: BFI.

Goodwin, P. (1998) *Television Under the Tories: Broadcasting Policy 1979–1997*, London: BFI.

Grainge, P. (2010) 'Elvis Sings for the BBC: Broadcast Branding and Digital Media Design', *Media, Culture and Society*, 31(1): 45–61.

——(2009) 'Lost Logos: Channel 4 and the Branding of American Event Television', in R.E. Pearson (ed.), *Reading Lost*, London: I.B.Tauris.

——(2008) *Brand Hollywood: Selling Entertainment in a Global Media Age*, London and New York: Routledge.

Grant, M., Colville, M., Eschenburg, M., Dickerson, S., Sturgeon, P., Mortensen, N. and Crawford, G. (2010) *An Econometric Analysis of the TV Advertising Market: Final Report*, Analysys Mason and Brand Science for Ofcom, 11 March 2010. Online. Available: <http://stakeholders.ofcom.org.uk/binaries/research/tv-research/report.pdf> (accessed 7 October 2010).

Gray, J. (2010) *Show Sold Separately: Promos, Spoilers, and Other Media Paratexts*, New York: New York University Press.

——(2005) *Watching with The Simpsons: Television, Parody, and Intertextuality*, London and New York: Routledge.

Green, J. (2007) 'What Does an American Television Network Look Like?' *Flow*, 16 November 2007. Online. Available: <http://flowtv.org/2007/11/what-does-an-american-television-network-look-like/> (accessed 22 December 2010).

Griffin, J. (2008) 'The Americanization of *The Office*: A Comparison of the Offbeat NBC Sitcom and its British Predecessor', *Journal of Popular Film and Television*, 35(4): 155–63.

Grossberger, L. (1997) 'Yellow Puerile', *Media Week*, 7(32), 1 September 1997. Online.

Haley, K. (2002) 'Rocking the Industry: HBO at 30', *Broadcasting and Cable*, 4 November 2002: 1A-22A.

Hankinson, G. and Cowking, P. (1993) *Branding in Action: Cases and Strategies for Profitable Brand Management*, London and New York: McGraw-Hill.

Harrison, I. (2008) *Britain From Above*, London: Pavilion.

Heard, A. (1986) ' ... and Pass the Contribution', *Channels of Communication*, 6(3), June 1986: 50–51.

Hearst Corporation (2009) 'Our Brands', Hearst Corporation website. Online. Available: <http://www.hearst.com/our-brands/index.php> (accessed 15 December 2010).

Hemingway, J. (2007) 'Viacom's Aggressive Online Plan', *Broadcasting and Cable*, 24 September 2007: 3.

Henrickson, P. (2001) *Cablevision*, 26(2), 23 July 2001: 20.

Hesmondhalgh, D. (2002) *The Cultural Industries*, London and California: Sage.

Hibberd, J. (2008) 'NBC has Damaged its Brand', *Hollywood Reporter*, 16 December 2008. Online. Available: <http://www.hollywoodreporter.com/blogs/live-feed/nbc-damaged-brand-51055> (accessed 23 December 2010).

Higgins, J.M. and Romano, A. (2004) 'The Family Business', *Broadcasting and Cable*, 1 March 2004: 1, 6, 31.

Hills, M. (2007) 'From the Box in the Corner to the Box Set on the Shelf: "TVIII" and the Cultural/Textual Valorisations of DVD', *New Review of Film and Television Studies*, 5(1): 41–60.

Hilmes, M. (2003) 'Protectionism, Deregulation and the Telecommunications Act of 1996', in M. Hilmes (ed.), *The Television History Book*, London: BFI.

Hollins, T. (1984) *Beyond Broadcasting: Into the Cable Age*, London: BFI.

Holt, J. (2003) 'Vertical Vision: Deregulation, Industrial Economy and Prime-time Design', in M. Jancovich and J. Lyons (eds), *Quality Popular Television*, London: BFI.

Huff, R. (1998) 'ABC Seeing Yellow Spots Again: Its Controversial Fall Ad Campaign is Coming Back', *NY Daily News*, 11 June 1998. Online. Available: <http://www.nydailynews.com/archives/entertainment/1998/06/11/1998-06-11_abc_seeing_yellow_spots_agai.html> (accessed 10 October 2010).

Hujic, A. (1999) *MTV Europe: An Analysis of the Channel's Attempt to Design a Programming Strategy for a Pan-European Youth Audience*, unpublished PhD thesis, Goldsmiths College (University of London).

Iosifidis, P. (2008) 'Top Slicing and Plurality in Public Service Broadcasting: a European Review', *Inter Media*, 36(1): 30–33.

Isaacs, J. (1989) *Storm over Four: A Personal Account*, London: Weidenfeld and Nicolson.

Jackson, M. (1999) 'Chief Executive's Report', *Report and Financial Statements 1999*, Channel 4 Television Corporation.

Jacobs, J. (2005) 'Violence and Therapy in *The Sopranos*', in L. Mazdon and M. Hammond (eds), *The Contemporary Television Series*, Edinburgh: Edinburgh University Press.

Jansson, A. (2002) 'The Mediatisation of Consumption: Towards an Analytical Framework of Image Culture', *Journal of Consumer Culture*, 2(1): 5–31.

Jaramillo, D.L. (2002) 'The Family Racket: AOL Time Warner, HBO, *The Sopranos*, and the Construction of a Quality Brand', *Journal of Communication Inquiry*, 26(1): 59–75.

Jenkins, H. (2006) *Convergence Culture: Where Old and New Media Collide*, New York and London: New York University Press.

Johnson, C. (2009) 'Trading Auntie: The Exploitation and Protection of Intellectual Property Rights During the BBC's Monopoly Years', *New Review of Film and Television Studies*, 7(4): 441–58.

——(2007) 'Tele-branding in TVIII: The Network as Brand and the Programme as Brand', *New Review of Film and Television Studies*, 5(1): 5–24.

Johnson, C. and Turnock, R. (2005) 'From Start-up to Consolidation: Institutions, Regions and Regulation Over the History of ITV', in C. Johnson and R. Turnock (eds), *ITV Cultures: Independent Television Over Fifty Years*, Maidenhead, Berkshire: Open University Press.

Jordan, J. (2007) 'Media: Double Standards – Delivering Huge Benefit to Consumer and Trade', *Campaign (UK)*, 12 October 2007.

Josephson, J. (1990) 'The World's Best Known Channel', *Television Business International*, 3(5): 20.

jw7579 (2009) 'Little Things TV Stations Do That Annoy You', *Television Without Pity*, 27 October 2009. Online posting. Available: <http://forums.televisionwithoutpity.com/index.php?showtopic=828600&st=2145> (accessed 7 October 2010).

Kallan, C. (1987) 'Fox on the Loose: Are the Networks Being Hounded?', *Emmy*, 9(3): 48–56.

Kelly, J.P. (2009) 'Beyond the Broadcast Text: New Economies and Ephemeralities of Online TV', paper presented to *The Promotional Surround: logos, promos, idents, trailers* conference, University of Nottingham, June 2009.

Kelso, T. (2008) 'And Now No Word From Our Sponsor: How HBO Put the Risk Back Into Television', in M. Leverette, B.L. Ott and C.L. Buckley (eds), *It's Not TV: Watching HBO in the Post-television Era*, New York and London: Routledge.

Kimmel, D.M. (2004) *The Fourth Network: How Fox Broke the Rules and Reinvented Television*, Chicago: Ivan R. Dee.

Klaassen, A. (2006a) 'Viacom Keys in on Comedy to Monetize Internet Video', *Advertising Age*, 77(49), 4 December 2006.

——(2006b) 'How MTV Plans to Triple Digital Revenue', *Advertising Age*, 77(18), 1 May 2006.

Klanten, R., Meyer, B., Jofré, C. and Lovell, S. (eds) (2005) *On Air*, Berlin: Die Gestaltenn Verlag.

The Knowledge Agency Ltd. (2005) *Television Promotions – What the Viewers Think: A Report of the Key Findings of a Qualitative and Quantitative Study*, Ofcom, 6 December 2005. Online. Available: <http://stakeholders.ofcom.org.uk/binaries/research/tv-research/promoviewers.pdf> (accessed 2 October 2010).

Koerner, S. (2005) 'Insight From the Inside Out', *The Hub Magazine*, 2 May 2005: 10–13. Online. Available: <http://www.hubmagazine.com/?s=koerner> (accessed 9 November 2010).

Kompare, D. (2006) 'Publishing Flow: DVD Box Sets and the Reconception of Television', *Television and New Media*, 7(4): 335–60.

——(2005) *Rerun Nation: How Repeats Invented American Television*, New York and London: Routledge.

Kunz, W.M. (2009) 'Prime-time Television Program Ownership in the Post-fin/syn World', *Journal of Broadcasting and Electronic Media*, 53(4): 636–51.

Lambie-Nairn, M. (1997) *Brand Identity for Television: With Knobs On*, Phaidon: London.

Leverette, M., Ott, B.L. and Buckley, C.L. (eds) (2008) *It's Not TV: Watching HBO in the Post-television Era*, New York and London: Routledge.

Light, J.J. (2004) *Television Channel Identity: The Role of Channels in the Delivery of Public Service Television in Britain, 1996–2002*, unpublished PhD thesis, University of Glasgow.

Lion Television (2010) *Britain From Above*. Online. Available: <http://www.liontv.com/London/Productions/Britain-From-Above> (accessed 2 November 2010).

Lippert, B. (1997) 'I Want My ABC', *New York*, 18 August 1997: 20, 82.

Lotz, A.D. (2007a) *The Television Will Be Revolutionized*, New York and London: New York University Press.

——(2007b) 'Must-See TV: NBC's Dominant Decades', in M. Hilmes (ed.), *NBC: America's Network*, Berkeley: University of California Press.

Lury, C. (2004) *Brands: The Logos of the Global Economy*, London: Routledge.

McCabe, J. (2005) 'Creating "Quality" Audiences for *ER* on Channel Four', in M. Hammond and L. Mazdon (eds), *The Contemporary Television Series*, Edinburgh: Edinburgh University Press.

McChesney, R.W. (2008) *The Political Economy of Media: Enduring Issues, Emerging Dilemmas*, New York: Monthly Review Press.

McDowell, W. and Batten, A. (2005) *Branding TV: Principles and Practices*, Burlington, MA and Oxford: Focal Press.

McMurria, J. (2003) 'Long-format TV: Globalisation and Network Branding in a Multi-channel Era' in M. Jancovich and J. Lyons (eds), *Quality Popular Television*, London: BFI.

Mandell, T. (2005) 'MTV Goes to Africa', *Black Filmmaker*, 8(33): 44–45.

Mark (2006) 'The Strange, Reality-blurring World of the Defaker Comments Section', Gawker website, 21 September 2006. Online. Available: <http://defamer.gawker.com/202388/the-strange-reality+blurring-world-of-the-defaker-comments-section> (accessed 9 November 2010).

Marsh, H. (1998) 'Agenda: Is ITV's Marketing Hitting the Right Buttons?', *Marketing*, 29 October 1998. Online. Available: <http://www.marketingmagazine.co.uk/news/64706/AGENDA-ITV-rsquos-marketing-hitting-right-buttons-One-year-ITV-rsquos-management-team-set-implement-coherent-strategy-improve-branding-programming-Harriet-Marsh-reviews-its-progress-finds-broadcaster/?DCMP=ILC-SEARCH> (accessed 23 December 2010).

Marshall, P.D. (2002) 'The New Intertextual Commodity', in D. Harries (ed.), *The New Media Book*, London: BFI.

Matthews, T. (2005) '*Top Gear* Celebrates Emmy Win', *Ariel*, 29 November 2005: 3.

Mawer, C. (2009) 'Red Bee Media', paper presented at *The Promotional Surround: logos, promos, idents, trailers* conference, University of Nottingham, June 2009.

Meehan, E. (2005) *Why TV Is Not Our Fault: Television Programming, Viewers, and Who's Really in Control*, Lanham, MD: Rowman and Littlefield.

Metz, W. (2004) 'Home Box Office', in H. Newcomb (ed.), *Encyclopedia of Television: Volume 2, D-L*, 2nd edn, New York: Fitzroy Dearborn.

Mills, B. (2010) 'Invisible Television: The Programmes No one Talks About Even Though Lots of People Watch them', *Critical Studies in Television*, 5(1): 1–16.

Morrissey, B. (2007) 'Social Media Replacing Microsites in Marketing Mix', *Brandweek*, 12 November 2007. Online. Available: <http://www.brandweek.com/bw/esearch/article_display.jsp?vnu_content_id=1003671048> (accessed 22 December 2010).

MTV (2010), 'Think MTV', MTV website. Online. Available: <http://www.mtv.com/thinkmtv/> (accessed 22 December 2010).

Mullen, M. (2008) *Television in the Multichannel Age: A Brief History of Cable Television*, Malden, MA and Oxford: Blackwell.

Murdoch, J. (2009) 'The Absence of Trust', the MacTaggart lecture at the Edinburgh Television Festival, 28 August 2009. Online. Available: <http://www.newscorp.com/news/news_426.html > (accessed 22 December 2010).

Murdock, G. (2004) 'Building the Digital Commons: Public Broadcasting in the Age of the Internet', The 2004 Spry Memorial Lecture, Vancouver, 18 November 2004, University of

Montreal. Online. Available: <https://pantherfile.uwm.edu/type/www/116/Theory_Other Texts/Theory/Murdock_BuildingDigitalCommons.pdf> (accessed 23 December 2010).

Murray, S. (2005) 'Brand Loyalties: Rethinking Content Within Global Corporate Media', *Media, Culture and Society*, 27(3): 415–35.

Myerson, J. (1997) 'Introduction', in Martin Lambie-Nairn, *Brand Identity for Television: With Knobs On*, Phaidon: London.

Nazerali, S. (2003) 'Brands? Bunkum ... ', *Broadcast*, 24 October 2003: 30.

Nelson, R. (2007) 'HBO Premium: Channelling Distinction Through TVIII', *New Review of Film and Television Studies*, 5(1): 25–40.

News Corporation (2010) 'Television Stations', News Corporation website. Online. Available: <http://www.newscorp.com/operations/tvstations.html> (accessed 22 December 2010).

Ofcom (2010) *Public Service Broadcasting: Annual Report 2010, D – PSB Viewing*, Ofcom, 8 July 2010. Online. Available: <http://stakeholders.ofcom.org.uk/binaries/broadcast/reviews-investigations/psb-review/psb2010/psbviewing.pdf> (accessed 23 December 2010).

Ofcom and Gfk (2010) *The Consumer's Digital Day*, Ofcom, 14 December 2010. Online. Available: <http://stakeholders.ofcom.org.uk/binaries/research/811898/consumers-digital-day.pdf> (accessed 11 February 2011).

O'Leary, N. (2009) 'Searching for Life on Hulu', *Adweek*, 25 May 2009. Online. Available: <http://www.adweek.com/aw/content_display/special-reports/other-reports/e3i15f4e 2b3b4a487b3cbb6ddcfb338c9e7> (accessed 23 December 2010).

O'Malley, T. (2009) 'Introduction' in T. O'Malley and J. Jones (eds), *The Peacock Committee and UK Broadcasting Policy*, London: Palgrave Macmillan.

Ouellette, L. (2008) 'Citizen Brand: Neoliberal Governmentality and Post-network Television Culture', paper presented at the Society for Cinema and Media Studies Conference, Philadelphia, March 2008.

Ouellette, L. and Hay, J. (2008) *Better Living Through Reality TV*, Malden, MA and Oxford: Blackwell.

Peacock, A. (1986) *Report of the Committee on Financing the BBC*, Cmnd 9824.

Peterson, T. (2002) 'The Secrets of HBO's Success', *Business Week*, 20 August 2002. Online. Available: <http://www.businessweek.com/bwdaily/dnflash/aug2002/nf20020820_2495.htm> (accessed 22 December 2010).

Powell, R. (1987) 'Do I Want My MTV?', *Televisual*, September 1987: 26–28.

Proctor, T. (2007) *Public Sector Marketing*, Harlow, Essex: Pearson Education Ltd.

Revoir, P. (2002) 'Family Fortunes', *Broadcast*, 28 June 2002: 17.

Reynolds, R. (1996) 'BBC World at One ... ', *Ariel*, 23 January 1996: 8–9.

Rixon, P. (2003) 'The Changing Face of American Television Programmes on British Screens', in M. Jancovich and J. Lyons (eds), *Quality Popular Television*, London: BFI.

Robertson QC, G. and Nicol QC, A. (2002) *Media Law*, 4th edn, London: Penguin.

Robinson, R.A. (1984) 'Special Report on MTV', *The Hollywood Reporter*, 281(12): S1–S14.

Rogers, J. (2007) 'Korean Broadcaster Buys *Top Gear* for Digital Service', *Broadcast*, 2 March 2007: 12.

Rogers, M.C., Epstein, M. and Reeves, J.L. (2002) '*The Sopranos* as HBO Brand Equity: The Art of Commerce in the Age of Digital Reproduction', in D. Lavery (ed.), *This Thing of Ours: Investigating The Sopranos*, London: Wallflower.

Ross, C. (1997) 'ABC's New Ads are Edgy, Risky', *Advertising Age*, 19 May 1997.

Ross, S.M. (2008) *Beyond the Box: Television and the Internet*, Malden, MA and Oxford: Blackwell.

Rosser, M. (2004) 'Spot the Difference', *Broadcast*, 15 October 2004: 2–3.

INDEX

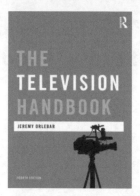

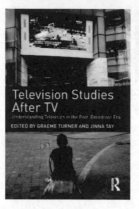